Mirror of Realization

'God Is a Percept – The Universe Is a Concept'

By

Mashhad Al-Allaf
Ph.D. in Philosophy

IIC - CLASSIC SERIES, USA

MIRROR OF REALIZATION

By:

MASHHAD AL-ALLAF
(Ph.D. in Philosophy)

© Mashhad Al-Allaf 2003
All rights reserved. No part of this publication may be reproduced, stored in a retrieved system, or transmitted in any form or by any means; electronic, mechanical, photocopying, web text, recording or otherwise, without the prior permission of the Copyright owner.

To Order please send an e-mail to:

iic_classic@yahoo.com

Islamic Information Center, USA

Comments and Suggestions please send an e-mail to:

mashhad9@yahoo.com
or
alallafm@slu.edu

Includes bibliography.

ISBN 0-9722722-2-4

1. Islamic-Religion
2. World-Religion
3. Religion-Philosophy
4. Islam-West

I. Al-Allaf, Mashhad, 1957-

CONTENTS

Introduction: A story of a Professor   7

Part One: Allah, The Story of Creation, and Revelation
1. Is Religion a Necessity?   9
2. The Meaning of the Word "Allah"   10
3. Knowing Allah –The Exalted-   12
   - 3.1. His Essence   12
   - 3.2. Divine Attributes   17
   - 3.3. His 99 Names   19
4. The Story of Creation   24
5. Structuring the Life of Man by Revelation   34
6. Prophet Abraham   39
7. The Meaning of the Word "Islam"   41
8. The Qur'an   43

Part Two: The Islamic Divine Law (Shari'ah)
9. Structuring the Life of Man by Divine Law (Shari'ah)
   - 9.1. The Five Ahkam or Regulations: 48
   - 9.2. Wajeb   51
   - 9.3. Mandoob   52
   - 9.4. Mubah   52
   - 9.5. Makrooh   53
   - 9.6. Haram   54
10. Sources of Shari'ah (Islamic Divine Law)
    - 10.1. The Qur'an   57
    - 10.2. The Sunnah   59
    - 10.3. Ijma'   74
    - 10.4. Qiyas   75
11. The Divisions of the Shari'ah (Islamic Divine Law)
    - 11.1. Fiqh (Jurisprudence)   78
    - 11.2. Usul al-Deen (Scholastic Theology)   80
    - 11.3. Akhlaq (Ethics & Purification of the Soul)   81
12. The Objectives (Maqasid) of the Islamic Divine Law
    - 12.1. The Abandoned Ship   82
    - 12.2. The Categories of Benefits   83
    - 12.3. The Maqasid Paradigm   85
    - 12.4. Al-Ghazali and the Abandoned Ship   93

Part Three: Last prophet, the seal of Prophethood
13. The Need for a Prophet   94
14. The Life of Muhammad (pbuh)   96
15. The Beginning of Revelation   104
16. The Struggle or Jihad   107

17. The Isra' and Mi'raj	137
18. The Migration or Hijra	143
19. The Establishment of The Islamic State	155
19.1. New Society and New Islamic Calendar	160
19.2. A Charter of Islamic Alliance	162
19.3. The Prophet Establishing Peace and Virtues	164
19.4. A Treaty With the Jews	166
19.5. The Battle With Quraish (Badr)	167
19.6. The Prisoners of War	172
19.7. An Attempt to Kill the Prophet	173
19.8. The Prophet Working for Peace	177
19.9. Last Ceremony	177
20. The Death of the Prophet Muhammad (pbuh)	179
21. His Physical and Moral Characters	187
22. The Miracles of Prophet Muhammad (pbuh)	190

Part Four: Islam, Iman, and Ihsan

23. **Hadith Gabriel:** Levels of Devotion	194
24. **Islam:** Pillars and Rituals of Islam	196
24.1. Shahada	197
24.2. Salat	198
24.3. Zakat	213
24.4. Sawm	215
24.5. Hajj	219
25. **Iman:** Articles of Faith	
25.1. Believing in Allah	225
25.2. His Angels	226
25.3. His Books	227
25.4. His Messengers	228
25.5. The Last Day	230
25.6. Divine Destiny (al-Qadar)	231
26. **Ihsan:** Sufism and the Marvels of the Heart	
26.1. To "Be" and to "Become"	234
26.2. The Heart and its Steps	235
26.3. How to Prepare the Heart?	236
26.4. Everyone is Unique in Spirituality	237

Part Five: Islamic Knowledge

27. Classification of Sciences	239
27.1. Revealed Sciences	239
27.2. Rational Sciences	240
28. 'Ilm al-Kalam (Scholastic Theology)	240
28.1. Kalam Argument: The Universe has a Cause	241
28.2. Schools of 'Ilm al-Kalam	243

29. Islamic Philosophy (Falsafa)
    29.1. Ma'rifah (Islamic Theory of Knowledge) 245
    29.2. Al-Kindi 246
    29.3. The Model of Islamic Conception of Reality 251
    29.4. Metaphysics (The Universe is not Eternal) 252
    29.5. Actual Infinity is Impossible 253
    29.6. Al-Kindi and David Hilbert on Infinity 257
    29.7. Proofs of the Existence of Allah 259

30. Al-Jabr (algebra)
    30.1. How to Divide Inheritance? 261
    30.2. Al-Khawarizmi's Logical System of Algebra 263

31. Dreams and Interpretation
    31.1. The Dream of the King of Egypt 266
    31.2. Different Kinds of Dreams 267
    31.3. Rules of Interpretation 267
    31.4. Good Dreams and False or Confused Dreams 268
    31.5. Requirements for a True Dream 269
    31.6. Examples of Dreams 270

Part Six: The Islamic State
32. The Supreme Authority of the Islamic State 272
33. The Legal Steps in Establishing the Islamic State 276
    33.1. Shura (Consultation) 276
    33.2. Musawat (Equality) 278
    33.3. 'Adl (Justice) 280
    33.4. Prescribing Good and Forbidding Evil 281

34. Legality and Principles from Jurisprudence 283
    34.1. Principles for the Aversion of Harm 284
    34.2. Principles Devised to Avoid Corruption 285
    34.3. Principles for Relief from Difficulties 286
    34.4. Principles of Necessities and Prohibition 287
35. Characteristics of Islamic Legislation 288
36. Islamic State and Leadership 289
    36.1. Who Appoints the Muslim Ruler? 290
    36.2. The Requirements of the Ruler 290
    36.3. How was the First Muslim Ruler Elected? 291
    36.4. Should Muslims Obey the Ruler Regardless? 293

Part Seven: Islamic Stories and Poetry
37. Qur'anic Story, the Story of prophet Joseph 295
38. Stories of the Companions of the Prophet 307
    38.1. Umm Salamah (Female Sahabia) 307
    38.2. Abu al-Darda' 311
39. Parables from Al-Ghazali 314
40. Short Poems   316,   **References**   317

The value of an action

depends on the intention

A man will be rewarded

only

for what he intended.[1]

---

[1] This saying is based on the famous Prophetic Hadith:
[The value of] an action depends on the intention behind it. A man will be rewarded only for what he intended.
The emigration of one who emigrates for the sake of Allah and His Messenger (may peace be upon him) is for the sake of Allah and His Messenger (may peace be upon him); and the emigration of one who emigrates for gaining a worldly advantage or for marrying a woman is for what he has emigrated. (Agreed upon: Narrated by Bukhari and Muslim)

Introduction: A Story of a Professor

I was about to leave my office in the philosophy department when I heard eastern music that sounded familiar to me. I listened carefully and found that it was coming from my colleague's office who teaches music. I arrived at his office as he turned the music off, probably preparing to go to class. I knocked on his door and said, 'I heard eastern music that I believe I recognize.'

He said: 'yes, that was a piece that I am preparing to present to my students in class, it is the Islamic call for prayer (Adhan).'

I told him this was not the Islamic call for prayer, but a song by an Iraqi singer who is very well known as an alcoholic, and some say that he is also a homosexual. Noticing that he was not interested in learning this from me, I told the professor he could find the Islamic call for prayer (Adhan) on the Internet.

This situation and many others like it need to be considered seriously. It is sad to see the universities, as the precious places of society, being trivialized. And how professors, as the elite of the society, become less knowledgeable and more careless about other cultures and religions.

Something like this is highly offensive to Muslims because it creates a misconception about the practice of Islam. However, the most important thing that concerns me, as a professor of philosophy, and one who has devoted his career to education, is that students pay a lot of money to universities, devote a lot of time to study, and put a lot of trust in these elites of society who are not giving them what they want or deserve.

My story with this professor did not end there. I decided to measure the progress of his learning and after two years I went to his office and talked to him about school, asking him about his students and what he was presenting to them about the Islamic call for prayer. I was surprised to find that he was still presenting the same song of the Iraqi singer as an Islamic call for prayer.

I had no intention in writing a book on the Islamic Religion, however, after this incident and other similar happenings I decided to write this book in order to help my readers, my students, my colleagues, and all seekers of the truth, to achieve a better understanding of reality.

"Allah is the Light of the heavens and the earth. The parable of His Light is as if there were a Niche and within it a Lamp: the Lamp enclosed in Glass; the glass as it were a brilliant star: lit from a blessed Tree, an Olive, neither of the East nor of the West, whose Oil is well-nigh luminous, though fire scarce touched it: Light upon Light! Allah guides to his light whom He wills. And Allah sets forth Parables for mankind, and Allah is All-Knower of everything." (Qur'an, 24:35)

"With Him are the keys of the Unseen, none knows them but He. And He knows whatever there is on the earth and in the sea. Not a leaf falls but with His knowledge: there is not a grain in the darkness [or depths] of the earth, nor anything fresh or dry [green or withered], but is [inscribed] in a Record clear [to those who can read]." (Qur'an: 6:59)

PART ONE

Allah, The Story of Creation, and Revelation

1. Is Religion a Necessity?
This question might seem to be too philosophical, however, it will be simplified and clarified through this book, and we will see later whether spirituality and religion are necessary or not.[2]

Islam is a revelation of a message from Allah (The God), through the angel Gabriel, to Prophet Muhammad, peace and blessings of Allah be upon him (pbuh)[3], to be delivered to mankind. Thus there are three major principles we need to discuss in this book:

> Allah -The Exalted-
> The Message itself or the Religion (Islam)
> Muhammad (pbuh) as a prophet and a messenger

---

[2] In the eighteenth century Kant (1724-1804) made his philosophical inquiry revolve around this question: Is metaphysics possible?
His answer was given in a negative way. He seemed to put metaphysical issues in the field of the "Nomina" or the "thing in itself", and thus they are outside our "experience" and outside the realm of "phenomenon" which means that they are outside rational demonstration.
In the twentieth century Muhammad Iqbal (1873-1938) in his book *The Construction of Religious Thought In Islam 1934*, raised a similar epistemological question: Is Religion Possible?
His answer was in affirmation. Iqbal thought that religious experience is possible especially in the light of the scientific achievements, also due to his conviction that Kant's position can be accepted only if we start with the assumption that all experience other than the normal level of experience is impossible. If this is the case then Kant has to show whether the normal level of experience is the "only" level of knowledge-yielding experience.
In this book I moved from the "possibility" to "necessity", in which I argue that there is something mysterious in the human existence that requires spirituality. Denying this need is denying one of the necessities that makes human; human in the first place.

[3] In Islamic religion if the name of the Prophet Muhammad or any other prophet is mentioned, then people should say:
Peace and blessings of Allah be upon him (pbuh), in Arabic: Salla Allahu 'Alaihi wa Sallam.

2. The Meaning of the Word Allah (The God):

In Islam ALLAH (The God) is the cause of existence and the source of the universe; its creation, its continuity, and its end. He is also the source of life, sustenance, knowledge, etc. But before I go any further I should clarify to you the meaning of the word "Allah".

The word "god" in Arabic language is: "ILAH", thus, ilah is a god, the definite article in Arabic is: "AL " meaning "The" in English.
By putting "AL" in front of "ILAH" the Arabic word becomes: AL-ILAH.
By the rules of abbreviation in the Arabic language the letter "I" was dropped and the word became: ALLAH.

By having the definite article "AL", meaning "The", the word "ALLAH" is no longer meaning *a god*, instead it means: *"The God"*, in fact it is a clear reference in the Arabic language to The One God, and thus the only One God.

Allah (The God)

Ilah = god
Al = The
Al + ilah = The + god
Alilah = The God

By dropping the letter "i" by rules of abbreviation the word becomes:

Alilah = Allah = The God or The One God and The Only One

The Oneness of Allah (The God) is central to Islamic religion and Islamic philosophy as we will see, in fact the declaration of faith in Islam is nothing more than an emphasis of this oneness by saying: "I bear witness that there is no god but Allah, and I bear witness that Muhammad is his messenger."

Notice that you may read in the Qur'an a verse with the plural pronoun in a form such as "We" saying:

"Say: "Come, I will rehearse what Allah hath (really) prohibited you from": join not anything as equal with Him; be good to your parents; kill not your children on a plea of want - **We** provide sustenance for you and for them - come not nigh to shameful deeds, whether open or secret; take not life, which Allah hath made sacred, except by way of justice and law: thus doth He command you, that ye may learn wisdom. (Qur'an, 6:151) (emphasis mine)

It is absolutely acceptable in the Arabic language to refer to a singular by using the plural pronoun "we" which is also called the "royal we", however, when the Qur'an addresses the issue of worshiping One God or talking about Islamic creed it is always presented in the singular pronoun "I" in Arabic: أنا or "Me" as in His saying –the Exalted-:

"Verily, **I am Allah**: there is no god but **I**: so worship **Me** (only), and establish regular prayer for celebrating **My** praise." (Qur'an, 20:14)

Or as in this verse both pronouns were used in clear reference to One God, Allah –the Exalted- says:

"Not a messenger did **We** send before you but We revealed to him (saying): that there is no god but **I**; therefore worship **Me**." (Qur'an, 21:25)

But who is Allah, how do Muslims think of Him, and what kind of Divine attributes does He have?

3. Knowing Allah –The Exalted-

His Essence, Divine Attributes, and His 99Names

3. 1. Knowing the Essence of Allah:[4]

First of all, knowing the essence of Allah - the Exalted – in Islam is not an issue of personal reflection or philosophical contemplation. The knowledge of Him –the Exalted- must be derived from the revelation itself and from what Allah said about Himself. This knowledge must be derived from the main sources of Islamic religion, and these sources are the Qur'an and Sunnah, as I will explain later. Since this is not an area of personal conjecture, Muslims usually quote the Qur'an or the Sunnah or a reliable Muslim scholar who presented this issue in the light of Qur'an and Sunnah. Here I am using Imam al-Ghazali's text on this topic.

The Oneness

First and most important in Islam is to know that Allah -the Mighty, the Glorified- is One without any equal. He is separate in creating and innovating; He is alone in bringing into existence and inventing. There are none like Him to rival or equal Him, and none opposite Him to contest or contend with Him. The proof is in His saying - the High -

"Had there been therein (in the heavens and the earth) aliha (gods) besides Allah, then verily, both would have been ruined. Glorified is Allah, the Lord of the Throne, (High is He) above all that (evil) they associate with Him!" (Qur'an, 21:22)

To explain, if there had been two gods and the first of them willed a certain thing, the second, if he were under compulsion to aid the first, would be a subordinate and impotent being rather than an

---

[4] In this discussion of the divine attributes and knowing the essence of Allah, it is recommended that a scholar who is not skilled in the field of Kalam to relay upon the writing of a well qualified Muslim Scholar. I am using mainly the famous text of Abu Hamed al-Ghazali (1058-1111) called *al-Risala al-Qudsiyya*; chapter two, volume one of his famous encyclopedia: *The Revival of Religious Science*. However, I have made some modifications and changes by adding or deleting some information as needed to fit my goal in this book.

almighty god; and if the second were able to contradict and oppose the first, he would be a powerful and dominating being, while the first would be weak and impotent rather than an almighty god. This verse from the Qur'an presents to humans a logical argument that is strongly consistent with the validity of logical reasoning

The logical form of the Qur'anic argument:
Premise 1: If there were gods in the heaven and earth besides Allah, then they (heaven and earth) will be destroyed and collapsed (every god seeking power and control)

Premise 2: But they are Not collapsed (the universe is systematically working)

Conclusion: Therefore, there is only one God.

The argument has this valid logical form of Modus Tollens:
If P......, then ..... Q
Not Q

Therefore, Not P

> **An example to clarify the Qur'anic argument**
>
> If you are in the USA, then you are in North America
> **(P)**   **(Q)**
> You are not in North America **(Not Q)**
>
> ---
>
> Therefore, you are not in the USA **(Not P)**

In another verse Allah-the High- says:

"Say: He is Allah, the One and Only" (Qur'an, 112:1)

The Oneness of Allah is very important and essential in Islamic belief. This is also called *Tawheed* as we will discuss later.

Ancient Eternity (Azali)
Allah is Azali, or Ancient from eternity. He has no beginning, but He is the beginning of everything and before anything living or dead.

"He is the First and the Last, the Evident and the Hidden: and He has full knowledge of all things." (Qur'an 57:3)

The proof of this is found in the supposition that if Allah had been originated and not ancient, He would have been in need of an originator. In turn His originator would also need an originator and so on in a chain of infinity. Those who would enroll in such a chain will never be found, or the chain reaches to an Ancient Originator and He would then be the First. This is the one whom we named the Maker, the Originator, the Fashioner, and the Creator of the Worlds.

Eternity (Abadi)
Allah, besides being without beginning, has no end to His existence (Abadi). He is the First and the Last. Since His eternity is established, His end is impossible.

Free From Substance
Allah - the High - is not a substance which has a physical dimension. Instead, He is Exalted above all dimensions.[5]

Free From Bodily Form
Allah - the High – does not have a body composed of different substances, since the body is that which is composed of substances. When His being a substance limited by place is refuted, His being a body is also refuted, because every body is limited by place and is composed of substances. But it is impossible for the substance to be

---

[5] The proof: every substance that is definite is limited by its own place and is inevitably either constant in it or moving away from it. Therefore it is not independent of motion or rest for both these are originated, and that which is not independent of originated phenomena is itself originated. If an ancient definite substance were conceivable, the eternity of the substances of the world would have been reasonable. And if a person should use the term substance and not mean thereby a resident substance, he would be mistaken as far as the use of the term is concerned, not as far as the meaning for which he had used it.

free from division, composition, motion, rest, form, and quantity, all of which are characteristics of originated phenomena. And if it were possible to believe that the Maker of the world is contained within a physical body, it would also be possible to believe in the divinity of the sun and the moon as well as other heavenly bodies.

Free from the Quality of Substance
Allah - the High - is not a quality of a substance that exists in a body or a condition in a place; because an accident is that which exists in a body. But every body is inevitably originated and as such its originator exists before it. How then could (Allah) exist in a body when He has existed in eternity alone, with no other beside Him, and He then originated the bodies and their qualities afterwards. Besides He is a Knowing, and Able, and the Willing Creator as shall be discussed later. It is impossible for these attributes to exist in substance or its quality. On the contrary they are impossible except in a Self-existent and Self-sufficient Creator.

The Creator (al-Khaliq)
Every originated phenomenon in the world is of His making, creation, and invention. There is no other creator of it besides Him, and there is no innovator of it except Him. He created the creation and fashioned them, and He brought into being their ability and movement. In His saying - the High –

"He is Allah, the Creator, the Inventor, the Bestower of Forms (or Colors). To Him belong the Most Beautiful Names: whatever is in the heavens and on earth glorify Him. And He is the Exalted in Might, the Wise." (Qur'an, 59:24)

And in His saying –the High-:

"That is Allah, your Lord! There is no god but He, the Creator of all things; so worship Him (Alone), and He is the Trustee (Disposer of affairs) over all things." (Qur'an, 6:102)

Nothing Whatever Like Unto Him
The eighth principle, which sums up the previous principles, is to know that Allah is One, Eternal, being neither a substance, nor a body, nor a quality of substance; that the whole world is made of substances, their quality, and bodies, and consequently He

resembles nothing and nothing resembles Him. He is the Living, the Subsisting, there is none like unto Him.[6]
Allah said in the Qur'an:

"(He is) the Creator of the heavens and the earth: He has made for you pairs from among yourselves, and pairs among cattle: by this means does He multiply you: **there is nothing whatever like unto Him**, and He is the One that hears and sees (all things)." (Qur'an: 42:11) (emphasis mine)

All bodies and their qualities were created and made by Him; hence it is impossible that they are like Him or resemble Him.

---

[6] Notice that, logically speaking, definitions could be offered in two ways: first by affirmation, such as Allah is One, He is merciful, He hears. Second, we can define by negation, such as Allah does not hear in a way similar to us or by ears like ours that get infected sometimes. While this verse from Qur'an applying the two method of definition in a very short way by saying, Exalted He is, that "there is nothing whatever like unto Him, and He is the One that hears and sees (all things)."

3.2. The Six Most Important of the Divine Attributes
These six attributes are: life, knowledge, will, power, hearing, and seeing. I will discuss each one briefly.

Life
The first principle is the knowledge that Allah - the High, the Glorified - is Alive. He is not a dead matter, exalted be He, such as stone or wood or other material substances, and He is not an idol.

"Allah! There is no god but He, the Ever Living, the Self-subsisting, Eternal. No slumber can seize Him nor sleep. His are all things in the heavens and on earth." (Qur'an 2:255)

Knowledge
The second principle is the knowledge that He - the High - is Knowledgeable, knowing all things and comprehending all creation; not even the weight of an atom in Heaven or on earth is ever hidden from His Knowledge. He is truthful in His saying:

"With Him are the keys of the Unseen, none knows them but He. And He knows whatever there is on the earth and in the sea. Not a leaf falls but with His knowledge: there is not a grain in the darkness (or depths) of the earth, nor anything fresh or dry (green or withered), but is (inscribed) in a Record clear (to those who can read)." (Qur'an: 6:59)

Furthermore evidence of His Truthfulness is found in His Saying - the High:

"Should not He Who has created know? And He is the One that understands the finest mysteries (and) is well-acquainted (with them)." (Qur'an: 67:14)

He has led you, through His creation, to comprehend the knowledge that you cannot doubt in proving the subtleness of creation and orderly creation, even in insignificant and meager things. This shows us the knowledge the Maker has to bring order and His ability to arrange. Muslims believe that what Allah - the Exalted - Himself said is the Last Word in guidance and in revealing knowledge.

Will
The third principle is the knowledge that He - the High – has the ability through his Will to bring about certain actions. Nothing exists which does not depend upon, and proceed from His Will. He is the Creator, the Restorer, the Doer of whatsoever He wills. Every deed that has proceeded from Him, has an opposite deed which could have proceeded from Him. He has the Will to render one of them into existence, and He alone decides the outcome of the deed.

"Verily, when He intends a thing, His Command is, "Be", and it is!" (Qur'an: 36:82)

He has the power over both deeds. Therefore, it is necessary that there should be a Will that directs His Power to one of the two possibilities.

Power or Ability
The fourth principle is the knowledge that the Maker of the world is Almighty and that He - the High - is Truthful in His saying:

"And it is He Who has power over all things," (Qur'an 5:120)

Because the world is perfect in its making and orderly in its composition. For he who would see a silk garment, fine in its weave and texture, symmetrical in its embroidery and ornamentation, and would imagine that it was woven by a dead person that has no life, or by a helpless person with has no power, would be completely lacking in intellect and utterly foolish and ignorant.

Hearing and Seeing
The fifth and the sixth principles are the knowledge that He - the High - is the Hearer and the Seer. Neither the whispers of the innermost heart nor the secret thoughts and reflections are hidden from His Sight. The sound of the creeping of the black ant upon the solid rock in the darkest night is not beyond His Hearing. And how could He not see and hear when seeing and hearing are attributes of perfection not of defect? Could the created be more perfect than its Creator, the thing made more magnificent and more complete than the Maker? Or how could they ever be equal, no matter how much He might diminish in perfection while His creation and work increase therein?

3. 3. The Ninety-Nine Names of Allah[7]: Explanation and Meaning
Allah in Islam has ninety-nine names. Each of them present His attributes, and He can be called by any of them, from these 99 names we cover only few of them as an example:

"He is Allah, besides Whom there is no other god; the Sovereign, the Holy One, the Source of Peace (and Perfection), the Guardian of Faith, the Preserver of Safety, the Exalted in Might, the Compeller, the Supreme: Glory to Allah! (High is He) above the partners they attribute to Him." (Qur'an, 59:23)

Allah:
"It is the Name of the True Existent, Who unites the Attributes of Divinity, the qualified by the Qualities of Lordship, the unique

---

[7] This is a short portion of a chapter from al-Ghazali, translated by R. C. Stade, as McCarthy mentioned. It begins with a Tradition attributed to Abu Hurayra: "The Messenger of Allah-Allah's blessing and peace be upon him- said: Allah -Great and Glorious-has nine and ninety Names, one hundred minus one: He is Odd [i.e. single, unique] and loves the odd; whoso enumerates them will enter the Garden." (Then follows the enumeration of the ninety-nine Names.) McCarthy gave the list, and translated Ghazali's comments on the first few by way of example. In the following are three Names of Allah and the explanation of their meaning. I am quoting al-Ghazali from his book: *al-Maqsad al-Asna fi Sharh Ma'ani Asma' Allah al- Husna* [*The Noblest of Aims in the Explanation of Allah's Fairest Names*] in McCarthy's translation, 1980, pp. 296-300.

possessor of true Existence. For every being other than He is not entitled to existence by its essence, but simply derives existence from Him. So it, with respect to its essence, is perishing, but from the aspect adjacent to Him it is existent. So every existent is perishable except Him.

Note [fa'eda]:
Know that this Name, of the nine and ninety, is the greatest of the Names of Allah-Great and Glorious! For it denotes the Essence comprehending all the Divine Attributes without exception, whereas all the other individual Names denote only individual meanings, such as: knowledge, power, action, or something else. Also because it is the most proper of the Names, since no one can apply it to another either literally or figuratively, whereas by the other Names another may be named [denominated], e.g. the Powerful and the Knowing and the Merciful etc. So for these two reasons it is clear that this Name is the greatest of these Names.

Precision [daqiqa: fine point]:
It is conceivable that the creature may be qualified by something of all the other Names so that the Name may be applied to or predicated of him, e.g. the Merciful and the Knowing and the Indulgent and the Patient and the Very Grateful, etc.; but the Name is applied to creature in another way different from its predication of Allah-Great and Glorious! As for the meaning of this Name, it is peculiar to God in a special sense, and it is inconceivable that there be any sharing in it either figuratively or literally. Because of this specialness all the other Names are described as being "the Name of Allah"--Great and Glorious!-and are defined in relation to Him. So one says: the Patient and the Very Grateful and the King and the Compeller [Almighty] are among the Names of Allah--Great and Glorious! But one does not say: Allah is among the Names of the Very Grateful and the Patient. For that [Allah], inasmuch as it is more indicative of the Essence of the divine meanings and more peculiar to them, is better known and more manifest; hence there is no need to define it by something else, but others are defined in relation to it.

Remark [tanbih: alerting]:
The man's portion respecting this Name ought to be al-ta'alluh [deification, divinization,]. By this I mean that his heart and ardor be wholly engaged by Allah-Great and Glorious! He sees none but

Him, attends to no other, hopes in and fears only Him. How could it be otherwise when it has been understood from this Name that He is the True, Real Existent, and everything else is transient and perishing and null except through Him. So man first of all sees himself as the first thing perishing and worthless, just as the Apostle of God-God's blessing and peace upon him! saw himself when he said: "The truest verse uttered by the Arabs is the statement of Labid:

"Sorely everything except God is worthless,
And every happiness [comfort] without doubt is fleeting."

The Merciful, the Compassionate: [al-Rahman, al-Raheem]

"And your God is One God: there is no god but He, Most Gracious, Most Merciful." (Qur'an, 2:163)

Two Names derived from mercy (al-rahma). Mercy requires an object of mercy "marhum: a mercified", and there is no such object save that it is in need. One because of whom the need of the needy is satisfied without any intent and will and concern for the needy is not called or named "compassionate." And one who wishes to satisfy a needy man's need but does not satisfy it, if he be able to satisfy it, is not called "compassionate"; for if his wish were fulfilled, he would satisfy the need. But if he be powerless to satisfy the need, he may be called "compassionate" with regard to the graciousness which affects and influences him, but he is imperfect and defective. Perfect mercy [al-rahma al-tamma] is simply the pouring forth of good upon the needs and *one's Allah's* will for them out of concern for them. And inclusive mercy [al-rahma al-tamma] is that which includes the deserving and the undeserving. The mercy of Allah--Great and Glorious!-is perfect and all-embracing. It is perfect in so far as He wills to fulfill the needs of the needy and actually fulfills them. It is all-embracing in so far as it comprehends the deserving and the undeserving, and embraces this life and the afterlife, and includes necessities and needs and the advantages outside of them. So He is in truth the Absolute Merciful [al-Raheem al-Mutlaq].

Precision:
Mercy is not devoid of a painful empathy which befalls the merciful [compassionate] and moves him to satisfy the need of the object of mercy. But the Lord-Praised and Exalted He!-is deemed far above that. So perhaps you will think that to be a defect is the meaning of mercy. Know, then, that that is a perfection and not an imperfection in the meaning of mercy. That it is not an imperfection is clear from the fact that the perfection of mercy is by the perfection of its fruit. So long as the need of the needy is fulfilled perfectly, the object of mercy has no share in the suffering and affliction of the merciful, but the suffering of the merciful is simply due to the weakness and imperfection of his soul. And its weakness adds nothing respecting the aim of the needy after his need is perfectly satisfied. And that it is a perfection in the meaning of mercy is that one who is compassionate out of sensitiveness and suffering, almost as good as intends by his action the removal of the pain of sympathy from himself and will have had a regard for himself and will have exerted himself for a personal end-and that diminishes the perfection of the meaning of mercy. Rather the perfection of mercy is that his regard be directed toward the object of mercy for the latter's sake, not for the sake of finding ease from the pain of sympathy.

Note:
Al-Rahman is more specific and particularized than Al-Raheem, and for that reason no one other than Allah-Great and Glorious!-is named by it, whereas al-Raheem may be applied to other than Allah. So from this viewpoint al-Rahman is close to the Name of Allah Most High which functions like a proper name [i.e. Allah], though this [al-Rahman] is certainly derived from al-rahma [mercy]. For that reason Allah--Great and Glorious!-united the two of them and said:

"Say (Oh, Muhammad): Pray to Allah or pray to the Merciful [al-Rahman]: by whatever name you invoke Him (it is the same), for to Him belongs the Best Names" (Qur'an, 17.110).

From this aspect, and inasmuch as we have forbidden synonymity in the enumerated Names, it follows necessarily that one must distinguish between the meanings of the two Names. To be exact, the meaning of Al-Rahman is a kind of mercy beyond creatures' objects of power. And this mercy is connected with the beatitude of the afterlife. So Al-Rahman is He Who is compassionate toward servants or humans, first by creation of them, and secondly by guidance to the Faith and the causes of happiness, and thirdly by making them happy in the afterlife, and fourth by granting them the favor of looking at His gracious and noble Face.

Remark:
The servant's [man's] portion of the Name Al-Rahman is that he be merciful to Allah's heedless servants and turn them from the way of heedlessness to Allah-Great and Glorious!-by preaching and counsel, gently and not harshly, and that he look upon sinners or the disobedient with the eye of mercy, not that of contempt, and that every sin taking place in the world be like his own personal sin so that he spares no effort to remove it as far as he can out of mercy [compassion] for that sinner lest he be exposed to Allah's wrath and merit being far from Allah's presence.

And his portion of the Name Al-Raheem is that he leaves no want of a needy person without trying to satisfy it to the best of his ability, and abandon no poor person in his neighborhood and his town without undertaking to care for him and to drive away his need either by his own wealth, or by his repute, or by striving for him through intercession with another. If he is unable to do all that, then he will help him by private prayer [du'a'] or by manifesting grief because of his need, out of compassion and sympathy for him, so that he is, as it were, a sharer of his in his hurt and his need.

I think what was presented is sufficient to give an idea about the 99 names and their meanings.[8]

---

[8] After al-Malek, McCarthy listed the remaining Names of God, each followed by Stade's translation and that of Asin Palacios in Spanish Language too.

4. The Qur'anic Story of Creation

The Universe
Allah –the Exalted- is the Creator of everything. He created the universe in six days:

"Indeed, your Lord is Allah, Who created the heavens and the earth in six Days, then He established Himself on the Throne (of authority): He draweth the night as a veil over the day, each seeking the other in rapid succession: He created the sun, the moon, and the stars, (all) governed by laws under His Command. Is it not His to create and to govern? Blessed be Allah, the Cherisher and Sustainer of the Worlds!" (Qur'an, 7:54)

The universe and every portion in it was created by Allah in a meticulous way, and is governed by laws of absolute mathematical precision. Some of these laws might be unveiled to human understanding and intellectual discoveries, but some of them might stay mysteriously unknown until the end of the human life on earth.

Adam
Allah -the Exalted- created Adam from dust. The word "Adam" in Arabic is either derived from the Arabic words (adeem and adamah) which means the surface of the earth, or it is derived from the Arabic word adamah means tanned skin color (and thus it is related to the color of the dust or the surface of the earth). Or it is derived from the Arabic word al-adam (= ilfa), which means intimacy, closeness, union, and harmony.[9]

Allah created Adam as a human with human aspect we are aware of today: two hands, two legs, heart, five senses with their faculties, and the faculty of reasoning …etc. Allah –the Exalted- after fashioning Adam in this form, breathed in him from His spirit.

"When I have fashioned him (in due proportion) and breathed into him of My spirit, then fall you [the angels] down in obeisance unto him." (Qur'an, 15:29)

---

[9] See al-Razai's Dictionary (1989): p. 9.

In What Form or Fashion was Adam Created?
Many people think that Allah created Adam in "His image", meaning God duplicating His eternal image in the human form. In Islam, this would not be correct. In the following narration, from the tradition of the Prophet (pbuh), we find clarification to this issue:

"Abu Hurairah, may Allah be pleased with him, reported: Allah's Messenger (may peace be upon him) said:

Allah, the Exalted and Glorious, created Adam in His own image with His length of sixty cubits, and as He created him He told him to greet that group, and that was a party of angels sitting there, and listen to the response that they give him, for it would form his greeting and that of his offspring. He then went away and said: Peace be upon you! They (the angels) said: May there be peace upon you and the Mercy of Allah, and they made an addition of "Mercy of Allah". So he who would get into Paradise would get in the form of Adam, his length being sixty cubits, then the people who followed him continued to diminish in size up to this day" (Agreed upon; narrated by both Bukhari and Muslim)

Allah created Adam in "His image" meaning in the very image of Adam himself. Otherwise, humans would have an eternal fashion, and would all appear exactly alike.

Knowledge and Language:
Allah gave Adam knowledge and taught him the names of every thing and gave him the ability of both reasoning and language; by which the descendents of Adam carried on further knowledge, communication, discoveries, and further naming of things. When Allah placed all things before the angels and asked them to name these things, the angels said:

"They (angels) said: "Glory be to You, we have no knowledge except what you have taught us. Verliy, it is You, the All-Knower, the All-Wise." (Qur'an, 2:32)

Then Allah –the Exalted- asked Adam to name them, and Adam did inform the angels about the names of all things.

Eve

Adam slept and while he was sleep Allah created Eve (Hawwa') from one of his ribs. The reason Eve was called Hawwa' because she was created from a living being (Hayy) which is an Arabic word derived from Hayat (life):

Allah said:

"O mankind! Be dutiful to your Lord, who created you from a single person (Adam), and from him (Adam) He created his wife (Eve), and from them both He created many men and women; and fear Allah, through Whom you demand your mutual (rights), and (reverence) the wombs (that bore you): for Allah ever watches over you." (Qur'an, 4:1)

Eve, then, was married to Adam. Abdullah Ibn Abbas said: "Proclaim marriage, for it is the custom of your father Adam. There is nothing more beloved to Allah than marriage and nothing more hateful in His sight than divorce."[10]

The Covenant of Humans with Allah:

Allah –the Exalted- said:

"And (remember) when your Lord brought forth from the Children of Adam, from their loins, their descendants, and made them testify concerning themselves, (saying): "Am I not your Lord?" They said: "Yes! we testify," lest you should say on the Day of Judgment: "Of this we were never mindful." (Qur'an, 7:172)

Islam teaches that within Adam was the sperm containing all future descendants, and by answering: "Yes! We do testify" all future generations entered in covenant of knowledge and realization with Allah, and admitted that He is their Lord. One of the consequences of knowing that Allah is their Lord is to be obedient to Him.

---

[10] Al-Kisa'i (1997): p. 33.

Fitra

Fitra means that every single human is born with a state of intuitive ability of knowledge and of natural disposition of knowing Allah as the Creator. Fitra means that humans intuitively know that there is a creator of them and of this universe, and that this creator is their Lord.

Allah –the Exalted- said:

"So direct your face steadily and truly to the Faith. [Adhere to] the Fitra (intuitive ability of mankind to know their Lord) of Allah upon which He has made mankind: no change should there be in the creation of Allah: that is the standard Religion: but most of people do not know." (Qur'an, 30:30)

This Fitra is the epistemological state of knowing Allah as the Creator of heavens and earth and the Lord of everything. This ability of intuitively knowing Allah consciously exists in every single human, having the ability to reason. But this general state of Fitra in knowing the Lord is common to all without being specified in any form of religion, as the Prophet (pbuh) said:

"Abu Hurairah, may Allah be pleased with him, reported: Allah's Messenger (may peace be upon him) said:

Every infant is born in the state of fitra. It is his parents who make him a Jew, a Christian, and Magian, just as an animal gives birth to its young ones. Do you find any deficiency in their limbs." (Agreed upon: Bukhari and Muslim)

Angels, Jinn, Satan, and Iblis

Among the creations of Allah were the Angels who were created from light to worship Allah and glorify Him. They do not have worldly desires or material interests. They have certain duties to perform in this universe; whether in heaven or on earth. All angels are obedient to Allah.

The Jinn were created from fire. Some of the jinn are obedient to Allah and some are not.

Satan is from jinn. Satan disobeyed Allah, and attempted to lead humans to the disobedience of Allah. Iblis is a name of a Satan who is a jinn.

Adam's Relationship with the Angels and Iblis
After Adam (pbuh) named all things before the Angels manifesting the knowledge that was given to him by Allah. Allah asked the angels to bow to Adam as a sign of respect. The Angels obeyed the command of their Lord, except Iblis, who refused the command of Allah –the High–.

"And behold, We said to the angels: "Bow down to Adam:" and they bowed down: except Iblis: he refused and was arrogant: he was of those who reject Faith." (Qur'an, 2:34)

Iblis was a jinn, and jinn are created from fire, so in his rejection to obey the command of his Lord, Iblis made this argument:

"(Allah) said: "What prevented you from bowing down when I commanded you?" He said: "I am better than him: You created me from fire, and him from clay." (Qur'an, 7:12)

This argument was the first of its kind as a reference to certain elements, making his level of existence superior to that of man.

Allah –the Exalted the Merciful– warned Adam and Eve of the evil of Iblis saying:

"Then We said: "O Adam! verily, this is an enemy to you and your wife: so let him not get you both out of the Paradise, so that you will land in misery." (Qur'an, 20:117)

Adam and Eve in the Paradise:
Then Allah –the Exalted– told Adam to enjoy paradise with his wife Hawwa' (Eve), and to eat of the bountiful things therein; but to not approach one particular tree, otherwise they would both run into harm and transgression.
Then Satan tempted them, trying to make them disobey the command of Allah, telling them that the reason the Lord forbade them to eat from this tree is:

"But Satan whispered to him: he said, "O Adam! shall I lead you to the Tree of Eternity and to a kingdom that never decays?" (Qur'an, 20:120)

Satan further tried to convince them to eat from this tree by saying:

"he said: "Your Lord only forbade you this tree, save that you should become angels or become of the immortals." (Qur'an, 7: 20)

Iblis tempted Adam and Eve in an attempt to get them out of paradise and to lower their high rank among the creatures in paradise, and to deprive them the state of absolute happiness they were in. As a result Adam and Eve ate from the tree. Immediately after eating from the tree, they became aware and conscious about their faults and also of their nakedness:

"So by deceit he brought about their fall: Then when they tasted of the tree, that which was hidden from them of their shame (private parts) became manifest to them, and they began to sew together the leaves of the Garden over their bodies. And their Lord called unto them: "Did I not forbid you that tree, and tell you that Satan was an avowed enemy unto you?" (Qur'an, 7:22)

Notice that the command of Allah was not: "You shall not eat from this tree." The command specifically was: "do not approach this tree" meaning do not come close to or near the prohibited area because He, the Creator and most High, knows that human nature usually struggles with temptation and sometimes fails to avoid temptation. Thus, it is better to stay away from this area.
In Islam this is applicable to any command of prohibition, as a means of prevention and protection.

By this temptation Satan was able to make Adam and Eve slip from paradise and get them out of it depriving them of eternal happiness. Allah –the Exalted-commanded them to follow a certain order and they failed. Thus, Divine commands have both moral and legal implications, and as a result Allah –the Exalted- sent them all (Adam, Eve, and Satan) down to earth, telling them that on earth they would live for a specific period of time during which they would struggle against each other as enemies.

Allah said:

"We said: "Get you down, all, with enmity between yourselves. On earth will be your dwelling place and your means of livelihood (with enjoyment) for a time." (Qur'an, 2: 36)

Then Allah –The Merciful- taught Adam how to pray and how to supplicate for forgiveness. When Adam did, Allah forgave him. Thus, the original sin of our father Adam ended there.

Who Ate from the Tree Adam or Eve?
Notice that Adam was mentioned in the Qur'an as listening to the whispering of the Satan, However, after that, both Adam and Eve ate from the tree.

"Then Satan whispered to him: he said, "O Adam! shall I lead you to the Tree of Eternity and to a kingdom that never decays?" (Qur'an, 20:120)

Another support for the above is this authentic narration from the saying of the Prophet (pbuh):

"Anas bin Malik, may Allah be pleased with him reported: Allah's Messenger (may peace be upon him) said:

Allah would gather people on the Day of Resurrection and they would be concerned about it, ...and would say: if we could seek intercession with our Lord, we may be relieved from this predicament of ours. He (the Holy Prophet) said: They would come to Adam and say: Thou art Adam, the father of mankind, Allah created thee with His own hand and breathed unto thee of His spirit and commanded the angels and they prostrated before thee, so intercede for us with thy Lord so that He may relieve us from this position of ours. He would say: I am not in a position to do this, and would recall his error, and would feel shy of his Lord on account of that; go to Noah the first Messenger (after me) sent by Allah...." (Agreed upon; narrated by Bukhari and Muslim)

What About the Original Sin

Also notice that there is no original sin in Islam. After Adam was sent down to earth, he asked his Lord for forgiveness and Allah forgave him saying:

"Then learned Adam from his Lord words (of inspiration), and his Lord pardoned him (accepted his repentance); for He is the One Who forgives, the Most Merciful." (Qur'an, 2:37)

This was the first guidance sent from Allah to humans on earth. The Qur'an tells that guidance and revelation continued after that in order to help people achieve the best possible life on earth and to protect them from evil until they go back to their Lord; individually by death, or collectively at the time of the day of judgment.

After the first sin of Adam (pbuh) was forgiven the situation of the descendents of Adam depend on the response of the individual commitment, and obedience to the revelation and the guidance of their Lord.

"We said: "Get down all of you from it (the Paradise), then whenever comes to you guidance from Me, and whoever follows My guidance, on them shall be no fear, nor shall they grieve." (Qur'an, 2: 38)

The following is the story of creation from the Qur'an chapter 2, however, in other chapters of the Qur'an there are many verses that shed light on some details of this story:

The Qur'anic Story of Creation
(Qur'an, 2: 30-38)

"30. And [mention, O Muhammad], when your Lord said to the angels, "Indeed, I will make upon the earth a successive authority." They said, "Will You place upon it one who causes corruption therein and sheds blood, while we declare Your praise and sanctify You?" He [Allah] said, "Indeed, I know that which you do not know."

31. And He taught Adam the names – all of them. Then He showed them to the angels and said, "Inform Me of the names of these, if you are truthful."

32. They said, "Exalted are You; we have no knowledge except what You have taught us. Indeed, it is you who is the Knowing, the Wise."

33. He said, "O Adam, inform them of their names." And when he had informed them of their names, He said, "Did I not tell you that I know the unseen [aspects] of the heavens and the earth? And I know what you reveal and what you have concealed."

34. And [mention] when We said to the angels, "Prostrate before Adam"; so they prostrated, except for Iblees. He refused and was arrogant and became of the disbelievers.

35. And We said, "O Adam, dwell, you and your wife, in Paradise and eat therefrom in [ease and] abundance from wherever you will. But do not approach this tree, lest you be among the wrongdoers."

36. But Satan caused them to slip out of it and removed them from that [condition] in which they had been. And We said, "Go down, [all of you], as enemies to one another, and you will have upon the earth a place of settlement and provision for a time."

37. Then Adam received from his Lord [some] words, and He accepted his repentance. Indeed, it is He who is the Accepting of repentance, the Merciful.
38. We said, "Go down from it, all of you. And when guidance comes to you form Me, whoever follows My guidance – there will be no fear concerning them, nor will they grieve."

Different Levels of the Creation of Allah –the Exalted-.

Creation of Allah -The Creator-

'Alam al-Shahada	**'Alam al-Ghaib**
('alam al-Mulk)	('alam al-Malakut)
↓	↓
The Universe	Other Possible Worlds
Human Beings	Angels
Animals	Jinn
Plants	Satan
Non-Living things such as: Water, Stones, Fire, and the like	The Unknown to our knowledge & imagination

5. Structuring the Life of Man by Revelation

Mankind and Satan on Earth
Allah according to his absolute knowledge, love, and mercy, kept sending guidance in the form of revelation to humans on earth in order to organize their life on earth; establishing their benefits, telling them how to achieve justice among themselves telling them what is prohibited and what is permitted, and the most important is to warn them about their enemy (Satan):

"O Children of Adam! let not Satan seduce you, in the same manner as he got your parents out of the Paradise, stripping them of their clothing, to expose their private parts. Indeed, he and his tribe watch you from a position where you cannot see them: We made the Evil Ones friends (only) to those without Faith." (Qur'an, 7:27)

Because Satan took an oath to destroy the offspring of Adam and Eve:

"He [Satan] said: "Because you have thrown me out of the Way. Surely I will lie in wait for them on Your Straight Way:
Then I will come to them from before them and behind them, from their right and their left: and You will not find most of them as thankful ones. " (Qur'an, 7: 16-17)

Allah –the Exalted- asked humans to follow the messengers:

"O Children of Adam! If there come to you Messengers from amongst you, reciting to you My Verses, then whosoever becomes pious and righteous, on them shall be no fear nor shall they grieve." (Qur'an, 7:35)

First Crime: The Story of the Two Sons of Adam
Among the children of Adam were Qabeel and Habeel (Cain and Abel). Cain was a farmer and Abel was a shepherd. Each one of them decided to offer a sacrifice to their Lord. Abel, as a shepherd, took the best and finest ram and sacrificed it. Cain, as a farmer, took the best grain and placed it as an offering. The sacrifice of Abel was accepted but not that of Cain. As a result Cain felt certain

envy toward his brother. Satan tempted him to kill his brother. The Qur'an describes this story:

"And recite to them the truth of the story of the two sons of Adam. When each offered a sacrifice (to Allah), it was accepted from one but not from the other. Said the latter: "I will surely kill you." The former said; "Verily, Allah accepts only from those who are righteous.
"If you do stretch your hand against me to kill me, I shall never stretch my hand against you to kill you: for I fear Allah, the Lord of the Worlds." (Qur'an, 5:27-28)

The worst form of evil is killing. The Qur'an teaches that killing a human soul is like killing the human race. Every human being is a unique representative of the human race. If all humans were dead except one, then he or she would be the representative of mankind on earth. Thus, every human deserves the rights and benefits enjoyed by the human race. Every single human deserves dignity.

Is it Evil or Veil?
Cain became more obsessed with the thought of killing his brother. As jealousy, envy, and anger erupt inside the human soul, the heart becomes stiff and the mind can become veiled and unable to see the consequences. The vision of Cain was limited by the effect of evil. His inner dialogue became his only source of knowledge. Within this selfish dialogue Satan find a conduit to talk to human. Cain consulted no one, sought no guidance, thinking that his offspring would be successful; his foresight was blocked by blind evil:

"So his soul encouraged him the murder of his brother, so he killed him and became among the losers." (Qur'an, 5:30)

This murder proved that humans on earth must be guided by revelation that establishes and achieves the benefits of humans equally. The human mind tends toward temporary benefits, which are the benefits of some over the other. Thus, Allah sent more messages and revelations to guide the life of man on earth.

Continuation of Revelation
The same message that was sent to the descendents of Adam was sent to Noah. One of Noah's sons was called Shem (Sam, in

Arabic), and the descendents of Shem are called Semite (Sami), and Semitic people are Jews and Arabs.

Names and Number of Prophets:
Allah sent many prophets and messengers to guide and regulate human life on earth; by establishing equality, justice, true spirituality, moral commitment, and happiness. The Qur'an mentioned the names of 25 prophets in specific, and many others were just mentioned with no names, Allah said:

"And We have already sent Messengers before you. Among them are those [whose stories] We have related to you, and among them are those [whose stories] We have not related to you. It was not for any Messenger to bring a Sign [or verse] except by the permission of Allah. (Qur'an, 40:78)

Names of Prophets Mentioned in the Qur'an
(Peace be upon them all)

	Qur'anic Name	Biblical Name
1.	Adam	Adam
2.	Idris	Enoch
3.	Nuh	Noah
4.	Hud	-------
5.	Salih	-------
6.	Ibrahim	Abraham
7.	Isma'eel	Ishmael
8.	Ishaq	Isaac
9.	Lut	Lot
10.	Ya'qub	Jacob
11.	Yusuf	Joseph
12.	Shu'aib	-------
13.	Ayyub	Job
14.	Musa	Moses
15.	Haroon	Aaron
16.	Dhul-Kifl	Ezekiel
17.	Dawud	David
18.	Sulaiman	Solomon
19.	Ilyas	Elias
20.	Al Yasa'	Elisha
21.	Yunus	Jonah
22.	Zakariyah	Zechariah
23.	Yahya	John
24. 'Isa	Jesus
25.	Muhammad	-------

Books of Allah
Among the messages and books that Allah sent to humanity are the followings:

The Suhuf of Abraham   (The Testament of Abraham)

The Taurat   (or Torah; The law of Moses)

The Zaboor   (The Psalms of David)

The Injeel   (The Gospel of Jesus)

The Qur'an

The Qur'an teaches that some of these books have disappeared, However, some of them still exist such as the Torah, The Psalms of David, and the Gospels of Jesus, but the Qur'an teaches also that the remaining books were modified and changed by people in order to serve the interest of the rich or the strong or those in authority or to show superiority of a nation over others, etc., and thus by this modification these books are no longer the exact word of God, and it can not achieve justice and equality in the life of people.

6. Prophet Abraham

Abraham (Ibraheem in Arabic), peace be upon him, was one of the descendants of Noah. He has a special place in religion and in the history of humanity. Allah gave Abraham special status by choosing him as a prophet to deliver His Divine message to humanity. The religion that Allah revealed to Abraham is called Islam, which I will discuss shortly after this paragraph.

Abraham married Sarah who did not bear children for him, so she suggested he marry their servant, Hager, as another wife. Hager gave birth to Ishmael (Isma'eel), and meanwhile Sarah conceived a child named Isaac (Ishaq). The son of Isaac was called Jacob also called Israel later on, Jacob (Ya'qob in Arabic) had twelve sons, one of them called Josef (Yusuf). The 12 sons made the twelve tribes of the children of Israel. Moses was one of the descendants, who received revelation from Allah, and other descendants such as David, Solomon received revelation. Jesus, the son of Mary, was also one of those who received revelation.

From Ishmael, the other son of Abram, came many descendents. The one who received revelation among them was Muhammad the Prophet, who received the last revelation from Allah and was the seal of prophethood.

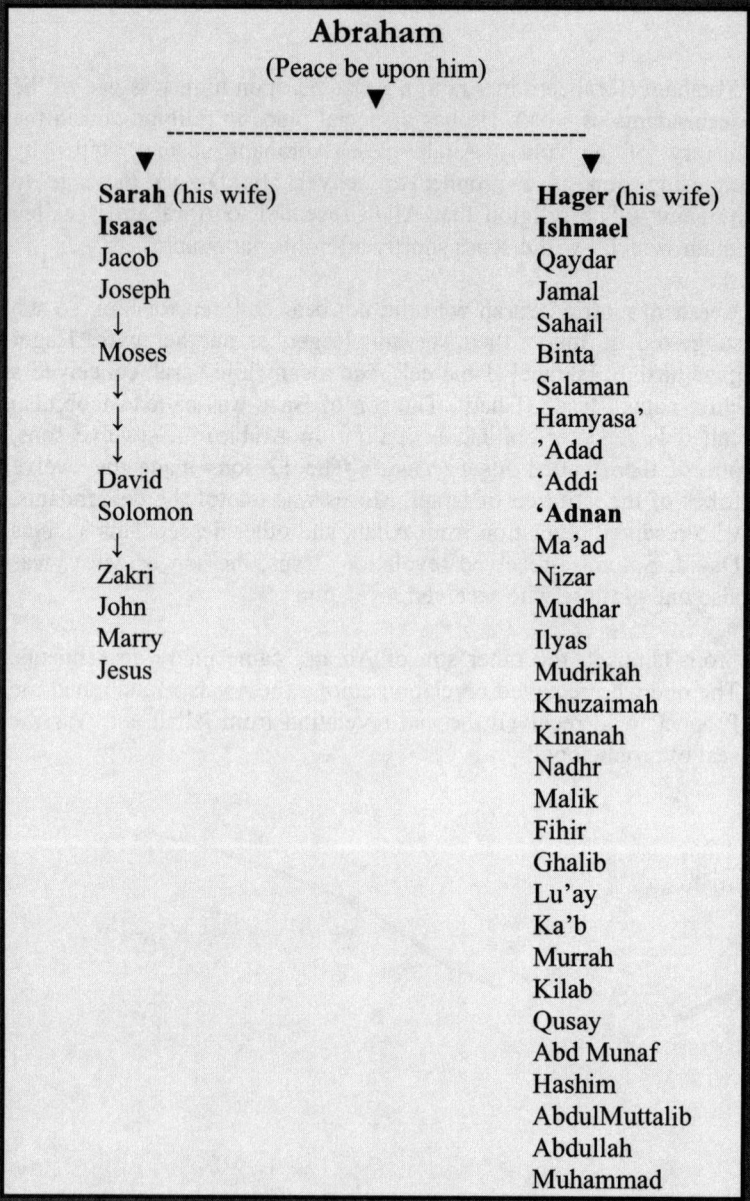

7. The Meaning of the Word "Islam"

The word "Islam" in the Arabic language has two cohesive meanings dynamically connected:

First: The word Islam derived from the Arabic root of three letters: (S.L.M.) which means "peace". However, the practice of Islam as a religion cannot be accomplished properly, in its full sense, unless the will of a worshiper is totally submitted to the will of the Creator: Allah (The God).

Second: The meaning of the word Islam refers to the total submission of the will of human beings to the will of God. The Arabic root for this submission is *Aslama* which means to turn oneself over to. By this submission, and only by this surrender and submission, a human can reach life with "peace" and happiness on spiritual, personal, and social levels.

Notice that if you work for a company and you refuse to submit your will to that of your employer, then you will not live in peace. If you live in a country and you refuse to submit your will to the will of its law, then peace will be out of your reach, and your life will be restless. Islam is similar to that; so if you live in this universe as a Muslim, then you should submit to the will of its creator.

Islam is the religion that Allah, the Creator Himself, gave to mankind, and the religion that He accepts from them: Allah said:

"The religion before Allah is Islam (submission to His Will)." (Qur'an, 3:19)

Islam can be the religion of any person male or female, who willingly accepts the faith by declaring the Shahada and testifies that there is no deity worthy of worship but Allah, and testifies that Muhammad is His messenger.

Can Muslims Force People to Accept Islam?
Notice that there is no compulsion in this religion; meaning that you cannot force or coerce people to accept Islam as their system of belief. There are good reasons showing why this is impossible in Islam:

First: forcing people to accept Islam as a religion is against the command of the religion itself; it is against the command of Allah – the Exalted- who clearly said in the Qur'an in one of the verses:

"**There is no compulsion in religion.** Verily, the Right Path has become distinct from the wrong path. Whoever disbelieves *Taghut* [false deities] and believes in Allah then he has grasped the most trustworthy hand-hold, that never breaks. And Allah is All-Hearer, All-knower." (Qur'an, 2:256) (emphasis mine)

Second: religion is a faith that settles deeply in the heart. People cannot be forced to believe something in their hearts. People can say something by tongues and have the exact opposite in their hearts.

Third: Allah wants people to worship Him out of their total acceptance and absolute devotion.

Fourth: Islam is a choice of voluntary surrender and submission of the human will to the will of the Creator. It would be, therefore, contradictory to force someone to submit his or her will to Allah.

The Overflowing Love: Three Dimensions of Submission
To submit one's will totally to the will of Allah is to absorb with love and manifest with devotion this religion in all aspects of one's life. When you love the Lord, the love overflows from your heart to the rest of your body. Thus, you act with love, and when you act with love you become a beloved person, and when you become a beloved person you live in peace. Living in peace is the ultimate happiness. Islam is rich and does enrich the life of man. Islam requires devotion on three levels:
- Saying by the tongue, articulating the belief: " I bear witness that there is no god but Allah, and I bear witness that Muhammad (pbuh) is His messenger."
- To believe in these words and have faith in them within the heart.
- Manifestation of this belief with action.

8. The Qur'an

Muslims believe that the Qur'an is the miraculous word of Allah, that is perfected and revealed to His messenger Muhammad (pbuh) in the Arabic language, transmitted to humans by continuous testimony (tawatur), and is protected from any change or modification.

"We have made it a Qur'an in Arabic" (Qur'an, 43:3)

The Qur'an was revealed in order to achieve justice and to realize the benefits of people on earth and to help people achieve their happiness in this life and in the hereafter.

By this definition we can attempt to elaborate and specify further points by logic of definition, noticing that every definition which affirms a certain thing negates other things at the same time:

1. Every revelation of Allah revealed to any messenger other than Muhammad (pbuh) is not Qur'an.

2. Every word or speech that is not the word of Allah is not Qur'an, even though it is in Arabic.

3. The Arabic interpretation (Tafseer) of the Qur'an is not Qur'an although it is in the Arabic language and deals solely with the Qur'an.

4. The translation of the Qur'an into other languages is not Qur'an; it is only the meanings of the Qur'an.

5. The Qur'an reveals a religion that is perfected and completed, Allah –the Exalted said:

"This day I have perfected your religion for you, completed. My favor upon you, and have chosen for you Islam as your religion. But as for him who is forced by severe hunger, with no inclination to sin, then surely, Allah is Oft-Forgiving, Most Merciful." (Qur'an, 5:3)

6. The Qur'an was gradually revealed in portions. Designated people among the companions of the Prophet wrote it down. Those people were called Kuttab al-Wahi, or writers of the revelation. Thus, its continuous testimony or tawatur presents its authenticity which is proven and accepted within Islam. Allah says in the Qur'an:

"And [it is] a Qur'an which We have divided [into parts], in order that you might recite it to men at intervals. And We have revealed it by stages [in 23 years]."(Qur'an, 17:106)

In addition to dealing with particular events, the Qur'an was revealed piecemeal for another reason, as Allah said:

"We shall make you to recite [the Qur'an], so you [O Muhammad] shall not forget [it]." (Qur'an, 87:6)

If people ask why it was not revealed all, at once, then the answer comes from the Qur'an itself:

"And those who disbelieve say: Why is the Qur'an not revealed to him all at once? Thus [it is sent down in parts], that We may strengthen your heart thereby. And We have arranged it in right order." (Qur'an, 25:32)

7. The Qur'an is protected from any change or modification, Allah said:

"We have, without doubt, sent down the Message; and We will assuredly guard it (from corruption)." (Qur'an, 15:9)

8. The Qur'an is the word of Allah and is impossible to be produced by humans and non-humans, in this sense it is miraculous. Allah said:

"Say: "If the whole of mankind and Jinns were to gather together to produce the like of this Qur'an they could not produce the like thereof, even if they helped one another." (Qur'an, 17:88)

9. The Qur'an is miraculous in challenging the ability of man to produce a similar chapter of it, no matter how short that chapter is. Allah said:

"And if you are in doubt as to what We have revealed to Our servant, then produce a Sura [chapter] of the like thereof and call your witnesses [supporters and helpers] besides Allah, if you are truthful.
But if you do not, and you can never do it, then fear the Fire whose fuel is men and stones which is prepared for the disbelievers." (Qur'an, 2:23,24)

10. The Qur'an was revealed to Muhammad (pbuh) in portions and parts or piecemeal over a period of 23 years in relation to particular events and spiritual teachings.

"And [it is] a Qur'an which We have divided [into parts], in order that you might recite it to men at intervals. And We have revealed it by stages [in 23 years]."(Qur'an, 17:106)

11. The Qur'an was revealed in two places: Mecca, where Muhammad (pbuh) was born and lived first, and Madina where he was forced to migrate.

12. The revelation of the Qur'an ended upon the death of the Prophet Muhammad (pbuh), and there was no revelation after that.

13. The Qur'an is the seal of revelation.

14. The Qur'an has 114 sura or chapters. Each sura has a specific name. The first sura is called: The Opening or al-Fatiha and the last sura is called: al-Nas. Among the names of other suras or chapters you can find: Mary, The Women, Abraham, Joseph, The Bees, The Light, and others.

15. Each sura consists of ayat or verses or signs, they vary in length -- some of them are two or three words and some are two lines or more. The total number of the all ayat in Qur'an is 6235.

16. Each ayah consists of words, and each word consists of letters. The total number of letters is 330733.

17. The recitation of the Qur'an is an act of worship; it is not like reading any other book. The recitation of each letter is rewarded the same as ten good deeds, according to the teaching of the Prophet (pbuh).

18. The word "Qur'an" in the Arabic language is derived from the root word qera'a which means: to read. Thus Qur'an means Reading or Recitation.

The first revelation to Muhammad (pbuh) was:

**"Read! In the name of your Lord who created,
Created man, from a clot [a piece of thick coagulated blood]
Read!
And your Lord is Most Generous,
Who taught [the writing] by the Pen,
Taught man that which he knew not." (Qur'an, 96:1-5)**

19. The Qur'an is the main source of legislating, organizing, and enhancing the life of Muslims; it is the source of spiritual teaching, moral responsibility, and legal obligations.

As far as being the source of regulation the Qur'an includes Ahkam or legal rules for the belief itself, the moral life such as right and wrong, and the practical part of rights and duties. I will discuss this later.

20. The Qur'an is also a source of healing in the physical sense. Whether it is a physical illness, psychological stress, depression, emotional instability, and the like. Allah –the Exalted- said:

"We send down in the Qur'an that which is a healing and a mercy to those who believe." (Qur'an, 17:82)

Since the time of the Prophet until the present time Muslims have been using certain verses from the Qur'an for healing and protection from magic and evil spells.

PART TWO

ISLAMIC DIVINE LAW (SHARI'AH)

9. Structuring the Life of Man by Divine Law

The Five Ahkam

Allah -the Exalted- said in the Qur'an:

"In the Law of Equality there is (saving of) Life to you, O you people of understanding; that you may become righteous." (Qur'an, 2: 179)

Rules and regulations are very beneficial to human life, but if they are not enforced they are seldom obeyed. Take for example regulation of speed limits, or prohibition of drinking and driving. These regulations are very beneficial to everyone; it saves the life of the driver, the lives of others, it protects the property of the driver, property of others, property of the state, family members, and many other things, but this regulation cannot achieve its goal without a law to enforce it on the society and then a system of legislation, courts, and punishments. Similar to that is the regulation of the benefits in the Qur'an; it is enforced by a set of punishments.

The regulations and the ruling values in Islam are called Ahkam. One ruling value or regulation of actions is called Hukm. There are five kind of Ahkam in the Islamic Divine Law. Let us discuss them in some detail.

9.1. Five Ahkam or Ruling Values in Shari'ah
These five categories of ahkam are legal and moral regulations and are related to the behavior of humans in their relationship with Allah.

What is a Hukm (a legal rule)?
Hukm is the word and command of Allah that is addressed and related specifically to the actions, or behaviors, or deeds of humans who are capable of performing these commands.

From this definition we can conclude that in Islam the ruling values of behavior and moral responsibility or legal obligation are derived from:
- The word of Allah (through the Qur'an)
- The tradition of the Prophet Muhammad (pbuh) (through the Sunnah)
- The consensus (Ijma') of 'Ulama' or scholars of Islamic law in light of the Qur'an and Sunnah
- From Qiyas.

This legal regulation, or hukm, commands either permission or prohibition. It is either in the form of a request or a demand (talab) to do a particular thing, or a demand to avoid doing a particular thing. This request or demand might also be in the form of a binding obligation or could be in a form of giving choice, as we will see in textual examples from the Qur'an and Sunnah.

The Hukm, or legal regulation, might give the believer the freedom of choice in making a decision whether to do a particular thing or not, without giving specific preference to the choice made by the believer. This is called takhieer in Arabic.

The Hukm or legal obligation might also be in the form of making one thing as a cause of the other or its condition or prevention.

For example the following Ayat are Hukm of prohibition:

"O you who believe! Enter not houses other than your own, until you have asked permission and greeted those in them: that is best for you, in order that you may remember." (Qur'an, 24:27)

"And do not come near to adultery. Indeed, it is ever an immorality and is evil as a way." (Qur'an, 17:32)

Hukm is the legal command establishing what is prohibited and what is not, for example this following verse is not a hukm; it is only a description about natural phenomenon:

"It is not permitted to the Sun to catch up the Moon, nor can the Night outstrip the Day: each (just) swims along in (its own) orbit (according to law)." (Qur'an, 36:40)

The following verse is a hukm because it regulates something, making it forbidden and obligatory on every Muslims to avoid:

"O you who believe! Intoxicants and gambling, [dedication of] stones, and [divination by] arrows, are an abomination of Satan's handiwork. So avoid that in order that you may be successful." (Qur'an, 5:90)

Who is Legally and Morally Obligated (Mukallaf)?
Every Muslim, male or female, who is mature by reaching the age of puberty, and mentally competent is obligated to follow the commands of Allah. For the Prophet Muhammad said:

"Allah's commands exclude those who are asleep till he wakes up, and the young until reaching puberty, and the insane till they become mentally competent."

Thus, there are three requirements for legal obligation and moral responsibility:

1. Islam; which excludes non-Muslims.
2. Maturity (having reached puberty); which excludes infants, babies, and children.
3. Sound Rationality, consisting of two parts:
    A. Consciousness; which exclude people in sleep, anesthetic, comatose people, and the like.
    B. Mental competence; which excludes the insane, mentally ill and similar cases.

The Nature of Allah's Commands
All the commands of Allah to humans are within the realm of human capability and capacity. There is not a single command in the Qur'an that humans cannot carry out or perform.

"Allah burdens not a person beyond his scope. He gets reward for that which he has earned, and he is punished for that [evil] which he has earned." (Qur'an, 2:286)

In the Islamic Divine law the Ahkam and the legal regulations in regard to all human behavior can be divided into five categories:

9.2. Wajeb or Fardh (Required, Obligatory):

This category would include obligations such as daily prayer, obligatory fasting, etc., which are obligatory on every Muslim, male or female, who have fulfilled the requirements of takleef, or the ability to do them. The requirements of takleef that every Muslim should fulfill in order to perform these obligations are:

First, being mature by reaching the age of puberty (children are not obligated in Islam, but they are encouraged).

Second: by having sound reasoning (insane, comatose people, or people in a similar unconscious states are not obligated).

This type of required behavior is binding and it is established by definitive proof in the Qur'an and Sunnah. The performance of Wajeb or Fardh acts is rewarded. According to the Qur'an and Sunnah, if a Muslim neglects performing these required behaviors they would be punished, both in this world and the hereafter.

The Fardh or obligations are divided into two kinds:

> One is called *Fardhu 'Ayn* which means individual or personal duties that every Muslim is responsible to do. Each Muslim is responsible for their own prayers, almsgiving and fasting and are held individually accountable for the performance of these duties.

> Second: are those called *Fardhu Kifaya*, which means collective duties, such as attendance at funeral prayers, or commanding the good and forbidding evil. If some member of the community did this fard in a way that fulfills the goal, then it is no longer obligatory on the rest of the community to do it, and they are absolved from this duty. Those who perform this duty are the ones who will be rewarded. If no one achieves this fard, then the whole community will be held accountable.

9.3. Mandoob (Recommended):

This hukm is also called: mustahabb, masnoon, and nafl. Mandoob is any act that is commendable but not required. While there is no punishment for the neglect of duties which are Mandoob, there is reward for performing them.

The Mandoob or recommended acts include extra prayers, fasting Monday and Thursday, praying sunat alfajr, charitable acts, and pious deeds of different kinds. For example:

"O you who believe! When you deal with each other, in transactions involving future obligations in a fixed period of time, reduce them to writing." (Qur'an, 2:282)

Documenting transactions and debt among people is not obligatory but recommended in order to protect the rights of people and their inheritances in cases of denial or forgetfulness. Although the Qur'anic word "write" gives the meaning of obligatory command in Arabic, writing down debts is not Wajeb but recommend, because in the rest of the ayah there is an explanation in the form of 'If you trust each other, then there is no need to the writing' which renders the action as only Mandoob. Since the command of Allah in the Wajeb or obligatory is not conditional, rather it is imperative.

9.4. Mubah (Permitted but Morally Indifferent):

This is also called: ja'ez and halal (lawful). Mubah is any act that is left to the personal decision and to individual liberty. Muslims can make the decision whether or not to perform any act that is considered Mubah. There is neither reward nor punishment for the performance or avoidance of the Mubah. For example Allah -the Exalted-said:

"This day are[all] things good and pure made lawful to you. The food of the People of the Book is lawful to you and yours is lawful to them. [Lawful to you in marriage] are [not only] chaste women who are Believers, but chaste women among the People of the Book, revealed before your time, when you give them their due dowers, and desire chastity, not lewdness, nor secret intrigues. If any one rejects faith, fruitless is his work, and in the Hereafter he will be in the ranks of those who have lost [all spiritual good]." (Qur'an, 5:5)

The Mubah is usually called halal (lawful), the reference to which is usually associated with the word halal or any other word similar in meaning in Arabic such as:

"It is no fault in the blind nor in one born lame, nor in one afflicted with illness, nor in yourselves, that you should eat in your own houses, or those of your fathers, or your mothers, or your brothers, or your sisters, or your father's brothers, or your father's sisters, or your mother's brothers, or your mother's sisters, or in houses of which the keys are in your possession, or in the house of a sincere friend of yours: there is no blame on you, whether you eat in company or separately. But if you enter houses, salute each other - a greeting of blessing and purity as from Allah. Thus does Allah make clear the Signs to you: that you may understand." (Qur'an, 24:61)

There is a rule in Islamic law that all things in their original or natural state are Mubah (halal or lawful) unless there is a regulation of their prohibition because Allah -the Exalted- said in the Qur'an:

"He is Who created for you all that is on earth [outside the earth or hidden inside it]." (Qur'an, 2:29)

Although there is neither reward for doing mubah nor punishment for avoiding it, the intention might turn a mubah act into a rewarding act. For example eating with the sincere intention to strengthen your body so you can work more and help your parents is an act of reward, because of the sincere intention toward the parents.

9.5. Makrooh (Discouraged or Abominable):
An act that avoiding its doing is preferable over doing it. One such act would be divorce, for the Prophet Muhammad (pbuh) said:

"The most abominable of permissible things in the sight of Allah is divorce."

However, for acts of doing makrooh there is no punishment, and for the avoidance of these acts there is reward.

Another example: the Prophet Muhammad (pbuh) made it clear that it is makrooh to offer to buy something for which another person has made an offer to purchase. Or trying to offer an engagement to a woman who was already engaged to another person.

Makrooh is the opposite of mandoob, meaning that the neglecting of a mandoob act is discouraged and leads to a makrooh.

9.6. Haram (Forbidden or Prohibited):

It is also called mahdoor. Haram is any act that is prohibited by the religion. These acts are binding by definitive proof in the Qur'an and Sunnah. For the performance of haram there is punishment and for the avoidance of haram there is reward.

Some examples of haram are killing, theft, unlawful sexual activity or adultery, drinking alcohol, and gambling.

The prohibited acts are clearly mentioned in Islam with the word of prohibition or other words similar in meaning in the Arabic language. An example is this verse from the Qur'an, where Allah - the Exalted- says:

"Prohibited to you (for marriage) are: your mothers, daughters, sisters; father's sisters, mother's sisters; brother's daughters, sister's daughters; foster-mothers (who gave you suck), foster-sisters; your wives' mothers; your step-daughters under your guardianship, born of your wives to whom you have gone, no prohibition if you have not gone in; (those who have been) wives of your sons proceeding from your loins; and two sisters in wedlock at one and the same time, except for what is past; for Allah is Oft-Forgiving, Most Merciful." (Qur'an, 4:23)

Another example from the Qur'an:

"Those who unjustly eat up the property of orphans, eat up a fire into their own bodies: they will soon be enduring a blazing fire!" (Qur'an, 4:10)

By doing what is haram or prohibited a person is subjecting himself to punishment; in this world or in the hereafter. Specific punishments are prescribed penalties and are applied according to

Islamic Divine law, and can only be performed by an Islamic court with qualified judges.

According to the tradition of the Prophets, abstaining from haram is an act that deserves the rewards that are enjoyable in the hereafter.

Every prohibited thing in Islam is prohibited, by the Qur'an and Sunnah, in order to secure benefits, the rights of people, to enhance the society, or to prevent harm.

Haram or the prohibited are of two kinds:

> The first type is haram *lidhatihi*, meaning that it is harmful itself, and it becomes forbidden for the harm that is intrinsically possessed. Harm will be inflicted on the user of such a thing. An example of this is found in the Qur'an, where Allah -the Exalted- said:
>
> "He has only forbidden you dead meat, and blood, and the flesh of swine" (Qur'an, 2:173)
>
> The meat of carrion is prohibited for the harm that it causes to the user. The same can be said about killing and stealing. Adultery, murder, and theft, are all forbidden for the same reason.
>
> The Second kind is haram *lighayrihi* or an act that is forbidden for a reason other than itself. This kind of haram is not harmful in itself, and might be very useful, but it is associated with something else that deprives it its value and turns it to haram. An example would be as follows: prayer is wajeb, but to pray in a house or on land that is taken illegally and unlawfully from others make the prayer itself unacceptable. A contract of business or sale that takes place during the time of the Friday congregational prayer is a haram of this kind, although sale and business is not forbidden, but during this specific time it becomes haram lighayrihi.

The Five Ahkam

Wajeb (Obligatory)   Haram (Forbidden)

Mubah (Permissible)

Mandoob (Recommended)   Makrooh (Discouraged)

10. The Sources of Islamic Divine Law (Shari'ah)

Shari'ah is the Islamic Divine Law. It is derived from the Arabic word Shara'a which means "to prescribe" or "to enact". Qur'an and the Sunnah of the Prophet Muhammad are the main sources of Shari'ah. However, Ijma' and Qiyas are also reliable sources of legislation in the area of unregulated benefits, thus, we can say that Shari'ah is derived from the following sources: Qur'an, Sunnah, Ijma', and Qiyas. I will discuss each one briefly.

10.1. Qur'an: The First Source of Islamic Shari'ah

The Qur'an is the main source Shari'ah. Thus it is the main source of Muslims' method of life in its total ranks and various aspects. Allah -Almighty- called this Qur'an: Huda meaning Guidance that leads people to the right path.

"This is the Book about which there is no doubt, a guidance for those conscious of Allah." (Qur'an, 2:2)

Allah also called the Qur'an Furqan meaning a criterion by which people can distinguish right from wrong, truth from falsehood, rights from duties, and the beneficial from the harmful.

The Qur'an covers many areas such as belief itself, moral responsibility, legal obligation, social justice, family, history, nature, benefits, spirituality, and happiness of people in this life and in the hereafter.

Although the Qur'an is not a legal document it includes within its regulation of what is beneficial, a portion that is deeply legislative. Among these aspects are the rights and duties of people toward each other, and their relation to their Lord. I will discuss this part with more details in the following chapter on the divisions of shari'ah.

The language of the Qur'an in regard to Ahkam and legal regulations is of two kinds:

First: it is specified clearly and prescribed with no need for interpretation; and thus it is definitive in meaning or *Qat'i*. An example of this qat'i is the command of praying or fasting, the prohibition of usury in both ways of lending money or borrowing money or the prescribed punishment of eighty lashes in cases of false accusation or Qadhf. The punishment of such harming acts are quantitatively set, and mathematics and numbers are so clear in references, therefore, there is no need for reflection and interpretation for this text.

Second: the text is not so definitive and it is open to interpretation. This kind of text is called speculative or *Dhanni*. In the case of speculative text the interpretation of such is only a duty and work of some 'Ulama or scholars who are authorized, and are highly qualified by reaching the highest rank of understanding the Qur'an, Qur'anic Sciences, the tradition of the Prophet, the Arabic language, and being able, skilled, and talented in logical inference. This person is called Mujtahid and his or her work is called Ijtihad. Ijtihad is encouraged in Islam in order to understand Shari'ah. An example of this is the command of Allah to rub or wipe the head during Wudu':

"O you who have believed! When you rise up for prayer, wash your faces, and your forearms to the elbows, and wipe over your heads and wash your feet to the ankles." (Qur'an, 5:6)

The command of rubbing the head is qat'i, however, how big is the area to be rubbed is speculative; is it the whole head or portion of it?

In this latter case Mujtahids can give their personal interpretation based on the understating of the Qur'an itself first, or on saying or doing of the Prophet, if he can find this as a support, and other available sources, as we will discuss later. As a result different Mujtahid might give different ideas, but the variety of such in jurisprudence is useful because it gives the individual and the community the liberty of choosing that which is most beneficial to them.

Who is the Mujtahid?
A Mujtahid is a Muslim scholar who have the knowledge, talent, skills of concluding or inferring Islamic legal opinions from detailed sources and evidence. A Mujtahid must be very well

acquainted with Qur'an and Sunnah and the objectives of the Islamic Divine law, as these two sources are the main sources of legislation. They also must be skilled in the Arabic language, history, literature, and life experience will be very supportive. This Mujtahid is also called Faqeeh (Jurist) or 'Alim (Scholar) or Mufti.

From the process of doing Ijtihad over the issues that needed to be speculated and interpreted there emerged in Islamic religion four schools of Ijtihad and jurisprudence that are still practiced today, and two other schools that are less followed in number. I will return to these schools under the divisions of Shari'ah.

Some of the Famous Mujtahids are:
Abu Hanifa
Malik Ibn Anas
Ja'far al-Sadiq
Ash-Shafe'i
Ahmad Ibn Hanbal
Al-Awza'i
Sufian ath-Thauri
Abu Hamid al-Ghazali
Ibnu Taimia
Ibn Hazm

10.2. Sunnah: The Second Source of Islamic Shari'ah
In this context of studying Shari'ah we can define Sunnah as the tradition of the Prophet Muhammad; what he said, what he did, and what he saw and approved of.

Sunnah is the second source of legislation in the Islamic Shari'ah. It comes after Qur'an; which is the first and the main source of legislation. The regulation of Muslims' lives according to Sunnah is necessary, especially when the Qur'anic text is speculative or brief; where the saying or the doing of the Prophet interprets, explains, or applies with spelling out the commands of Allah in daily life. While the Qur'an has more than six thousand ayat (verses), the ayat of legal regulations are about two hundred. The prophetic hadiths, or sayings of the Prophets, in regard to legal regulations are about four thousand. Thus, Sunnah is the best explanatory source of the Qur'an, Allah said:

"And We have sent down to you the Message; that you may make clear to the people what was sent down to them, and that they may give thought." (Qur'an, 16:44)

The Sunnah of the Prophet explains and expounds the principles of the Qur'an and the legal commands in it in the following ways:

> Specifying the common,
> Limiting the absolute,
> Detailing the general, and
> Clarifying the obscure.

For example: prayer is regulated in the Qur'an as obligatory, however, how many raka'as in each and how to pray is not mentioned in the Qur'an. It is the Sunnah that made this general command specific, through the saying and the action of the Prophet himself. The Prophet led Muslims in prayer, so they observed him praying, and he told them:

> "Do your regular prayer after my example."

By saying and doing things, especially in explaining the Qur'an, the Prophet was inspired and instructed by revelation. He does not speak on his own, nor does he bring personal opinions, Allah says:

"Nor does he speak from [his own] inclination. It is no but a revelation revealed [to him]." (Qur'an, 53:3-4)

Following the Sunnah of the Prophet, especially in the area of legislation, is obligatory, and the obligation is derived from the Qur'an itself:

"And whatever the Messenger has given you – take; and what he has forbidden you – refrain from. And fear Allah; indeed, Allah is strict in Punishment." (Qur'an, 59:7)

Another Ayah:

"O you who have believed, obey Allah, and obey the Messenger, and those charged with authority among you. And if you disagree over anything, refer it to Allah and His Messenger, if you should believe in Allah and the Last Day. That is best [way], and most suitable for final determination." (Qur'an, 4:59)

However, following the whole Sunnah of the Prophet in regard to legal regulation or general daily practice is recommended since the Prophet, peace be upon him, is the best example, Allah said:

"You have indeed in the Messenger of Allah a beautiful pattern (of conduct) for any one whose hope is in Allah and the Final Day, and who engages much in the praise of Allah." (Qur'an, 33:21)

All prophets are of very high standard of morality. Allah described the Prophet Muhammad as having a great standard of moral values:

"And indeed, you are of a great moral character." (Qur'an, 68:4)

Is Sunnah One Part or More?
Sunnah is constituted of whatever word, deed, report, decision, and physical or moral description that is attributed to the Prophet Muhammad even his movements and patterns of rest.

Sunnah could be divided into three parts:

A- The saying of the Prophet, also called Hadith:
Hadith in Arabic language means speech or discourse. The Prophet's speech is called Prophetic Traditions. This includes what the Prophet said on different occasions concerning different matters. Hadith of the Prophet is a source of legislation only when it is said in regard to issues of legislation. His saying or Hadith in regard to issues of non-legislative matters are not a source of Shari'ah, but they might still be a source of moral example but not of legal obligation. Thus they are in the area of mandoob and mubah, but not Wajeb.

B- The deeds of the Prophet:

This includes what the Prophet did; for example, the way he performed prayers. Exempt from this are these kinds of action:

> First, his own natural way of doing things that are not revelation such as walking, sitting, these are not legislative, however, following the Prophet and imitating him as best example, is mubah, and mustahab.
>
> Second: what was specified for him, but not permissible to Muslims such as continuous fasting.

C- What he approved of:

The approval or the saying or practice that was tacitly approved of by the Prophet; if he saw or heard something and he accepted it with no denial or rejection.

Recording The Prophetic Tradition or Hadith

The Prophet Muhammad, peace be upon him, appointed scribes to write down the revelation of the Qur'an during his lifetime, however, he prohibited the recording of his own Hadith, fearing that people might confuse the Qur'anic text with Prophetic Hadith.

All the Sunnah of the Prophet or Hadith are narrated to us and transmitted through the companions (Sahaba) of the Prophet, who lived with him, observing him, seeing, and hearing him. The Prophetic Hadith was transmitted further by the successors or the followers (Tabe'een) of the companions of the Prophet and then by the followers of the followers, generation after generation, being collected and written.

The Caliph Omar Ibn Abdul Aziz, reigned 99-101 A.H. noticed that the companions of the Prophet and their successors were dying, and he was afraid that the tradition of the Prophet would vanish. He requested his representative in Madina and in other provinces to collect and write down the Prophetic traditions. The recording of Hadith might have started earlier in an individual attempts, but it was more organized with the command of the Caliph.

The Science of the Prophetic Tradition and the Components of Hadith

In the process of collecting and writing down the Prophetic Tradition a need for checking the authenticity of these sayings and the way of narration, and the qualification of the narrators arose. As a result a new field of knowledge was born in the Islamic civilization, called: 'Ilm al-Hadith (The Science of Prophetic Tradition). It is a specific science for studying the tradition of the Prophet. This science developed its own methodology that uses many of the procedures that we use in science today; such as observation, collecting data, comparison, confirmation, falsification, and so forth. In this science each Hadith of the Prophet has been divided into two parts:

1. Sanad: The uninterrupted chain of the narrators and authorities who transmitted the prophetic Hadith. Sanad must be traced back with no interruption to the first authority of the tradition, i.e., the Prophet.

2. Matn: The text itself or what the Prophet (pbuh) said.

In the sanad the scholars of Hadith study the narration such as the way of transmitting Hadith; whether in any of these forms that has different references: "said", "told", " I heard", "I heard him saying", "it has been narrated", "told me", "told us", etc.

It also studies the chain of narrators; whether the chain of the narrators presents continuity, discontinuity in verifying the ascending link in which the succeeding person received the tradition from the preceding one, showing that there is no gap separating two narrators in time or space that prevented their meeting or reception.

Also the state of the narrators themselves, such as justness and invalidation is considered. Also if the narrator is Muslim, adult, mature, mentally competent, morally and religiously known as free from committing major or grave sin, nor persistent on committing minor sins.

According to the above a narrator would be classified as "very trustworthy", "trustworthy", "truthful", or "liar".

There is also the narrator's memory and mental ability in order to ensure ability of memorization and retrieving information, also showing that a person is free from error or illusion. This requirement is called exactitude, which covers two areas:

First, ability to memorize and communicate knowledge by heart, for example if one of the narrators starts losing their memory in older age the narration is not accepted.

Second, the ability of exactitudes in writing, which means that the narrator preserves what he has written after rectifying and verifying it. Also to make sure that the narrator's books and writings were well preserved and safeguarded against distortion and modification by other people before the narrator communicated the information to students or colleagues.

Imam Malik said about the requirements of the information collected: "Information is rejected when it comes from the following four people: the incompetent and foolish, those who have heretical tendencies and call on people to their side, those who forge lies on people's speeches, though they have done nothing of the like to the prophet's tradition, and old people known for virtue and their worship of Allah, but have no knowledge of what they are reporting."[11]

This method of analyzing these and other requirements help in making a sound judgment about the Hadith in regard to acceptance and rejection.[12]

---

[11] Tabbarah, Afif (1993): p.473.

[12] In regard to the Sanad, Hadith is classified to the following categories:
"Al-Mutawatir (successive). It is a tradition transmitted uninterruptedly by many or successive authorities or people who are not liable to meet on falsehood; in this way, the Isnad is regularly traced back till the chain arrives at the first authority, the Prophet.
Al-Mashhour (well-known). It is one reported by three or more reputed people, and there are many of this kind in the Sunna, both in letter and spirit.
Al-Aziz (dear). It is a tradition reported by two people.
Al-Ahad (single). It is a tradition reported by a single person." See Tabbarah (1993): pp. 474-475.

Degrees of Authenticity of Hadith

Scholars of Hadith classify hadiths in regard to their authenticity and truthfulness into three categories:

Sahih (true or authentic),
Hasan (sound or good), and
Da'eef (weak.)

A. Sahih (Authentic or True) Hadith

"It is a tradition free of falsity and in the Isnad of which there is no defect; it is transmitted by a reputed and trustworthy person from one like him with no deviation or defectiveness along the entire chain which goes back to the first authority."[13] This type can be used by the Mujtahid to derive legal opinions and legal regulations.

B. Hasan (Good) Hadith

"It is one in the Isnad of which no transmitter is guilty of falsehood however in the chain of authorities there is one blamed for shortcomings in his memory and precision, from whom following transmitters carry on the chain without themselves being guilty of falsehood. The critical scholar feels certain that this tradition has a well-known origin." This type can also be used by the Mujtahid to derive legal opinions and legal regulations.

C. Da'eef (Weak) Hadith

"It is one concerning which there is doubt as regards its context or in the Sanad of which some transmitters are not reliable or have been guilty of some sort of innovation." This type of Hadith can be used in deriving legal regulations, however, they might be useful in, and limited to the area of morality and encouraging noble deeds.

---

[13] For these three kinds see: Tabbarah (1993): pp. 475-476. Tabbarah noted also in regard to the tradition which is forged or falsely ascribed to the Prophet, it is called a fabricated one; in fact, it is no tradition, and its transmission is prohibited unless this is done to distinguish it and warn people against it.

Kinds and Categories of Hadith
According to

The Narrators of the Sanad (Chain of Narration)	**According to Authenticity** (Narration and Text)
Mutawatir (Successive)	Sahih (Authentic or True)
Mashhoor (Well-Known)	Hasan (Good)
Aziz (Dear)	Da'eef (Weak)
Ahaad (Single)	

Example of Analyzing a Hadith

Let us take this hadith as an example: **Abu 'Abd ar-Rahman 'Abdullah**, the son of 'Umar ibn al-Khattab (may Allah be pleased with them both), said: **I heard the Messenger** of Allah (may the blessings and peace of Allah be upon him) **say**: "............."

[Person (s) sying]: (I heard the Prophet say): "............."
      Sanad   ***Matn***

First: This Hadith has a sanad, which is a chain of authority transmitting the Hadith. Abu 'Abd ar-Rahman 'Abdullah is the narrator of this Hadith.

Second: Does the narrator fulfill the requirements mentioned above? Yes, he is a very well known scholar, with a great intellectual ability and moral values, also this specific person is well known of his following literally in the footsteps of the Prophet.

Third: In his narration he said: "I heard the Messenger."
Was he alive at the time of the Prophet? Yes. He was the son of 'Umar Ibn al-Khattab, a companion of the Prophet. Was he able to hear? (physical ability of hearing and socialization with the prophet) Yes, he was a companion of the prophet, who was continuously attending the Prophet's speech, associating himself with him in public actions, carefully listening to the Prophet, and intelligently observing his minute acts.

Fourth: Did he personally hear the Prophet, or did he hear someone else who heard the Prophet? No, he personally heard the Prophet, directly in his case.

Fifth: Was the narration itself transmitted in the form of: "we have been told" or "so and so said" or "the Messenger said"... or other forms of narration? No, it was in the form: "the Messenger of Allah said" which is a very strong form of narration.

Sixth: It can be concluded from the strong authority of transmitting this Hadith, that this is highly strong Hadith.

The Most Authentic Collections of Hadith of the Prophet (pbuh):

Among the earliest was the collection of Imam Malik Ibn Anas (d. 179 A.H.) which is called al-Muwatta' of Imam Malik. Other famous collections of Hadith and reliable books are:

1. Saheeh al-Bukhari, compiled by Mohammed Ibn Ismail al-Bukhari (d. 256 A.H.)

2. Saheeh Muslim, compiled by Moslem Ibn Al-Hajjaj (d.261 A.H.)

3. Sunan al-Termithi, complied by Mohammed Ibn 'Isa At Termithi (d. 279 A.H).

4. Sunan al-Nasa'i, compiled by Abu Abdul Ruhman Ahmed Ibn Shou'aib An-Nasa'i (d. 303 A.H.)

5. Sunan Ibn Majah, compiled by Abu Abdullah Mohammed Ibn Al-Kazwini (d. 273 A.H.)

6. Sunan Abi Da'ood compiled by Abu Dawood Suleiman Ibn Al-Ash'ath (d.275 A. H.)

Notice that the highest level of Hadith is the one that is agreed upon; meaning that the two great scholars of Hadith Bukhari and Muslim agreed upon it is a saheeh Hadith. In the second level is the one narrated by Bukhari only. In the third level is that narrated by Muslim only. Fourth is the Hadith that comply with Bukhari and Muslim's conditions and requirements although it is not transmitted by them. Fifth is the one complying with Bukhari's conditions. Sixth is the Hadith that comply with Muslim's conditions. Seventh is that which is revised by a reliable Scholar of Prophetic Hadith.

Samples of Prophetic Hadith

HADITH 1.

On the authority of Abu 'Abd ar-Rahman 'Abdullah, the son of 'Umar ibn al-Khattab (may Allah be pleased with them both), who said: I heard the Messenger of Allah (may the blessings and peace of Allah be upon him) say:

Islam has been built on five [pillars]: testifying that there is no god but Allah and that Muhammad is the Messenger of Allah, performing the prayers, paying the zakat, making the pilgrimage to the House, and fasting in Ramadan.

(It was related by al-Bukhari and Muslim)

HADITH 2.

On the authority of Abu 'Abd ar-Rahman 'Abdullah ibn Mas'ud (may Allah be pleased with him), who said: The Messenger of Allah (may the blessings and peace of Allah be upon him) and he is the truthful, the believed, narrated to us:

Verily the creation of each one of you is brought together in his mother's belly for forty days in the form of seed, then he is a clot of blood for a like period, then a morsel of flesh for a like period, then there is sent to him the angel who blows the breath of life into him and who is commanded about four matters' to write down his means of livelihood, his life span, his actions, and whether happy or unhappy.

HADITH 3.

On the authority of Abu Huraira (may Allah be pleased with him), who said: The Messenger of Allah (may the blessings and peace of Allah be upon him) said:

Each person's every joint must perform a charity every day the sun comes up: to act justly between two people is a charity; to help a man with his mount, lifting him onto it or hoisting up his belongings onto it is a charity; a good word is a charity; every step you take to prayers is a charity; and removing a harmful thing from the road is a charity.

(It was related by al-Bukhari and Muslim.)

Hadith Qudsi, Prophetic Hadith, and the Qur'an

Hadith, as we noted above, is about narrating the sayings or the actions or the approval of the Prophet. The saying of the Prophet is not Qur'an, in spite of the fact that he is the messenger of Allah and he speaks in Arabic. The words of the Prophet regarding different matters is not Qur'an, it is not the word of Allah; it is his own utterance. This saying or utterance is called Hadith and is divided into two kinds:

1. Hadith Qudsi (Sacred or Divine Tradition)
2. Regular Hadith (Prophetic Tradition). This has been already discussed.

Hadith Qudsi (Sacred or Divine Tradition)

Al-Sharif al-Jurjani (died 816 A.H.) in his book *The Lexicon* or *Al-Ta'reefat* defines this kind of Hadith as follow:

"A Sacred Hadith is, as to the meaning, from Allah the Almighty; as to the wording, it is from the Messenger of Allah, may the blessings and peace of Allah be upon him. It is that which Allah the Almighty has communicated to His Prophet through revelation or in dream, and he, peace be upon him, has communicated it in his own words. Thus the Qur'an is superior to it, because, besides being revealed, it is His wording."[14]

Another more comprehensive definition is provided by a scholar of jurisprudence named al-Mulla 'Ali ibn Muhammad al-Qari, (died 1016 A.H.) in which he says about Sacred Hadith:

"It is that which is related by the foremost of relaters and the most reliable of authorities, the best of blessings and salutations be upon him, from Allah, may He be glorified, sometimes through the medium of Gabriel, upon whom be blessings and peace, and sometimes by revelation, inspiration and dreams, Allah having entrusted to him the expressing of it In such words as he wished. It differs from the Holy Qur'an in that the revelation of the latter was only through the medium of the Upright Soul and is restricted to the wording specifically revealed from the Preserved Tablet, which was

---

[14] Al-Jurjani (1969): al-Ta'reefat, p. 88, also see the useful introduction of The Forty Hadith Qudsi (1980): selected and translated by Ezzeddin Ibrahim and Denys Johnson-Davies, p. 8.

then passed on by tawatur, absolutely unchanged in every generation, age and time. Many and well known are the consequences that flow from this: that [unlike the Holy Qur'an] Sacred Hadith are not acceptable for recitation in one's prayers; they are not forbidden to be touched or read by one who is in a state of ritual impurity, or by a menstruating woman or one confined to childbed; if repudiated, such repudiation does not result in the person so doing being guilty of unbelief; and they are not characterized by the attribute of inimitability."[15]

What is the Difference between Sacred Hadith and Prophetic Hadith?[16]

The chain of narration or authorities (Sanad) ends with the Prophet in the prophetic hadith, while in Sacred Hadith the final attribution is to the Almighty. Also, Sacred Hadiths are to be found recorded in the first person.

Sacred Hadith, moreover, are subject, in regard to establishing their authenticity, to the same stringent rules as are Prophetic Hadith, being regarded as sound and good or as weak and of doubtful authenticity according to whether they comply with the demands of these rules.

What is the Difference between Sacred Hadith and the Qur'an?

1. The Holy Qur'an has been handed down through the centuries in its revealed wording by tawatur, whereas Sacred Hadith have been transmitted in versions recorded by chains of individuals.
2. The Holy Qur'an is divided into chapters and verses; the Sacred Hadith is not.
3. He who recites the Qur'an is rewarded tenfold for every letter recited, as the Prophet said, while this is not applicable to Sacred Hadith.
4. Allah the Almighty has promised that Qur'an will be preserved from change and alteration, while there is no such assurance in regard to Sacred Hadith.
5. As all Muslim scholars agreed that when Qur'an is quoted, the exact words should be given and not merely the meaning, while it is possible to quote Sacred Hadith by meaning.

---

[15] See Forty Hadith Qudsi (1980): pp. 8-9.

[16] In the following distinctions I mainly relied upon the introduction of the Forty Hadith Qudsi (1980): pp. 9-12.

The Forms in which Sacred Hadith are Recorded:
Two main forms, among others, have been singled out by scholars for relating Sacred Hadith: the first-and that preferred by early Muslim scholars-being that the Sacred Hadith should start with the words "the Prophet, may the blessings and peace of Allah be upon him, says from among the sayings he relates from his Lord, may He be glorified", while the second form opens with the words "Allah the Almighty has said, from among the sayings related from Him by the Messenger of Allah, may the blessings and peace of Allah be upon him." The meaning is one and the same.

However, there are some more forms such as: "The Messenger of Allah, may the blessings and peace of Allah be upon him, said that Allah, may He be glorified, said". This is a commonly used form.

Samples of HADITH QUDSI (Sacred Hadith)

HADITH 1.

On the authority of Abu Hurayrah (may Allah be pleased with him), who said that the Messenger of Allah (may the blessings and peace of Allah be upon him) said: Allah (glorified and exalted be He) said:

I am so self-sufficient that I am in no need of having an associate. Thus he who does an action for someone else's sake as well as Mine will have that action renounced by Me to him whom he associated with Me. (It was related by Muslim, also by Ibn Majah).

HADITH 2.

On the authority of the son of 'Abbas (may Allah be pleased with them both), from the Messenger of Allah (may the blessings and peace of Allah be upon him), that among the sayings he related from his Lord (glorified and exalted be He) is that He said:

Allah has written down the good deeds and the bad ones. Then He explained it [by saying that] he who has intended a good deed and has not done it, Allah writes it down with Himself as a full good deed, but if he has intended it and has done it, Allah writes it down with Himself as from ten good deeds to seven hundred times, or many times over. But if he has intended a bad deed and has not done it, Allah writes it down with Himself as a full good deed, but if he has intended it and has done it, Allah writes it down as one bad deed. (It was related by al-Bukhari and Muslim.)

HADITH 3.

On the authority of Abu Dharr al-Ghifari (may Allah be pleased with him) from the Prophet (may the blessings and peace of Allah be upon him) is that among the sayings he relates from his Lord (may He be glorified) is that He said:

O My servants, I have forbidden oppression for Myself and have made it forbidden amongst you, so do not oppress one another.
(It was related by Muslim, ibn Majah, and Tirmidhi)

10.3. Ijma' or Scholarly Consensus: The Third Source of Islamic Shari'ah:

Ijma' is the agreement among all Muslim scholars who are Mujtahids in regard to a legal issue or a ruling matter (Hukum Shar'i) made after the death of the Prophet.

There are some opinions whether Ijma' is valid regardless if one or few of the Muslim scholars disagree. A majority of the scholars of Usul al-Fiqh (The principles of Jurisprudence) require the consensus of all the Mujtahids on a ruling matter in order for it to be accepted as a binding authority or hukum. According to them the disagreement of one nullifies the hukum as a Wajeb or obligatory. Others think that if the majority of the Mujtahids agree on a ruling matter or hukm, then the consensus is valid regardless of the disagreement of the few who oppose it.[17]

When Ijma', or consensus, is concluded and achieved it becomes a source of Islamic legislation, thus it becomes a binding authority or Wajeb -- meaning it is obligatory on every Muslim to follow it. Even the Ijtihad of other scholars from subsequent ages cannot nullify it.

Notice that the agreement of many Muslims who are not Mujtahid on any legal issue is not Ijma' and does not count as consensus. Their decision is not binding as a source of legislation.
Also the Ijma' of Muslim scholars on an issue that is not legal, such as an issue of language, is not a legally binding Ijma'. Ijma' must be performed after the Prophet's death.

Proof and Evidence of Ijma' (Hujjiyyat al-Ijma')
If Ijma' meets the requirements, then it is a valid source of Islamic law or Islamic legislation. The proof of its validity is derived from the following:
Qur'an:

"O you who believe! Obey Allah, and obey the Messenger, and those charged with authority among you. If you differ in anything among yourselves, refer it to Allah and the Messenger,

---

[17] For more details on this issue please see Abdul Kareem Zaidan (1987), Al-Wajeez fi Usul al-Fiqh, pp.179-193.

if you do believe in Allah and the Last Day: That is best, and most suitable for final determination." (Qur'an, 4:59)

Those who are in charge of affairs are called in this ayah 'Ulu al-Amr, Ibnu Abas said that this verse refer the 'Ulama or Muslim scholars, also in the same chapter ayah 83 Allah says:

"When there comes to them some matter touching (public) safety or fear, they divulge it. If they had only referred it to the Messenger or to those charged with authority among them, the proper investigators would have understood it from them (directly)" (Qur'an 4:83).

These ayat are proof of establishing Ijma' as a valid source of Islamic law.

Sunnah also establishes Ijma' as a valid source, the Prophet (pbuh) said:
"My community shall never agree on an error."

10.4. Qiyas or Analogical Deduction: The Fourth Source of Islamic Shari'ah

Qiyas can be also called analogical syllogism. Since syllogism is a form of deductive reasoning, it is then sufficient to call it analogical deduction. In general Qiyas means measurement, which means measuring something by something else, such as measuring the size of the room by yardstick or similar measurement. In this process of measurement one thing is being taken as a criterion for measuring or evaluating the other.

However, Qiyas has a more technical meaning as a source of Islamic Shari'ah. It is used to understand and regulate that for which there is no textual support (from Qur'an, Sunnah, Ijma') in the light of the one that is textually supported, in order to apply the same legal regulation because the effective cause ('illa) of the hukm or regulation is being shared. Thus, by this kind of analogy the hukm is established. For example:

The Qur'an forbids alcohol in sura (chapter) 5, verse 90, By analogy this prohibition is extended to anything that causes intoxication, whether it is made from grapes or other sources, whether it is liquid or powder or another form, since the effective cause or 'illa, which is intoxication, is common to all of them. Although this specific substance is not mentioned in the Qur'an, Qiyas makes a binding prohibition about it.

The Qur'an forbids selling or buying during Friday prayer in Sura 62:9. By analogy this prohibition could be extended to other kinds of transactions since the effective cause or 'illa is being shared; the cause of prohibition is diversion from prayer.

Example of Qiyas

1. Everything that causes intoxication is prohibited
2. Wine causes intoxication
---
3. Therefore, wine is prohibited

1. Vodka causes the same effects as wine (that is intoxication)
2. Wine is prohibited
---
3. Therefore, Vodka is prohibited too

Wine and Vodka share the same effective cause ('illa) or they have a common result, which is intoxication, thus, the prohibition was the same in each case.

Notice that this form of qiyas is based on a form of logical syllogism. Syllogism is a form of deductive reasoning that consists of two related premises and a conclusion. Qiyas might also be called personal opinion or R'iy. According to a prophetic hadith the Prophet asked Mu'adh ibn Jabal when he sent him to Yemen, and before he departed:

"How will you reach a judgment when a question arises?
A cording to the word of Allah (Qur'an), replied Mu'adh.
And if you find no solution in the word of Allah (Qur'an)?
Then according to the Sunnah of the Messenger of Allah.
And if you find no solution in the Sunnah of the Messenger of Allah, nor in the Word of Allah?
Then I shall take a decision according to my own opinion (R'ayi). The Prophet was pleased with this answer.

The Sources of the Islamic Shari'ah (The Islamic Divine Law)

1. The Qur'an

2. The Sunnah (The Tradition of the Prophet Muhammad, pbuh)

   A. What he said
   B. What he did
   C. What he saw and approved of

3. Ijma'

4. Qiyas

11. THE DIVISIONS OF ISLAMIC SHARI'AH

The Islamic Divine law or Shari'ah is divided into three major parts in regard to fields of knowledge and investigation. These areas are:

Fiqh, or jurisprudence that deals with legal requirements and regulations of the Islamic religion; such as the five pillars of Islam and how to apply them, their legal and religious requirements.

Usul al-Deen, or scholastic theology deals with Iman and the related issues of faith or 'Itiqad, the articles of faith, life after death and resurrection.

Akhlaq or ethics or sufism deals with the purification of the soul and reaching higher standards in spirituality, and love of Allah.

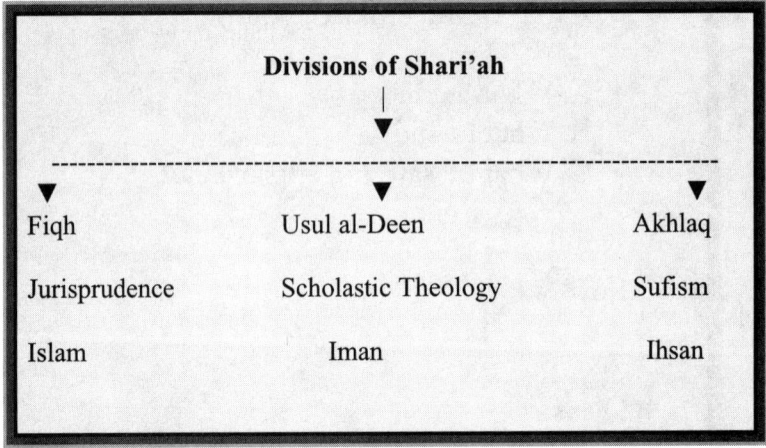

Fiqh (Jurisprudence or Legal Study):
It is also called Islamic law. Fiqh is a field of Islamic science in which the faqeeh (the jurist) infers an Islamic legal opinion from its valid sources such as the Qur'an and Sunnah. Jurisprudence covers the two aspects of human life in regard to rights and duties:

1. The area of worshipping or 'Ibadat: covers the relationship between humans and their Creator in terms of the rights of Allah over His creatures, and duties of man in worshipping Allah.

2. The area of human interaction or Mu'amalat: regulates and covers the relationship among humans in a social setting, in terms of rights and duties. It also regulates the relationship between humans and the rest of nature (animals, plants, natural resources, and the environment).

In regard to legal doctrines and inferring legal opinions (Ijtihad) there are four major schools of law or jurisprudence that are followed by Muslims, and two schools that are followed by fewer Muslims. These schools also called Madhaheb of Fiqh or legal doctrines in law or jurisprudence, they are:

Al-Hanafi Madhhab, named after Abu Hanifa (699-767).
The Hanafi school of law was officially adopted by the state during the 'Abbasid caliphate and continued to be officially the madhheb of the Ottoman Empire until 1924.
Today the Hanafi School of Islamic law is widely accepted and followed by Muslims and practiced in their daily life in the following regions and countries: Pakistan, Afghanistan, India, Balkans, Transcaucasia, the central Asian republics, and China.

Al-Maliki Madhhab, named after Malik Ibn Anas al-Asbahi (713-795)
The Maliki Islamic School of Law was established in Madina in the Arab peninsula and spread to the Hijaz and the Gulf area. It was accepted and practiced by Muslims in Sudan, Andalusia, in Spain, and northwest Africa. It is now the daily practice of many Muslims and the dominant school of fiqh in Sudan, Morocco, Algeria, Tunisia, Libya, and Spain.

Al-Shafe'i Madhhab, named after its founder Muhammad Ibn ldris al-Shafe'i (767-820).
This school was established in Baghdad by al-Shafe'i, then al-Shafe'i moved to Egypt where his school found acceptance, however, after the Ottoman conquest in 1517 the Hanafi Madhheb become the official school of jurisprudence in Egypt. Currently the legal opinion of al-Shafe'i is the daily practice of many Muslims in these regions: Malaysia, Indonesia, Egypt, Palestine, Jordan, the coastlands of Yemen, and among populations in Pakistan, and India.

Al-Hanbali Madhhab, named after Ahmad Ibn Hanbal (780-855) Ibn Hanbal born in Baghdad and traveled to Syria, Yemen, and Mecca. He died in Baghdad. Although he is the founder of this school of jurisprudence, his major work was in Hadith. Ibn Khallikan said that Imam Ahmad memorized one million prophetic hadiths by heart.
This school is now widely accepted and practiced in Saudi Arabia and some Middle Eastern countries.

Al-Ja'fari Madhhab, named after Ja'far al-Sadiq (80-148 A.H./ 699-765A.D.)
He was a descendent of the Prophet (pbuh) and the sixth Imam from the descendents of Ali. He was a great scholar in the Islamic religious sciences. In fact, Abu Hanifa and Malik ibn Anas both studied with him in Madina. The Shi'ah who believe in the Twelve Imams consider Ja'far al-Sadiq to be the founder of their school of jurisprudence or Islamic law that is called Ja'fari School.
The Shi'ah, especially in Iran and some countries in the Middle East and Africa, follow this school.

Al-Dahiri Madhhab established by Abu Da'ood al-Dahiri and enhanced by Ibn Hazm al-Andalusi.

11.2. Usul al-Deen (Scholastic Theology)
Deals with Matters of Faith ('Aqa'ed). Islamic scholastic theology ('Ilm al-Kalam)[18] was established to achieve these goals:
First, to clarify the accepted foundations (usul) or 'Aqa'ed of Islam such as believing in One God, One Creator, Prophecy, etc...

---

[18] It was called Kalam (talk) for the following reasons:
- In their books they usually start the chapters by saying: "al-kalam in regard to this issue..."
- Or that talking (kalam) about these issues (such as Divine attributes...) was not preferable as the Prophet and his companions did not talk about it and silence in regard to these issues (which is metaphysically futile) is a must since reason cannot reach any conclusion about it and was not commanded by religion, since the Mutakallimun talked about it they were called people of kalam.
- Or because those theologians talked about and discussed "kalam Allah" and whether it is eternal or created by Allah.

Second, to prove these foundations (Usul) by rational proof or demonstration and argumentation.
Third, to defend these foundations (Usul) against any attack, criticism, or doubt. Their defense is also through rational demonstration.

What are The Subjects of Islamic Theology?
Theology covers:

1. Existence of Allah, and Divine attributes. (Tawheed)
2. Prophecy (Nubuwwa)
3. Life after death or eschatology (Ma'ad)

Islamic Theology (Usul al-Deen) deals with knowing Allah as the creator, knowing that to Him we will return (al-Ma'ad), and knowing the source of obligation, which is revelation and prophecy.

Using prayer as an example, how to pray is an issue of Jurisprudence, how to derive a legal opinion about the correctness of the prayer is an issue of principles of jurisprudence, and how Muslims are obligated to pray, is an issue from Usul al Deen, through revelation from The Qur'an and Sunnah. Why Muslims are obligated is an issue of Usul al Deen, because Allah is the creator and He legislates what is beneficial to man.

In 'Ilm al-Kalam, or Islamic scholastic theology, there are some schools, the most famous are: Mu'tazila, Ash'ariyyah, and Maturydiyyah. A detailed discussion about Kalam will be in part five.

11.3. Purification of the Soul (Ethics and Tasawwuf or Mysticism)
This covers the realms of what is an important aspect in the search for perfection and the moral and aesthetical values that are the most adherent to the spiritual essence of man in his relationship with his Creator. It also deals with how to live a life of happiness and satisfaction through purifying the soul and preparing the heart to deal with spiritual reality in the most efficient and proper way.

12. The Maqasid (Objectives) of the Divine Law

12.1. The Abandoned Ship as a Case Study:
Three hundred people were in a boat sailing on the sea. They realized that their safety was at risk, and the lives of the majority could only be saved by throwing 10 people overboard. Would it be morally right to kill 10 people in order to save 290?

The case of the ship was actually presented by Imam al-Ghazali (450-505 A.H./ 1058-1111 A.D.) in his book on the principles of Islamic Jurisprudence called *"al-Mustasfa Min 'lm al-Usul."*

Let us look at the objectives of Islamic Divine Law before attempting to answer this question. The justification of moral and legal actions in Islam is not based on personal reflection, or personal desire or the benefits of the majority; it is only justified by the Qur'an and Sunnah or the Islamic legislative system (Shari'ah).

Why Allah Revealed a Divine Law (Shari'ah)?
Some Muslim scholars of jurisprudence, especially Ibn Taimia (661-728 A.H./1263-1328 A.D.), said that Allah revealed such a legislative system or Shari'ah in order to achieve Justice.
Other jurists said it is for the purpose of achieving happiness. And still some others, especially al-Ghazali, said it is only for the achievement and the realization of the very benefits of man on earth.

A closer look at these three approaches to Shari'ah shows that they complement each other: happiness of mankind cannot be achieved at large without justice, and justice is one of the essential benefits and interest of people on earth.

The Maqasid Model of the Existential Structure
The Islamic Divine Law or Shari'ah was revealed for one basic universal purpose: to realize or to make real the best interests of humans on earth.

Benefit or Maslaha in Arabic language, which literally translates as benefit or interest, is defined by Imam al-Ghazali as that which secures a benefit or prevents harm.[19]

Human nature tends naturally to seek happiness and to live as good as possible, but this cannot be achieved unless people cooperate with each other, but cooperation is impossible unless people live a peaceful life. Peace and security cannot be achieved unless there are rules to protect the rights of all equally. However, rules and legal regulation are useless without a source of authority to enforce them and apply them equally. For the above reasons the Divine wisdom made the Islamic law or Shari'ah achieves the masalih or benefits of people in the two following ways:

First, by procuring these masalih (or by bringing them about). Since people cannot bring about the benefits of mankind equally; they discriminate against each other, they kill each other, they steal from each other, they humiliate others just because they are different in color, ethnicity, power, social status and the like. In one word they present their interest as central and others are only means to achieve their own ends. Allah is an absolute justice who legislates to mankind what is beneficial to all.

Second, the Islamic Divine Law achieves its goal by preserving or protecting these human universal benefits by setting rules and regulations with sets of prescribed punishments.

The Islamic Divine Law then has a two-fold function.

12.2. Categories of Benefits in Islam

As we just mentioned Imam al-Ghazali defined Maslaha as that which secures a benefit or prevents harm.[20] However, benefits mentioned in the Islamic Divine Law are of three kinds:

> First: *accredited benefits* (Masalih Mu'tabarah), which are regulated by The Lawgiver in the sense that a textual authority from the divine law could be found to prove their validity.

---

[19] Al-Ghazali (al-Mustasfa 1997): Vol.1. p. 416.
[20] Al-Ghazali: (1997): Vol. 1, p. 416.

Second: *nullified benefits* (Masalih Mulghat): there are also other kinds of benefits and interests that the Shari'ah neglected because they lead to harm and hardship (Mafsadah), such as stealing or usury.

Third: *unregulated benefits* (al-Masalih al-Mursalah), since the benefits of people can be as numerous as their public interests, we find that the divine law did not regulate a number of these benefits. So it provides no indication as to their validity. In the principles of jurisprudence these kinds of benefits are called the *unregulated benefits*, and it is left for legal scholars or jurists to work on them.

Benefits and the Objectives of Shari'ah

According to Imam al-Ghazali, masalih or benefits should be harmonious and consistent with the objective (Maqasid) of the Shari'ah, since the basic purpose of legislation (tashri') is to protect the interest of people against harm.

In regard to their importance and priority, benefits were divided by Muslim scholars into three kinds:

- The essentials (Daruriyyat),
- The complementary (Hjiyyat), and
- The embellishments (Tahsiniyyat)

In relation to the masalih and its division, the existential model will consist of four circles, three of them orbiting around the central one which represents the Islamic creed and the main source of legislation:

- The circle of the Shari'ah,
- The circle of the essentials (Daruriyyat),
- The circle of the complementarity (Hajiyyat), and
- The circle of the embellishments (Tahsiniyyat),

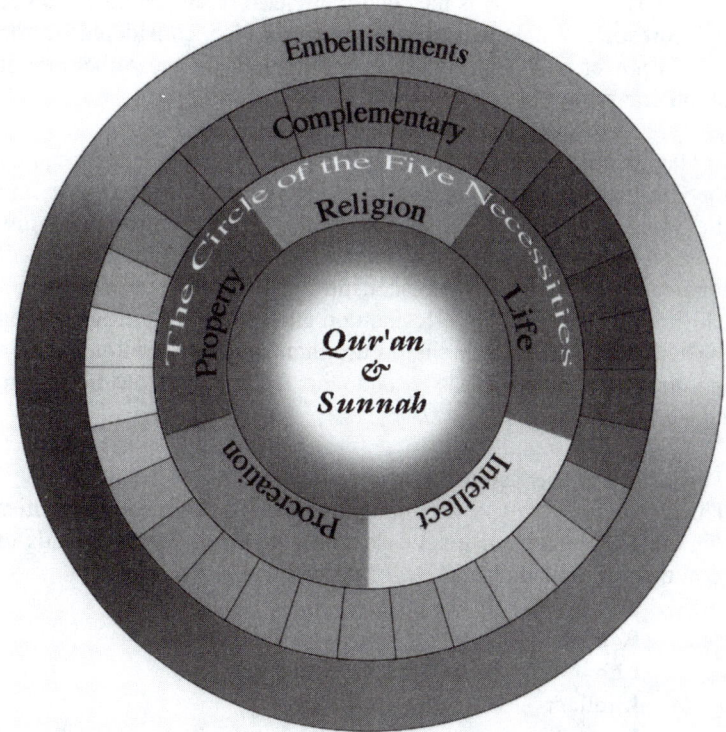

The Maqasid Model

12.3. The Maqasid Paradigm:
The following considers the objectives of the Islamic Divine Law in a concentric model (many circles with one common center).[21] This model has two important characteristics:

1- The circles are not only concentric, but all of them beyond the center may also be regarded as orbiting the center -- the core. They orbit in the manner of a solar system.

2- If we consider the radiuses as representing the pull or force of gravity toward the center, then the pull of gravity will be inversely proportional to the length of the radius; the shorter the radius the greater the pull of gravity and the longer the radius the less the pull.

---

[21] See Al-Allaf, Mashhad (1988): pp. 298-302.

The First Circle: This is the central circle. It represents the heart or the core of the Islamic culture and it is also considered as the central power of its activity and continuation. It is also the core of all other circles.

In Islamic culture this circle represents the Islamic belief especially the Creed ('*Aqidah*) as this 'Aqidah is presented in the Qur'an and the Sunnah or the tradition of the prophet. The Islamic Divine law represented in this core also emphasizes what is beneficial to all humans. It is like the supreme constitution of necessitation.
This circle is the source of legislation and practicality of preserving existence. Human beings should use their maximum rationalization to understand the wisdom and the benefits of such Divine legislation.

The Circle of the Essentials (Daruriyyat):
This circle includes five basic and universal necessities or priorities "on which the lives of people depend, and whose neglect leads to total disruption and chaos."[22] These five necessities are:

- Religion
- Life
- Intellect
- Procreation
- Property

These five necessities are derived from Shari'ah as necessary and basic for human existence. Therefore, every society should preserve and protect these five necessities; otherwise human life would be harsh, brutal, poor, and miserable here and in the hereafter.

For example, in order to establish the first necessity, **religion**, all the required things that are needed as beneficial tools to establish and attain the necessity of spirituality were already contained in the divine law, such as: all the principles, the rituals, the belief in angels, messengers, the day of judgment, and so on. All these things were mentioned to serve the purpose of establishing spirituality as a necessity in the existence of humans on earth. In addition to that another set of rules exists to maintain this necessity

---

[22] See Kamali (1991): p.271.

of spirituality and to protect it against destruction.

The second necessity, **life,** is secured by obtaining lawful means of sustenance such as food, marriage, medicine, shelter, etc. The way to protect it is through the enforcement of prescribed penalties provided by the Divine Law. For example, adultery, false accusation, killing, and suicide are prohibited.

A Logical Argument on Prohibition of killing and Suicide
Some may ask, what about a culture in which suicide itself is being justified as morally right?

The answer to this question is: a culture in which suicide or killing is a justified moral value is a culture that does not exist. Why?

Because life is the underlying value of human existence itself. If life were nullified, then, existence itself would be nullified too. Since these cultures exist, existence is not nullified, thus, killing or suicide was not encouraged as a value of any existent culture. This argument has the valid form of conditional syllogism as Modus Tollens:

If life had been nullified, then existence itself would have been nullified too.
But existence is not nullified (we are talking about a culture that exists now)

Therefore, killing or suicide was not a value of any existent culture.

If someone said that some people in some cultures commit suicide, then they actually were answering themselves, because the action of a minority who committed suicide does not make it a universal value of that given culture.

According to the Islamic Divine Law life is a necessity and it is one of the top priorities that must be preserved at all costs. After all killing is prohibited in Islam, and whomever kills a person it is as if he or she has killed all humans, or the human race. Every human is a unique representative of mankind; if all people died except one, then that person is the only one who represents mankind among other existences such as animals and trees. For this importance of life Islam ranked it as a top priority to be necessarily preserved and protected. Since humans do not always respond to the rules of legislation and sometimes act against their own interests, thus the legislature made strict legislation to punish the act of killing.

The same holds true for the third necessity, **intellect**. It is necessary and essential to the existence of the human race. The benefit of reason to the human existence might be beyond reason. Thus, it is secured by lawful means of sustenance, and protected against destruction by a set of rules and punishments. For example, anything that diminishes the intellect's ability to function properly such as alcohol or any similar substance is prohibited. I will give further elaboration on intellect when I discuss reason and revelation.

In regard to **property**, which is very beneficial and necessary to the human life, divine law facilitates all lawful means for its acquisition, and secures it by defending the right of ownership through penalizing theft.

Reason and Revelation:
Is it possible for moral values that relied upon religion to be consistent with moral values derived from pure reasoning?
In Islamic there is no contradiction between reason and revelation, sincere and deep reasoning will definitely lead to the truth of revelation. Let us take the example of intellect:
Revelation, the Islamic Divine Law mentioned clearly that intellect is a necessity and must be preserved, since alcohol nullifies the ability of intellectualization, alcohol and any other substance similar to its effects, becomes prohibited. Now we all know that alcohol has some benefits in it, Allah –the All Knowing- mentioned in the Qur'an that alcohol has some benefits, however, it is mentioned also that the harm of alcohol overweighs its benefits, and thus it is prohibited. Its use must be prevented by a set of legislations because it inflicts harm on all: society, family, and individuals. Allah, in His absolute wisdom, legislates for human beings benefits that sometimes they can't anticipate for themselves. Since alcohol causes harm the command of prohibition was stated so clearly that no skill of interpretation or exegesis is needed.
Reason, might prefer its own way of stating benefit and harm, however, reason is limited to its methodology, which is either

deductive or inductive. Since deductive reasoning can't predict the future, then inductive reasoning is what we are looking for. The golden key for knowing benefits and harm is "experience", and the only road to it is "trial and error". Society from history and experience discovered that alcohol caused harm to individuals, young and old, causing illness, and as a fruit of experience the reason started to restrict the consumption of alcohol. Going further in rationality and experience society realized that alcohol caused financial harm, by affecting both health and wealth of the society; reason sought more regulation of alcohol. Going further with rationality, reason realized that drinking and driving caused terrible damage to the life of people, property, family, and the society, thus rational legislation went further in restricting alcohol. Going further in experience being advanced more in science and medicine the harm of alcohol starts to manifest itself with more acceleration, therefore, physicians realized that pregnant women who consume alcohol are destroying their fetuses physically and mentally, and the harm inflicted on the fetus, the mother, the family, procreation, and society, therefore, more restriction is placed on alcohol. However, although the restriction of alcohol is ongoing, but not yet in a form of prohibition as that in divine law.[23] After all the route of reason in seeking more restrictions on consuming alcohol is continually confirming the beneficial aspect of the divine law legislation; showing no contradiction between reason and revelation in morality.

---

[23] In 1929 alcohol was prohibited in the United States.

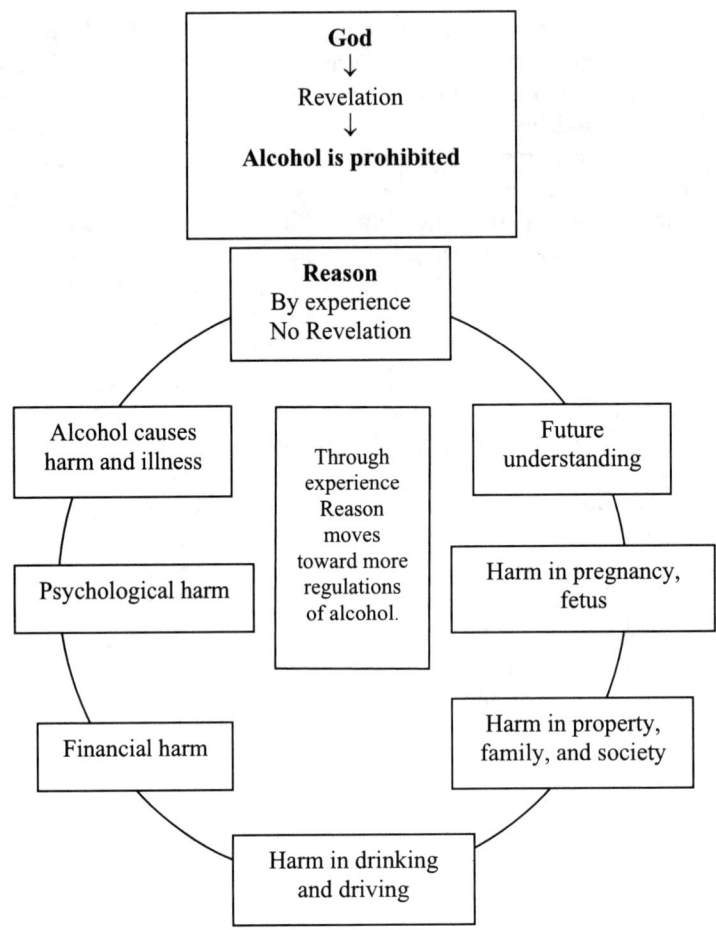

The Circle of the Complementarity:
The complementary things are matters that people need in order to remove restrictions and difficulties in applying the five necessities. In The Qur'an:

"Allah does not want to place you in a difficulty, but He wants to purify you, and to complete His favor to you, that you may be grateful." (Qur'an, 5:6)

In another chapter we read:

"Allah intends for you ease, and He does not want to make things difficult for you." (Qur'an, 2:185)

Thus complementary are intended to facilitate practicing and applying the necessities, therefore, a great benefit reside in them because they supplement the five essential values. However, there are two things that need to be mentioned here: first, there is no specific model for acquiring and fulfilling them, except being lawfully obtained. If food is complementary to preserving life as one of the main objectives, thus it is not necessary that it be a specific kind of food, such as fast food. In this sense diversity of cultures could be preserved too.
Language is necessary to enhance the intellect, but it is not necessary to be the English language, the native language of the culture must be preserved and protected, because language itself is culture, it is the medium through which identity can be preserved by linking the past and the present.

Second, the divine law also grants people some concessions *(rukhas)* in cases of hardship such as sickness, and traveling. Also people in other climates and cultures in which the time zone is very different; making a very long day or night, the divine law permits them to estimate what is similar to an average day time to break the fast. The same holds true for rules concerning commercial transactions.
Neglecting these complementary things will lead to hardships in life but not to chaos and collapse.

The Circle of the Embellishments:
The embellishments are intended to render human affairs or conditions more suited to the requirements of the highest standards of moral conduct. They "denote interests whose realization leads to improvement and the attainment of that which is desirable."[24]

Thus, the observance of cleanliness in personal appearance and in spirituality, the cultivation of moral virtues, the avoidance of wastefulness in consumption, and moderation in the enforcement of

---

[24] Kamali, M. H. (1991): p. 272.

penalties, fall within the scope of embellishments.[25]

General Legal Principles:
From thinking about these benefits a systematic set of legal rules and principles being deduced, such as:

1- Harm is removed.
2- Public harm or loss is averted by the private assumption of loss.
3- The greater of two harms is averted by assumption of the lesser.
4- Averting harm is to be preferred over procuring benefits.
5- Cases of necessity make permissible what is normally forbidden or restricted.
6- Necessity is determined by the particular circumstances.
7- Hardship secures lenience.
8- It is not permissible to do what will harm one's self.

---

[25] There are some logical implications, priorities, and characteristics for these three circles:
1- The central circle represents the source of legislation, and the source of establishing and procuring benefits.
2- The second circle is universal and dynamic; its global vitality resides in the fact that these five necessities are necessary to every single culture regardless of whether it is Islamic or not. The failure to preserve these necessities results in chaos for that culture, regardless of its identity.
3. The five necessities must be preserved according to their priorities- religion, life, intellect, procreation, and property.
4. Changing the priorities of these necessities will lead to perplexity in the moral life by changing the priorities in the standard of moral values. Thus property, or money, for example, can't be valued more than intellect or life.
5. The lower in the standard of necessities must be used to serve the higher, thus money or property should be used to serve intellect or life for example.
6. The third and fourth circles are the most lenient toward diversity. They are open to interaction with other cultures. Both circles keep the uniqueness of other cultures to be used and enhanced; the ways of gaining property are left to the economic system of that country on condition that it does not harm the property of others or put them at risk of harm. Second, it must be obtained by lawful means, of course. The tradition of the cultures culinary, and so on.
7. The circles themselves must be applied in their logical order and priority. Embellishments shouldn't be achieved before necessities.
8. These circles complement each other.

12.4. Al-Ghazali and the Question about the Abandoned Ship

According to al-Ghazali, and on the basis of Shari'ah, it is morally wrong to kill some people in order to save others. Why?

Al-Ghazali gave three reasons against the justification of killing in this case of the abandoned ship:

1. Universality: the benefit of people, in this case the majority, is not a universal benefit, it is only the interest of of small community who are going to use others as means to their end.
2. Necessity: the benefit of those people on the boat is not necessary to a degree to break another necessity and kill humans.
3. Certainty: we are not certain that killing those people is going to save the rest. What if they killed them and after that they faced another problem at sea, should they kill another 10 people to save the rest? This is morally unjustifiable and becomes out of control.

In Islam the life of every single human is unique and precious; it is one of the five necessities and must be preserved and protected. Allah commanded Muslims in the Qur'an that killing is prohibited, and to kill one soul is as if you killed the entire human race and to save one soul is as if you saved the entire human race.

From the above discussion we can easily conclude two moral rules in the realm of Islamic ethics:

First: The consequences, no matter how good, and no matter how much, do not justify any immoral act.

Second: The ends, no matter how noble, do not justify the means.

PART THREE

The last Prophet: The Seal of Prophethood Muhammad (pbuh)

13. The Need for a Prophet
Reason is not sufficient to establish equally the benefits of people on earth, it might be enough to establish benefits for some people such as the strong, the rich, the one who is in power, a certain color, race, ethnicity, or gender. But this is not real benefit since it inflicts harm on other people.
Most important is that human reason does not guide people to a specific system of legislation that is comprehensive and beneficial in achieving the interest of all people in this life and in the hereafter.

Humans are in need of the guidance of revelation that comes through prophets.

"Allah - the Exalted - has sent Prophet Muhammad - the praise and peace be upon him - as the seal of the prophets, and supported him with miracles and wonderful signs such as the splitting of the moon, the praise of the pebbles, and causing the dumb animal to speak, as well as water flowing from between his fingers and the unmistakable sign of the Glorious Qur'an with which he challenged the Arabs.

The Arabs, in their struggle with the Prophet, did everything to counteract him, but despite their distinguished ability and excellence in eloquence and rhetoric, they were not able to oppose him with anything like the Qur'an, because it was not within the power of human beings, to combine the succinctness of the phrases of the Qur'an and the smoothness of its style together with what it contained of the news of the ancient generations and the fact that the Prophet - the praise and peace be upon him - himself was unlettered having no experience with books, with the prediction of unknown future events the subsequent occurrence of which established the truthfulness of the Prophet - may praise and peace be upon him.

Examples of this are found in the Words of Allah:

"The Romans have been defeated in a land close by; but after their defeat, in a few years they shall become the victors." (Qur'an 30:2-3).

The reason why a miracle attests the truthfulness of the messengers is because everything which human beings cannot do must be the work of Allah."[26]

Was Muhammad a Prophet or a Messenger?
In order to answer this question we have to clarify these two concepts:

Nabi (Prophet):
The word prophet in the Arabic language means Nabi. Nabi is derived from the Arabic word Anba'a. A person is called a Nabi or prophet because he communicates to people something from Allah. Thus a prophet, or Nabi, is a human being who was chosen and inspired by Allah in order to revive and remind people of a divine message that was previously sent to them from Allah.

A Nabi or a prophet is endowed by Allah with certain powers and the ability to see the future, and this ability is an attribute of prophets that stands as the very proof of their prophethood. The Nabi brings no holy book.

Rasool (Messenger):
The word messenger in the Arabic language means Rasool. Rasool or a Messenger is also a human being who was chosen by Allah, but a Rasool was chosen in order to deliver a new message that establishes the benefits of people on earth. The message they deliver is usually talking about the hereafter and foreseeing the future. The Rasool usually brings from Allah a holy book, such as the Books of Moses known as the Torah.

In this sense every Rasool (messenger) is a Nabi (prophet), but not every Nabi is a Rasool. Muhammad was a Rasool and thus a Nabi too.

---

[26] Al-Ghazali: al-Risalah al-Qudsiyya, Ihya', Vol. 1.chapter 2.

14. The Life of the Prophet Muhammad[27]
(Blessings and Peace of Allah be Upon Him)

His Parents

Muhammad the son of 'Abdullah was born in Mecca on Monday the 9th of Rabee' al-Awwal (April 20, 571 A.D.) His father 'Abdullah was the youngest son of Abdul Muttalib, the most respected person in the tribe of bani Hashim. 'Abdullah married Amina, daughter of Wahab bin 'Abd Munaf. Amina thus, in the light of this ancestral lineage, stood eminent in respect of nobility of position and descent. Her father was the chief of Bani Zahra to whom great honor was attributed.

'Abdullah and Amina were married in Mecca, and soon after, Amina was pregnant and 'Abdullah went on a trade journey. On his way back he died in Madina. 'Abdullah was twenty-five years old when he died. 'Abdullah died two months before the birth of his son, Muhammad [pbuh].

'Abdullah left very little wealth —five camels, a small number of goats, a she-servant, called Barakah – Umm Ayman – who would later serve as the Prophet's nursemaid.

His Birth

Muhammad [pbuh] was born in Bani Hashim lane in Mecca on Monday morning, the 9th of Rabi' Al-Awwal, i.e., the twentieth or twenty-second of April 571 A.D.

His mother immediately sent someone to inform his grandfather 'Abdul-Muttalib of the happy event. Happily he came to her, and

---

[27] This short biography (Seerah) of the Prophet Muhammad (pbuh) is the most authentic. It is derived from many traditional sources that are very well known of their importance and reliability in this field. The authors of some of these sources are: Ibn Ishaq, Ibn Hisham, Ibn al-Qayyem, Sahih Bukhari, and Saheeh Muslim. Since all these sources with different narrations being nicely implemented in a great book in this regard called *Al-Raheeq al-Makhtoom (The Sealed Nectar)* by Safyy al-Rahaman al-Mubarkpuri, Dar al-Wafaa', Egypt, 1420 A.H. / 2000 A.D. Thus I decided to make a very condensed summary of the seerah of the Prophet based on his book.

carried Muhammad [pbuh] to Al-Ka'bah, prayed to Allah and thanked Him. 'Abdul-Muttalib called the baby Muhammad, a name not then common among the Arabs. He circumcised him on his seventh day, as was the custom of the Arabs.

Babyhood
It was the general custom of the Arabs living in towns to send their children away to bedouin wet nurses so that they might grow up in the free and healthy surroundings of the desert, where they would develop a robust frame and acquire the pure speech and manners of the bedouins, who were noted both for purity of their language and for being free from those vices which usually develop in sedentary societies. Muhammad [pbuh] was later entrusted to Haleemah from Bani Sa'd bin Bakr.
Traditions relate how Haleemah and the whole of her household were favored by successive strokes of good fortune while the baby Muhammad [pbuh] lived under her care. Ibn Ishaq states that Haleemah narrated that she along with her husband and a suckling

babe, set out from her village in the company of some women of her clan in quest of children to suckle. She said:

It was a year of drought and famine and we had nothing to eat. I rode on a brown she-ass. We also had with us an old she-camel. By Allah we could not get even a drop of milk. We could not have a wink of sleep during the night for the child kept crying on account of hunger. There was not enough milk in my breast and even the she-camel had nothing to feed him. We used to constantly pray for rain and immediate relief. At length we reached Mecca looking for children to suckle. Not even a single woman amongst us accepted the Messenger of Allah [pbuh] offered to her. As soon as they were told that he was an orphan, they refused him. We had fixed our eyes on the reward that we would get from the child's father. An orphan! What are his grandfather and mother likely to do? So we spurned him because of that. Every woman who came with me got a suckling and when we were about to depart, I said to my husband:
"By Allah, I do not like to go back along with the other women without any baby. I should go to that orphan and I must take him."
He said: "There is no harm in doing so and perhaps Allah might bless us through him."
So I went and took him because there was simply no other alternative left for me but to take him. When I lifted him in my arms and returned to my place I put him on my breast and to my great surprise, I found enough milk in it. He drank to his heart's content, and so did his foster brother and then both of them went to sleep although my baby had not been able to sleep the previous night. My husband then went to the she-camel to milk it and, to his astonishment; he found plenty of milk in it. He milked it and we drank to our fill, and enjoyed a sound sleep during the night. The next morning, my husband said: "By Allah Haleemah, you must understand that you have been able to get a blessed child." And I replied: "By the grace of Allah, I hope so."

Muhammad [pbuh] stayed with Haleemah for two years until he was weaned as Haleemah said:
We then took him back to his mother requesting her earnestly to have him stay with us and benefit by the good fortune and blessings he had brought us. We persisted in our request, which we substantiated by our anxiety over the child catching a certain infection peculiar to Mecca. At last, we were granted our wish and

Muhammad [pbuh] stayed with us until he was four or five years of age.

When Muhammad was four or five years old, as told by Anas in *Sahih Muslim*, Gabriel came down and ripped Muhammad's chest open and took out his heart. He then extracted a blood-clot out of it and said: "That was the part of Satan in thee." And then he washed it with the water of Zamzam in a gold basin. After that the heart was joined together and restored to its place. The boys and his playmates came running to his mother, i.e. his nurse, and said: "Verily, Muhammad [pbuh] has been murdered." They all rushed towards him and found him all right only his face was white.

Back to His Passionate Mother
After this event, Haleemah was worried about the boy and returned him to his mother with whom he stayed until he was six.
 In respect of the memory of her late husband, Amina decided to visit his grave in Yathrib (Madina). She set out to cover a journey of 500 kilometers with her orphan boy, woman servant Umm Ayman and her father-in-law 'Abdul-Muttalib. She spent a month there and then made her way back to Mecca. On the way, she became severely ill and died.

To His Compassionate Grandfather
'Abdul-Muttalib brought the boy to Mecca. He had warm feelings towards the boy, his orphan grandson, whose recent disaster (his mother's death) added more to the pains of the past.

When Muhammad [pbuh] was eight years, his grandfather 'Abdul-Muttalib passed away in Mecca. The charge of the Prophet [pbuh] was now passed on to his uncle Abu Talib, who was the brother of the Prophet's father.

To His Uncle
Abu Talib took the charge of his nephew in the best way. He put him with his children and preferred him to them. He singled the boy out with great respect and high esteem. For the remainder of his life, Abu Talib cherished his nephew and extended all possible protection and support to him. His relations with others were determined in the light of the treatment they showed to the Prophet [pbuh].

Bahira, the Monk

When Muhammad was twelve years old, he went with his uncle Abu Talib on a business journey to Syria. When they reached Busra they met a monk called Bahira (his real name was Georges), who showed great kindness, and entertained them lavishly. He had never received or entertained them before. He readily enough recognized the Prophet [pbuh] and said while taking his hand: "This is the master of all humans. Allah will send him with a Message which will be a mercy to all beings." Abu Talib asked: "How do you know that?" He replied: "When you appeared from the direction of 'Aqabah, all stones and trees prostrated themselves, which they never do except for a Prophet. I can recognize him also by the seal of Prophethood which is below his shoulder, like an apple. We have got to learn this from our books."

Muhammad's Early Job

Muhammad [pbuh], had no particular job in his early youth, but it was reported that he worked as a shepherd for Bani Sa'd in Mecca. At the age of 25, he went to Syria as a merchant for Khadijah [R].

Khadijah, daughter of Khwailid, was a business-woman of great honor and fortune. She employed men to do her business for a certain percentage of the profits. Quraish people were mostly trade's people, so when Khadijah was informed of Muhammad [pbuh], his truthful words, great honesty and kind manners, she sent for him. She offered him money to go to Syria and do her business, and she would give him a higher rate than the others. She would also send her hireling, Maisarah, with him. He agreed and went with her servant to Syria for trade.

His Marriage to Khadijah

When he returned to Mecca, Khadijah noticed more profits and blessings than she used to. Her hireling also told her of Muhammad's good manners, honesty, deep thought, sincerity and faith. Khadijah realized that she wanted to marry Muhammad [pbuh]. Many prominent men had asked for her hand in marriage, but she always spurned their advances. She disclosed her wish to her friend Nafisa who immediately went to Muhammad [pbuh] and broke the good news to him. He agreed and requested his uncles to go to Khadijah's uncle and talk on this issue. Subsequently, they were married. The marriage contract was witnessed by Bani Hashim and the heads of Mudhar. This took place after the Prophet's return from Syria. He gave her twenty camels as a dowry. She was, then, forty years old and was considered the best woman of her folk in lineage, fortune and wisdom. She was the first woman whom the Messenger of Allah [pbuh] married. He did not get married to any others until she had died.

Khadijah bore all his children, except one: Al-Qasim, Zainab, Ruqaiyah, Umm Kulthum, Fatimah and 'Abdullah who was called Taiyib and Tahir. The only child she did not bear was Ibrahim. All his sons died in childhood and all the daughters except Fatimah died during his lifetime. Fatimah died six months after his death. All his daughters witnessed Islam, embraced it, and emigrated to Madina.

Rebuilding al-Ka'bah and the Arbitration Issue
Five years before Prophethood, there was a great flood in Mecca that swept towards Al-Ka'bah and almost demolished it. Quraish was obliged to rebuild it to safeguard its holiness and position. When Muhammad [pbuh] was thirty-five, Quraish started rebuilding Al-Ka'bah. It was a low building of white stones no more than 6.30 meters high, from the days of Ishmael. It was also roofless and that gave the thieves easy access to its treasures inside. It was also exposed to the wearing factors of nature — because it was built a long time ago — that weakened and cracked its walls. The chiefs of Quraish decided to use only legal money in rebuilding Al-Ka'bah; so all money that was derived from harlotry, usury or unjust practices was excluded. They were, at first, too awed to knock down the wall, but Al-Waleed bin Al-Mugheerah Al-Mukhzumi started the work. Seeing that no harm had happened to him, the others participated in demolishing the walls until they reached the basis laid by Abraham. When they started rebuilding its walls, they divided the work among the tribes. Each tribe was responsible for rebuilding a part of it. The tribes collected stones and started work. The work went on in harmony till the time came to put the sacred Black Stone in its proper place. Then strife broke out among the chiefs, and lasted for four or five days, each contesting for the honor of placing the stone in its position. Daggers were on the point of being drawn and great bloodshed seemed imminent. Luckily, the oldest among the chiefs Abu Omaiyah bin

Mugheerah Al-Makhzumi made a proposal which was accepted by all. He said: "Let him, who enters the Sanctuary first of all, decide on the point." It was then Allah's Will that Muhammad [pbuh] should be the first to enter the Mosque. On seeing him, all the people on the scene, cried with one voice: "*Al-Ameen* (the trustworthy) has come. We are content to abide by his decision." Calm and self-possessed, Muhammad [pbuh] received the commission and at once resolved upon an answer which was acceptable to them all. He asked for a mantle which he spread on the ground and placed the stone in its center. He then asked the representatives of the different clans among them, to lift the stone all together. When it had reached the proper place, Muhammad [pbuh] laid it in the proper position with his own hands. This is how a very tense situation was eased and a grave danger averted by the wisdom of the Prophet [pbuh].

Away from Evil
Ibn al-Atheer reported Muhammad [pbuh] as saying: "I have never tried to do what my people do except for two times. Every time Allah intervened and checked me from doing so and I never did that again. Once I told my fellow-shepherd to take care of my sheep when we were in the upper part of Mecca. I wanted to go down to Mecca and entertain myself as the young men did. I went down to the first house of Mecca where I heard music. I entered and asked:

'What is this?'
Someone answered:
'It is a wedding party.'
I sat down and listened but soon went into a deep sleep. I was awakened by the heat of the sun. I went back to my fellow-shepherd and told him of what had happened to me. I have never tried it again."

The Trustworthy
He was the most gentle-hearted, chaste, hospitable man and always impressed people by his piety-inspiring countenance. He was the most truthful and the best to keep a covenant. His fellow-citizens, by common consent, gave him the title of *Al-'Ameen* (trustworthy). The Mother of believers, Khadijah, once said: He unites familial relations, he helps the poor and the needy, he entertains guests and endures hardships in the path of truthfulness.

The Value of Silence

Prophet Muhammad [pbuh] was, in his youth, a combination of the best social attributes. He was an exemplary man of weighty mind and faultless insight. His long silence helped favorably in his habit of meditation and deep investigation into the truth. He shunned superstitious practices but took an active part in constructive and useful dealings. He kept himself aloof from drinking wine, eating meat slaughtered on stone altars, or attending idolatrous festivals. He held idols in extreme aversion and most abhorrence. Allah's providence, no doubts, detached him from all abominable or evil practices.

In The Cave of Hira'

When Muhammad [pbuh] was nearly forty, he often passed long hours in retirement meditating and speculating over all aspects of creation around him. This meditative temperament helped to widen the mental gap between him and his compatriots. He used to provide himself with *Sawiq* (barley porridge) and water and then immediately head for the hills and ravines in the neighborhood of Mecca. One of these in particular was his favorite resort — a cave named Hira', in the Mount An-Nour. It was only two miles from Mecca, a small cave 4 yards long and 1.75 yard wide. He would always go there and invite wayfarers to share his modest provision. He used to devote most of his time, and Ramadan in particular, to worship and meditation on the universe around him. His heart was restless about the moral evils and idolatry that were rampant among his people; he was as yet helpless because no definite course, or specific approach had been available for him to follow and rectify the ill practices around him. Solitude attended with this sort of contemplative approach must be understood in its Divine perspective. It was a preliminary stage to the period of grave responsibilities that he was to shoulder very soon.

Privacy and detachment from the impurities of life were two indispensable prerequisites for the Prophet's soul to come into close communion with the Unseen Power that lies behind all aspects of existence in this infinite universe. It was a rich period of privacy that lasted for three years and ushered in a new era of indissoluble contact with that Power.

15. The Beginning of Revelation
Gabriel brings down the Revelation

When he was forty, signs of his Prophethood started to appear and twinkle on the horizon of life; they were the true visions he experienced for six months. The period of Prophethood was 23 years; so the period of these six months of true visions constituted an integral part of the forty-six parts of Prophethood. In Ramadan, in his third year of solitude in the cave of Hira', Allah's Will desired His mercy to flow on earth and Muhammad [pbuh] was honored with Prophethood, and the light of Revelation burst upon him with some verses of the Noble Qur'an.

As for the exact date, careful investigation into circumstantial evidence and relevant clues point directly to Monday, 21st. Ramadan at night, i.e. August, 10, 610 A.D. with Prophet Muhammad [pbuh] exactly 40 years, 6 months and 12 days of age, i.e. 39 Gregorian years, 3 months and 22 days.

Forerunners of the Revelation assumed the form of true visions that would strikingly come true all the time. After that, solitude became dear to him and he would go to the cave, Hira', to engage in *Tahannuth* (devotion) there for a certain number of nights before returning to his family, and then he would return for provisions for a similar stay. At length, unexpectedly, the Truth (the angel) came to him and said:

"Read."
"I cannot read," he (Muhammad [pbuh]) said.
The Prophet [pbuh] described: "Then he took me and squeezed me vehemently and then let me go and repeated the order:

'Read.'
'I cannot read' said I, and once again he squeezed me and let me go till I was exhausted. Then he said:

'Read.'
I said 'I cannot read.'
He squeezed me for a third time and then let me go and said:

"Read! In the name of your Lord who created,

Created man, from a clot [a piece of thick coagulated blood]
Read! And your Lord is Most Generous,
Who taught [the writing] by the Pen,
Taught man that which he knew not." (Qur'an, 96:1-5)

The Prophet [pbuh] repeated these verses. He was trembling with fear. At this stage, he came back to his wife Khadijah, and said, "Cover me, cover me." They covered him until he restored security. He apprised Khadijah of the incident in the cave and added that he was horrified. His wife tried to soothe him and reassured him saying, "Allah will never disgrace you. You unite familial relations; you bear the burden of the weak; you help the poor and the needy, you entertain the guests and endure hardships in the path of truthfulness."
She set out with the Prophet [pbuh] to her cousin Waraqa bin Nawfal who had embraced Christianity in the pre-Islamic period, and used to write the Bible in Hebrew. He was a blind old man.

Khadijah said:
"My cousin! Listen to your nephew!"
Waraqa said: "O my nephew! What did you see?"
The Messenger of Allah [pbuh] told him what had happened to him.
Waraqa replied:
"This is 'Namus' i.e. (the angel who is entrusted with Divine Secrets) that Allah sent to Moses. I wish I were younger. I wish I could live up to the time when your people would turn you out."
Muhammad [pbuh] asked:
"Will they drive me out?"
Waraqa answered in the affirmative and said:
"Anyone who came with something similar to what you have brought was treated with hostility; and if I should be alive till that day, then I would support you strongly."
A few days later Waraqa died and the revelation also subsided.

Interruption of Revelation
Ibn Sa'd reported on the authority of Ibn 'Abbas that the Revelation paused for a few days. [Fath al-Bari 1/27,12/360]

Once more, Gabriel brings Allah's Revelation

Ibn Hajar said: 'That (the pause of Allah's revelation for a few days) was to relieve the Messenger of Allah [pbuh] of the fear he experienced and to make him long for the Revelation. His waiting and longing for the coming of the revelation constituted a good reason for his steadfastness and self-possession on the arrival of Allah's inspiration, Al-Bukhari reported on the authority of Jabir bin 'Abdullah that he had heard the Messenger of Allah [pbuh] speak about the period of pause as follows:

"While I was walking, I heard a voice from the sky. I looked up, and surely enough, it was the same angel who had visited me in the cave of Hira'. He was sitting on a chair between the earth and the sky. I was very afraid of him and knelt on the ground. I went home saying: 'Cover me ..., Cover me ...'. Allah revealed to me the verses:

'O you (Muhammad [pbuh]) enveloped (in garments)! Arise and warn! And your Lord (Allah) magnify! And your garments purify! And keep away from *Ar-Rujz* (the idols)!'" [Qur'an 74:1-5]

After that the revelation started coming strongly, frequently and regularly. [Bukhari, The Book of Tafseer, 2/733][28]

---

[28] Ibn Al-Qayyim, mentioning the stages of the Revelation, said:
The First: The period of true vision. It was the starting point of the Revelation to the Messenger of Allah [pbuh].
The Second: What the angel invisibly cast in the Prophet's mind and heart. The Messenger of Allah [pbuh] said: "The Noble Spirit revealed to me 'No soul will perish until it exhausts its due course, so fear Allah and gently request Him. Never get so impatient to the verge of disobedience of Allah. What Allah has can never be acquired but through obedience to Him.'"
The Third: The angel used to visit the Messenger of Allâh [pbuh] in the form of a human being and would speak to him directly. This would enable him to fully understand what the angel said. The angel was sometimes seen in this form by the Prophet's Companions.
The Fourth: The angel came to him like the toll of a bell and this was the most difficult form because the angel used to seize him tightly and sweat would stream from his forehead even on the coldest day. If the Prophet [pbuh] was on his camel, the camel would not withstand the weight, so it

16. Jihad in Mecca or the Peaceful Intellectual Effort (Jahd)

Phases and Stages of the Call
The Call to Islam could be divided into two phases distinctively demarcated:

The Meccan phase: nearly thirteen years.
The Madinese phase: fully ten years.

Each of the two phases included distinctive features easily discernible through accurate scrutiny into the circumstances that characterized each of them.

The Meccan phase can be divided into three stages:

The stage of the secret Call: three years.
The stage of the proclamation of the Call in Mecca: from the beginning of the fourth year of Prophethood to almost the end of the tenth year.

The stage of the call to Islam and propagating it beyond Mecca: it lasted from the end of tenth year of the Prophethood until Muhammad's [pbuh] emigration to Madina.

---

would immediately kneel down on the ground. Once the Messenger of Allâh [pbuh] had such a revelation when he was sitting and his thigh was on Zaid's, Zaid felt the pressure had almost injured his thigh.

The Fifth: The Prophet [pbuh] saw the angel in his actual form. The angel would reveal to him what Allâh had ordered him to reveal. This, as mentioned in (Qur'an), in *Sûrah An-Najm* (Chapter 53 - The Star), happened twice.

The Sixth: What Allâh Himself revealed to him in heaven i.e. when he ascended to heaven and received Allâh's behest of *Salât* (prayer).

The Seventh: Allâh's Words to His Messenger [pbuh] at first hand without the mediation of an angel. It was a privilege granted to Moses and clearly attested in the Qur'ân, as it is attested to our Prophet [pbuh] in the *Sûrah Al-Isrâ'* (Chapter 17 - The Journey by Night) of the Noble Qur'an.

The First Stage: Strife in the Way of the Call
Three Years of Secret Call

It is well-known that Mecca was the center for the Arabs, and housed the custodians of Al-Ka'bah. Protection and guardianship of the idols and stone graven images that received veneration on the part of all the Arabs lay in the hands of the Meccans. Hence the difficulty of hitting the target of reform and rectitude in a place considered the den of idolatry. Working in such an atmosphere no doubt required unshakable will and determination, that is why the call unto Islam assumed a clandestine form so that the Meccans would not be enraged by the unexpected surprise.

The Early Converts

The Prophet [pbuh] naturally initiated his sacred mission right from home and then moved to the people closely associated with him.

Khadijah, the Prophet's spouse, was the first to enter the fold of Islam followed by his freed slave Zaid bin Haritha, his cousin, 'Ali bin Abi Talib, who had been living with him since his early childhood, and next came his intimate friend Abu Bakr As-Siddiq (Abu Bakr the truth verifier). All of those professed Islam on the very first day of the call.

The Prophet [pbuh] used to meet and teach the new converts Islam in privacy because the call to Islam was still running on an individual and secret basis. Revelation accelerated and continued after the first verses of "*O you wrapped in garments.*" The verses and pieces of *Sûrah* (chapters) revealed at this time were short ones with wonderful strong pauses and quite fascinating rhythms in full harmony with a delicate whispering setting. The central topic running through them focused on sanctifying the soul, and deterring the Muslims from falling prey to the deceptive glamour of life. The early verses were used as well to give a highly accurate account of the Hell and the Garden (Paradise), leading the believers down a new course diametrically opposed to the ill practices rampant among their compatriots.

The Quraishites learn about the Call

News of this stage of the Call leaked out, even though it was conducted in a clandestine manner and on an individual basis, and gathered a public interest all over Mecca. In the beginning, the

Meccan leaders were not interested in Muhammad [pbuh] and took no heed of his teachings.

After three underground years of activism, a group of believers emerged stamped by a spirit of fraternity and cooperation with one definite objective in their mind: propagating and deeply establishing the call unto Islam. For a full three years Muhammad [pbuh] had been content to teach within a rather narrow circle. The time had, however, come to preach the faith of the Lord openly.

The angel Gabriel had brought down a further Revelation of Allah's Will to confront his people, invalidate their falsehood and crush their idolatrous practices.

Calling the Closest Kinspeople
In obedience to Allah's Commands, Muhammad [pbuh] rallied his kinsmen of Bani Hashim with a group of Bani Al-Muttalib bin 'Abd Munaf. The audience counted forty-five men.

Abu Lahab immediately took the initiative and addressed the Prophet [pbuh]: "These are your uncles and cousins, speak on to the point, but first of all you have got to know that your kinspeople are not in a position to withstand all the Arabs. Another point you have got to bear in mind is that your relatives are sufficient unto you. If you follow their tradition, it will be easier for them than to face the other clans of Quraish supported by the other Arabs. Verily, I have never heard of anyone who has incurred more harm on his kinspeople than you." The Messenger of Allah [pbuh] kept silent and said nothing in that meeting.

Another Meeting
He invited them to another meeting and managed to secure an audience. He then stood up and delivered a short speech explaining quite cogently what was at stake. He said:

"I celebrate Allah's praise, I seek His help, I believe in Him, I put my trust in Him, I bear witness that there is no god to be worshipped but Allah with no associate. A guide can never lie to his people. I swear by Allah, there is no god but He, that I have been sent as a Messenger to you, in particular and to all the people, in general. I swear by Allah you will die just as you sleep, you will be resurrected just as you wake up. You will be called to account for your deeds. It is then either Hell forever or the Garden (Paradise) forever."

Abu Talib replied: "We would love to help you, accept your advice and believe in your words. These are your kinspeople whom you have collected and I am one of them but I am the fastest to do what you like. Do what you have been ordered. I shall protect and defend you, but I can't quit the religion of 'Abdul-Muttalib."

Abu Lahab then said to Abu Talib:
" I swear by Allah that this is a bad thing. You must stop him before the others do."
Abu Talib, however, answered:
"I swear by Allah to protect him as long as I am alive."

On Mount As-Safa
After the Messenger of Allah [pbuh] became sure of Abu Talib's commitment to his protection while he called the people unto Allah, he stood up on Mount As-Safa one day and called out loudly:
"O *Sabahah!* [This is an Arabic expression used when one appeals for help or draws the attention of others to some dangers] "Sects of Quraish came to him. He called them to testify to the Oneness of Allah and believe in his Messengership and the Day of Resurrection. Al-Bukhari reported part of this story on the authority of Ibn 'Abbas. He said: "When the following verses were revealed:
"And warn your tribe (O Muhammad [pbuh]) of near kindred." [Qur'an 26:214]

The Messenger of Allah [pbuh] ascended Mount As-Safa and started to call: "O Bani Fahr! O Bani 'Adi (two septs of Quraish)." Many people gathered and Abu Lahab was also present. The Prophet [pbuh] said:

"You see, if I were to tell you that there were some horsemen in the valley planning to raid you, will you believe me?"
They said: "Yes, we have never experienced any lie from you."
He said: "I am a warner to you before a severe torment."

Abu Lahab promptly replied: "Perish you all the day! Have you summoned us for such a thing?" The verses were immediately revealed on that occasion:

"Perish the two hands of Abi Lahab..." [Al-Qur'an 111:1].

It was verily a loud suggestive Call stating unequivocally to the closest people that belief in his Message constituted the cornerstone of any future relation between him and them, and that the blood-relation on which the whole Arabian life was based, had ceased to exist in the light of that Divine ultimatum.

Shouting the Truth and the Polytheists' Reaction
The Prophet's voice kept reverberating in Mecca until the following verse was revealed:

"Therefore proclaim openly (Allah's Message — Islamic Monotheism), that which you are commanded, and turn away from *Al-Mushrikûn* (polytheists)." [Qur'an 15:94]

He then commenced discrediting the superstitious practices of idolatry, revealing its worthless reality and utter impotence, and giving concrete proof that idolatry per se or taking it as the medium through which an idolater could come in contact with Allah, is manifest falsehood.

The Meccans, on their part, burst into outrage and disapproval. Muhammad's [pbuh] words created a thunderbolt that turned the Meccan time-honored ideological life upside down. They could ill afford to hear someone attaching to polytheists and idolaters the description of straying people. They started to rally their resources to settle down the affair, quell the onward marching revolution and deal a pre-emptive strike to its devotees before it devours and crushes down their consecrated traditions and long standing heritage.

What would they do?
Following careful deliberation, they hit upon the only target available, i.e. to contact the Messenger's uncle, Abu Talib and request him to intervene and advise his nephew to stop his activities.

"O Abu Talib! Your nephew curses our gods; finds faults with our way of life, mocks at our religion and degrades our forefathers; either you must stop him, or you must let us get at him. For you are in the same opposition as we are in opposition to him; and we will rid you of him."

Abu Talib tried to appease their wrath by giving them a polite reply. The Prophet [pbuh], however, continued on his way preaching Allah's religion and calling men hitherto, heedless of all their desperate attempts and malicious intentions. [Ibn Hisham 1/265]

Advisory Council to bar Pilgrims from Muhammad's Call
During those days, the Quraish had another serious concern; the proclamation of the Call had only been a few months old when the season of pilgrimage was soon to come. The Quraish knew that the Arab delegates were coming within a short time. They agreed that it was necessary to contemplate a device that was bound to alienate the Arab pilgrims from the new faith preached by Muhammad [pbuh]. They went to see Al-Waleed bin Al-Mugheerah to deliberate on this issue. Al-Waleed invited them to agree on a unanimous resolution that could enjoy the approbation of them all. However, they were at odds. Some suggested that they describe him as *Kahin*, i.e., soothsayer; but this suggestion was turned down on grounds that his words were not so rhymed. Others proposed *Majnun*, i.e., possessed by jinn; this was also rejected because no insinuations peculiar to that state of mind ware detected, they claimed. "Why not say he is a poet?" Some said. Here again they could not reach a common consent, alleging that his words were totally outside the lexicon of poetry. "OK then; let us accuse him of practicing witchcraft," was a fourth suggestion. Here also Al-Waleed showed some reluctance saying that the Prophet [pbuh] was known to have never involved himself in the practice of blowing on the knots, and admitted that his speech was a sweet tasting root and branch. He, however, found that the most plausible charge to be leveled against Muhammad [pbuh] was witchcraft. The ungodly company adopted this opinion and agreed to propagate one uniform formula to the effect that he was a magician so powerful and commanding in his art that he would successfully alienate son from father, man from his brother, wife from her husband and man from his clan.

The most wicked of them was Abu Lahab, who would shadow the Prophet's steps crying aloud, "O men, do not listen to him for he is a liar; he is an apostate." Nevertheless, Muhammad [pbuh] managed to create a stir in the whole area, and even to convince a few people to accept his Call.

Attempts made to check the Onward March of Islam

Having fully perceived that Muhammad [pbuh] could never be deterred from his Call, the Quraish, in a desperate attempt to quell the tidal wave of the Call, resorted to other cheap means acting from base motives: Scoffing, degrading, ridiculing, belying and laughter-instigating cheap manners, all of which were leveled at the new converts in general, and the person of Muhammad [pbuh] in particular, with the aim of dragging the spirit of despair into their morale, and slackening their ardent zealotry. They used to denounce the Prophet [pbuh] as a man possessed by a jinn, or an insane person:

"And they say: O you (Muhammad [pbuh]) to whom the *Dhikr* (the Qur'an) has been sent down! Verily, you are a mad man." [Qur'an 15:6]

Or a liar practicing witchcraft,

"And they (Arab pagans) wonder that a warner (Prophet Muhammad [pbuh]) has come to them from among themselves! And the disbelievers say: "This (Prophet Muhammad [pbuh]) is a sorcerer, a liar." [Qur'an 38:4].

Among the early converts, there was a group who had unfortunately no strong clan at their back to support them. These innocent souls were ridiculed and jeered in season and out of season. Referring to such people, the highbrow Quraish aristocrats used repeatedly to ask the Prophet [pbuh], with jest and scorn:

"Allah has favored from amongst us?" [Qur'an 6:53]

And Allah said:

"Does not Allah know best those who are grateful?" [Qur'an 6:53]

"Verily! (During the worldly life) those who committed crimes used to laugh at those who believed; and whenever they passed by them, used to wink one to another (in mockery); and when they returned to their own people, they would return jesting; and when they saw them, they said: 'Verily! These have indeed gone astray!' But they (disbelievers, sinners) had not been sent as watchers over them (the believers)." [Qur'an 83:29-33]

With respect to the Qur'an, they used to allege that it was:

"Tales of the ancients, which he (Muhammad [pbuh]) has written down, and they are dictated to him morning and afternoon." [Qur'an 25:5]

The iniquitous went on ceaselessly inculcating in people's ears that the Qur'an was not a true Revelation:

"This (the Qur'an) is nothing but a lie that he (Muhammad [pbuh]) has invented, and others have helped him at it." [Qur'an 25:4]

The pagans and those who were hostile to the revelation of Allah and Islam, could not understand how such wonderful verses could flow from the tongue of the Prophet [pbuh] without having someone to teach, and claimed:

"It is only a human being who teaches him." [Qur'an 16:103]

They also raised another baseless and superficial objection:
"Why does this Messenger (Muhammad [pbuh]) eat food and walk about in the markets (like ourselves)?" [Qur'an 25:7]

They could not perceive that a teacher for mankind is one who shares their nature, mingles in their life, is acquainted with their doings, and sympathizes with their joys and sorrows.

The Qur'an has vehemently refuted their charges and allegations and has explained that the utterances of the Prophet [pbuh] are the Revelations of the Lord and their nature and content provides a bold challenge to those who attribute his Prophetic expressions to some base origin, at times to the mental throes of a dreaming reformer, at others to the effusion of a frenzied poet or the incoherent driveling of an insane man.

In a fresh attempt to dissuade Muhammad [pbuh] from his principled stand, the Quraish invited him to compromise on his teachings and come to terms with their pre-Islamic practices in such a way that he would quit some of his religion and the polytheists do the same. Allah, the All-High says:

"They wish that you should compromise (in religion out of courtesy) with them, so they (too) would compromise with you." [Qur'an 68:9].

The idolaters offered that Muhammad [pbuh] worships their gods for a year, and they worship his Lord for a year. The prophet (pbuh) rejected this offer.

Persecutions
At the beginning of the fourth year of the Call, and for a period of some months, the polytheists confined their harassment tactics to the above-mentioned ones. But on realizing the futility of these procedures, they decided to organize a full-scale opposition campaign. They called for a general meeting and elected a committee of twenty-five men of Quraish notables with Abu Lahab, the Prophet's uncle, as a chairman. Following some lengthy deliberations, they reached a decisive decision to take measures deemed to stop the tidal wave of Islam through different channels. They were determined to spare no effort, in combating the new faith. They decided to malign the Messenger of Allah [pbuh] and put the new converts to different sorts of torture using all available resources. It was easy to put the resolutions relating to the new converts who were deemed weak into effect. As for the Prophet [pbuh], it was not easy to malign him because he had Abu Talib, his uncle, who came from a noble descent and had an awe-inspiring clan to support him.

Abu Lahab himself took the initiative in the new series of persecutions, and started to mete out countless aspects of harmful deeds, hatred and spite against Muhammad [pbuh], starting with flinging stones at him, forcing his two sons to divorce their wives Ruqaiya and Umm Kulthum, the Prophet's daughters. His wife, Umm Jameel bint Harb, the sister of Abu Sufyan also had her part in this ruthless campaign. She proved that she was not less than her husband in the enmity and hatred she harbored for the Prophet [pbuh]. She used to tie bundles of thorns with ropes of twisted palm-leaf fiber and strew them about in the paths which the Prophet [pbuh] was expected to take, in order to cause him bodily injury. She was a real shrew, bad-tempered with abusive language, highly skilled in the art of hatching intrigues, and enkindling the fire of discord and sedition. She was deservedly stained as *'the carrier of firewood'* in the Noble Qur'an. On receiving this news, she directly proceeded to the Mosque with a handful of pebbles to hurl at the Prophet [pbuh]. Allah, the Great, took away her sight and she saw only Abu Bakr who was sitting immediately next to the Prophet [pbuh]. She then addressed Abu Bakr most audaciously threatening to break his Companion's mouth with her handful of pebbles, and recited a line of verse pregnant with impudent defiance: "We have disobeyed the dispraised one, rejected his Call, and alienated ourselves from his religion." When she had left, Abu Bakr turned to the Prophet [pbuh] and inquired about the matter. The Prophet [pbuh] assured him that she did not see him because Allah had taken away her sight.

Abu Lahab and his household used to inflict those shameful examples of torture and harassment in spite of the blood relation that tied them for he was the Prophet's uncle and both lived in two contiguous houses. Actually, few of the Prophet's neighbors abstained from maligning him. They even threw the entrails of a goat on his back while he was performing his prayers.

Torturing New Muslims
The uncle of 'Uthman bin 'Affan used to wrap 'Uthman in a mat of palm leaves, and set fire under him. When Umm Mus'ab bin 'Umair heard of her son's conversion, she put him to starvation and then expelled him from her house. He used to enjoy full luxurious easy life, but in the aftermath of the tortures he sustained, his skin got wizened, and he assumed a horrible physical appearance. [Rahmat-ul-lil'alameen 1/57; Talqeeh Ahl-al-Athar p.60]

Another victim
Another victim of the highhandedness of the Quraish was 'Ammar bin Yasir, a freed slave of Bani Makhzoum. He, along with his mother and father, embraced Islam in its early phase. They were

repeatedly made to lie on the burning sand and were beaten severely. 'Ammar was at times tossed up on embers. The Prophet [pbuh] was greatly moved by the atrocities which were being perpetrated upon 'Ammar and his family. He always comforted them and raised his hand in prayer and said: "Be patient, you will verily find your abode in the Paradise." Yasir, the father, died because of repeated tortures. Sumaiyah, 'Ammar's mother was bayoneted to death by Abu Jahl himself, and thus merited the title of the first woman martyr in Islam. 'Ammar himself was subjected to various modes of torture and was always threatened to sustain severe suffering unless he abused Muhammad [pbuh] and recanted to Al-Lat and 'Uzza. In a weak moment, he uttered a word construed as recantation though his heart never wavered and he came back once to the Prophet [pbuh], who consoled him for his pain and confirmed his faith. Immediately afterwards the following verse was revealed:

"Whoever disbelieved in Allah after his belief, except him who is forced thereto and whose heart is at rest with Faith." [Qur'an 16:106]

Even the women converts were not spared, and the list is too long to include all of them. Zanira An-Nahdiyah and her daughter, Umm 'Ubais and many others had their full share of persecution at the hand of the oppressors — 'Umar bin Al-Khattab included — of course before his conversion to Islam. [Ibn Hisham 1/319]

The House of al-Arqam
In the light of these inhuman persecutions, the Prophet [pbuh] deemed it wise to advise his followers to conceal their conversion, in both word and deed. He took the decision to meet them secretly lest the Quraish learn of his designs, and so takes measures that might foil his goals.
The Prophet [pbuh], on the other hand, used to proclaim the Islamic Faith and preach it openly with deep devotion and studious pursuit, but for the general welfare of the new converts and in consideration of the strategic interest of Islam, he took Dar Al-Arqam, in As-Safa mountain, in the fifth year of his mission, as a temporary center to meet his followers secretly and instruct them in the Qur'an and in the Islamic wisdom.

The First Migration to Abyssinia (Ethiopia)

The series of persecutions started late in the fourth year of Prophethood, slowly at first, but steadily accelerated and worsened day by day and month by month until the situation got so extremely grave and no longer tolerable in the middle of the fifth year, that the Muslims began to seriously think of feasible ways to avert the painful tortures meted out to them. It was at that gloomy and desperate time that *Surat Al-Kahf* (Chapter 18 - The Cave) was revealed comprising definite answers to the questions with which the polytheists of Mecca constantly pestered the Prophet [pbuh]. It comprises three stories that include highly suggestive parables for the true believers to assimilate. The story of the Companions of the Cave implies implicit guidance for the believers to evacuate the hot spots of disbelief and aggression pregnant with the peril of enticement away from the true religion:

"(The young men said to one another): "And when you withdraw from them, and that which they worship, except Allah, then seek refuge in the Cave, your Lord will open a way for you from His Mercy and will make easy for you your affair (i.e. will give you what you will need of provision, dwelling, etc.)" [Qur'an 18:16].

Surat Al-Zumar (Chapter 39, The Crowds) was then revealed pointing directly to migration and stating that the earth is spacious enough and the believers must not consider themselves constrained by the forces of tyranny and evil:

"Good is (the reward) for those who do good in this world, and Allah's earth is spacious (so if you cannot worship Allah at a place, then go to another)! Only those who are patient shall receive their rewards in full without reckoning." [Qur'an 39:10].

The Prophet [pbuh] had already known that Ashamah Negus, king of Abyssinia (Ethiopia), was a fair ruler who would not wrong any of his subordinates, so he permitted some of his followers to seek asylum there in Abyssinia (Ethiopia).

In Rajab of the fifth year of Prophethood, a group of twelve men and four women left for Abyssinia (Ethiopia). Among the emigrants were 'Uthman bin 'Affan and his wife Ruqaiyah (the daughter of the Prophet [pbuh]). With respect to these two emigrants, the Prophet [pbuh] said:

"They are the first people to migrate in the cause of Allah after Abraham and Lot."

They sneaked out of Mecca under the heavy curtain of a dark night and headed for the sea where two boats happened to be sailing for Abyssinia (Ethiopia), their destination. News of their intended departure reached the ears of the Quraish, so some men were sent in their pursuit, but the believers had already left Shuaibah Port towards their secure haven where they were received warmly and accorded due hospitality.

In Ramadan of the same year, the Prophet [pbuh] went into the Holy Sanctuary where there was a large host of Quraish polytheists, including some notables and celebrities. Suddenly he began reciting *Surat An-Najm* (Chapter 41 - The Star). The awe-inspiring Words of Allah descended unawares upon them and they immediately were stunned by them. It was the first time for them to be shocked by the truthful Revelation. It had formerly been the favorite trick of those people who wished to dishonor Revelation, not only not to listen to it themselves but also to talk loudly and insolently when it was being read, so that even the true listeners would not be able to hear. Allah's Voice can never be silenced, "And those who disbelieve say:

"Listen not to this Qur'an, and make noise in the midst of its (recitation) that you may overcome." [Qur'an 41:26].

When the Words of Allah came into direct contact with their hearts, they were entranced and became oblivious to the materialistic world around them and were caught in a state of full attentiveness to the Divine Words to such an extent that when the Prophet [pbuh] reached the stormy heart-beating ending:

"So fall you down in prostration to Allah and worship Him (Alone)." [Qur'an 53:62]

The idolaters, unconsciously and with full compliance, prostrated themselves in absolute god-fearing and pure devotion. It was in fact the wonderful moment of the Truth that cleaved through the obdurate souls of the haughty and the attitude of the scoffers. They stood aghast when they perceived that Allah's Words had conquered their hearts and did the same thing that they had been trying hard to annihilate and exterminate. Their co-polytheists who had not been present on the scene reproached and blamed them severely.

However, due to the news that transpired to the Meccans about the good hospitality and warm welcome that the Muslims were accorded in Abyssinia (Ethiopia), the polytheists became terribly indignant and started to mete out more severe and horrible maltreatment and torture on the Muslims. Thereupon the Messenger of Allah [pbuh] deemed it imperative to permit the helpless creatures to seek asylum in Abyssinia (Ethiopia) for the second time. Migration this time was not as easy as it was the previous time, for the Quraish were on the alert to the least suspicious moves of the Muslims. In due course, however, the Muslims managed their affairs too fast for the Quraishites to thwart their attempt to escape. The group of emigrants this time comprised eighty-three men and nineteen or, in some versions, eighteen women. Whether or not 'Ammar was included is still a matter of doubt. [Tafheem-ul-Qur'an 5/188; Zad al-Ma'ad 1/24; Ibn Hisham 1/364; Rahmat-ul-lil'alameen 1/61]

Quraish's Machination against the Emigrants
The Quraish could not tolerate the prospect of a secure haven available for the Muslims in Abyssinia (Ethiopia), so they sent two staunch envoys to demand their extradition. They were 'Amr bin Al-'As and 'Abdullah bin Abi Rabi'a — before embracing Islam. They had taken with them valuable gifts for the king and his clergy, and had been able to win some of the courtiers over to their side. The pagan envoys claimed that the Muslim refugees should be expelled from Abyssinia (Ethiopia) and given over to them, on the ground that they had abandoned the religion of their forefathers, and their leader was preaching a religion different from theirs and from that of the king.

The king summoned the Muslims to the court and asked them to explain the teachings of their religion. The Muslim emigrants had decided to tell the whole truth, whatever the consequences. Ja'far bin Abi Talib stood up and addressed the king in the following words:

"O king! we were plunged in the depth of ignorance and barbarism; we adored idols, we lived in unchastity, we ate the dead bodies, and we spoke abominations, we disregarded every feeling of humanity, and the duties of hospitality and neighborhood were neglected; we knew no law but that of the strong, when Allah raised among us a man, of whose birth, truthfulness, honesty, and purity we were aware; and he called to the Oneness of Allah, and taught us not to associate anything with Him. He forbade us the worship of idols; and he enjoined us to speak the truth, to be faithful to our trusts, to be merciful and to regard the rights of the neighbors and kith and kin; he forbade us to speak evil of women, or to eat the substance of orphans; he ordered us to fly from the vices, and to abstain from evil; to offer prayers, to render alms, and to observe fast. We have believed in him, we have accepted his teachings and his injunctions to worship Allah, and not to associate anything with Him, and we have allowed what He has allowed, and prohibited what He has prohibited. For this reason, our people have risen against us; have persecuted us in order to make us forsake the worship of Allah and return to the worship of idols and other abominations. They have tortured and injured us, until finding no safety among them, we have come to your country, and hope you will protect us from oppression."

The king was very much impressed by these words and asked the Muslims to recite some of Allah's Revelation. Ja'far recited the opening verses of *Surat Maryam* (Chapter 19 — Mary) that tells the story of the birth of both John and Jesus Christ, down to the account of Mary having been fed with the food miraculously. Thereupon the king and the bishops of his realm were moved to tears. Here, the Negus exclaimed: "It seems as if these words and those which were revealed to Jesus are the rays of the light which have radiated from the same source." Turning to the crest-fallen envoys of Quraish, he said, "I am afraid, I cannot give you back these refugees. They are free to live and worship in my realm as they please."

The next day, the two envoys again went to the king and said that Muhammad [pbuh] and his followers blasphemed Jesus Christ.

Again the Muslims were summoned and asked what they thought of Jesus. Ja'far again stood up and replied:

"We speak about Jesus as we have been taught by our Prophet [pbuh], that is, he is the servant of Allah, His Messenger, His spirit and His Word breathed into Virgin Mary." The king at once remarked, "Even so do we believe. Blessed be you, and blessed be your master."

Then turning to the frowning envoys and to his bishops who got angry, he said:

"You may fret and fume as you like but Jesus is nothing more than what Ja'far has said about him."

He then assured the Muslims of full protection. He returned to the envoys of the Quraish, the gifts they had brought with them and sent them away. The Muslims lived in Abyssinia (Ethiopia) unmolested for a number of years till they returned to Madina. [Ibn Hisham 1/334-338]

In this way the Quraish's malicious intentions recoiled on them and their machination met with utter failure.

The pagans of Mecca therefore decided to approach Abu Talib for the second time and insisted that he put a stop to his nephew's activities, which if allowed unchecked, they said, would bring him into severe hostility. Abu Talib was deeply distressed at this open threat and the breach with his people and their enmity, but he could not afford to desert the Messenger too. He sent for his nephew and told him what the people had said, "Spare me and yourself and put not a burden on me that I can't bear." Upon this the Prophet [pbuh] thought that his uncle would let him down and would no longer support him, so he replied:
"O my uncle! by Allah if they put the sun in my right hand and the moon in my left on condition that I abandon this course, until Allah has made me victorious, or I perish therein, I would not abandon it."

The Prophet [pbuh] got up, and as he turned away, his uncle called him and said, "Come back, my nephew," and when he came back, he said, "Go and preach what you please, for by Allah I will never forsake you."

The Tyrants' Decision to kill the Prophet (pbuh)
Now that all the schemes and conspiracies of the Quraish had failed, they resorted to their old practices of persecution and inflicting tortures on the Muslims in a more serious and brutal manner than ever before. They also began to nurse the idea of killing the Prophet [pbuh]. In fact, contrary to their expectations, this new method and this very idea served indirectly to consolidate the Call to Islam and support it with the conversion of two staunch and mighty heroes of Mecca, i.e. Hamzah bin 'Abdul-Muttalib and 'Umar bin al-Khattab[R].

'Utaibah bin Abi Lahab once approached the Prophet [pbuh] and most defiantly and brazenly shouted at him, "I disbelieve in: "By the star when it goes down." [53:1] and in "Then he (Gabriel) approached and came closer." [53:8] In other words: "I do not believe in any of the Qur'an." He then started to deal highhandedly with Muhammad [pbuh] and laid violent hand on him, tore his shirt and spat into his face but his saliva missed the Holy face of the Prophet [pbuh]. Thereupon, the Prophet [pbuh] invoked Allah's wrath on 'Utaibah and supplicated:
"O Allah! Set one of Your dogs on him."

More details reported by Ibn Ishaq testify to the tyrants' deeply-established intentions of killing the Prophet [pbuh]. Abu Jahl, the archenemy of Islam, once addressed some of his accomplices: "O people of Quraish! It seems that Muhammad [pbuh] is determined to go on finding fault with our religion, degrading our forefathers, discrediting our way of life and abusing our gods. I bear witness to our god that I will carry a too heavy rock and drop it on Muhammad's head while he is in prostration to rid you of him, once and for all. I am not afraid of whatever his sept, Banu 'Abd Munaf, might do." The terrible unfortunate audience endorsed his plan and encouraged him to translate it into a decisive deed.

In the morning of the following day, Abu Jahl laid waiting for the arrival of the Messenger of Allah [pbuh] to offer prayer. The people of Quraish were in their assembly rooms waiting for news. When the Prophet [pbuh] prostrated himself, Abu Jahl proceeded carrying the big rock to fulfill his wicked intention. No sooner had he approached closer to the Prophet [pbuh] than he withdraw pale-faced, shuddering with his hands strained the rock falling off. Thereupon, the people watching hurried forward asking him what the matter was. He replied: "When I approached, a male-camel unusual in figure with fearful canines intercepted and almost devoured me." Ibn Ishaq reported that the Prophet [pbuh], in the context of his comment on the incident, said "It was Gabriel [AWS], if Abu Jahl had approached closer, he would have killed him. [Ibn Hisham 1/298]

'Urwa bin Az-Zubair narrated: I asked Abdullah bin 'Amr bin Al-'As to tell me of the worst thing that the pagans did to the Prophet [pbuh]. He said: "While the Prophet [pbuh] was praying in Al-Hijr of Al-Ka'bah, 'Uqbah bin Al-Mu'ait came and put his garment around the Prophet's neck and throttled him violently. Abu Bakr came and caught him by his shoulder and pushed him away from the Prophet [pbuh] and said: "Do you want to kill a man just because he says, My Lord is Allah?" [Bukhari 1/544]

The Conversion of Hamzah bin 'Abdul-Muttalib

The conversion of Hamzah bin 'Abdul-Muttalib was in the sixth year of Prophethood. It is recorded that the Prophet [pbuh] was one day seated on the hillock of Safa when Abu Jahl happened to pass by and accused the religion preached by him. Muhammad [pbuh], however, kept silent and did not utter a single word. Abu Jahl went on unchecked, took a stone and cracked the Prophet's head which began to bleed. The aggressor then went to join the Quraishites in their assembly place. It so happened that shortly after that, Hamzah, while returning from a hunting expedition, passed by the same way, his bow hanging by his shoulder. A slave-girl told him the whole story of the attack on the Prophet [pbuh]. On hearing that, Hamzah was deeply offended and hurried to Al-Ka'bah and there, in the courtyard of the Holy Sanctuary, found Abu Jahl sitting with a company of Quraishites. Hamzah rushed upon him and struck his bow upon his head violently and said: "Ah! You have been abusing Muhammad [pbuh]; I too follow his religion and profess what he preaches." The men of Bani Makhzum came to his help, and men of Bani Hashim wanted to render help, but Abu Jahl sent them away saying: "Let Abu 'Ummarah alone, by Allah I did revile his nephew shamelessly. [Ibn Hisham 1/291; Rahmat-ul-lil'alameen 1/68; Mukhtasar Seerat Ar-Rasool p.66]

The Conversion of 'Umar bin al-Khattab

Another significant addition to the strength of Islam was the conversion of 'Umar bin Al-Khattab in the sixth year of Prophethood, three days following the conversion of Hamzah. He was a man of dauntless courage and resolution, feared and respected in Mecca, and hitherto a bitter opponent of the new religion. The traditional account reveals that the Prophet [pbuh] once raised his hands in prayer and said: "O Allah! Give strength to Islam especially through either of two men you love more: 'Umar bin al-Khattab or Abu Jahl bin Hisham." 'Umar, obviously, was the one who merited that privilege. [At-Tirmidhi 2/209]

In fact, 'Umar's conversion created a great deal of stir in Mecca that some people denounced him as an apostate, yet he would never waver in Faith, on the contrary, he persisted in his stance even at the peril of his life.

Suhaib bin Sinan, in the same context, said that it was only after 'Umar's conversion, that we started to proclaim our Call, assemble around and circumambulate the Sacred House freely. We even dared retaliate against some of the injustices done to harm us.

Quraish's Representative Negotiates with the Messenger [pbuh]

Shortly after the conversion of these two powerful men, Hamzah and 'Umar bin Al-Khattab, the clouds of tyranny and oppression started to clear away and the polytheists realized that it was no use meting out torture to the Muslims. They consequently began to direct their campaign to a different course. The authentic records of the biography of the Prophet [pbuh] show that it had occurred to the Meccan leaders to credit Muhammad [pbuh] with ambition. They, therefore, time and again plied him with temptation. One day some of the important men of Mecca gathered in the enclosure of Al-Ka'bah, and 'Utbah bin Rabi'a, a chief among them, offered to approach the Prophet [pbuh] and contract a bargain with him whereby they give him whatever worldly wealth he asks for, on condition that he keep silent and no longer proclaim his new faith. The people of Quraish endorsed his proposal and requested him to

undertake that task. 'Utbah came closer to Muhammad [pbuh] and addressed him in the following words:
We have seen no other man of Arabia, who has brought so great a calamity to a nation, as you have done. You have outraged our gods and religion and taxed our forefathers and wise men with impiety and error and created strife amongst us. You have left no stone unturned to estrange the relations with us. If you are doing all this with a view to getting wealth, we will join together to give you greater riches than any Quraishite has possessed. If ambition moves you, we will make you our chief. If you desire kingship we will readily offer you that. If you are under the power of an evil spirit which seems to haunt and dominate you so that you cannot shake off its yoke, then we shall call in skilful physicians to cure you.
"Have you said all?" asked Muhammad [pbuh]; and then hearing that all had been said, he spoke forth, and said:

"In the Name of Allah, the Most Beneficent, the Most Merciful. Hâ-Mîm. [These letters are one of the miracles of the Qur'an, and none but Allah (Alone) knows their meanings]. A revelation from Allah, the Most Beneficent, the Most Merciful. A Book whereof the verses are explained in detail; - a Qur'an in Arabic for people who know. Giving glad tidings [of Paradise to the one who believes in the Oneness of Allah (i.e. Islamic Monotheism) and fears Allah much (abstains from all kinds of sins and evil deeds.) and loves Allah much (performing all kinds of good deeds which He has ordained)], and warning (of punishment in the Hell-fire to the one who disbelieves in the Oneness of Allah), but most of them turn away, so they listen not. And they say: Our hearts are under coverings (screened) from that to which you invite us ..." [Qur'an 41: 1-5]
The Messenger of Allah [pbuh] went on reciting the Chapter while 'Utbah sitting and listening attentively with his hand behind his back to support him. When the Messenger reached the verse that required prostration, he immediately prostrated himself. After that, he turned to 'Utbah saying:
"Well Abu Al-Waleed! You have heard my reply, you are now free to do whatever you please."
'Utbah then retired to his company to apprise them of the Prophet's attitude. When his compatriots saw him, they swore that he had returned to them with a countenance unlike the one he had before meeting the Prophet [pbuh]. He immediately communicated to

them the details of the talk he gave and the reply he received, and appended saying: "I have never heard words similar to those ones he recited. They definitely relate neither to poetry nor to witchcraft nor do they derive from soothsaying. O people of Quraish! I request you to heed my advice and grant the man full freedom to pursue his goals, in which case you could safely detach yourselves from him. I swear that his words bear a supreme Message. Should the other Arabs rid you of him, they will then spare you the trouble, on the other hand if he accedes to power over the Arabs, then you will bask in his kingship and share him his might." These words of course fell on deaf ears, and did not appeal to the infidels, who jeered at 'Utbah and claimed that the Prophet [pbuh] had bewitched him. [Ibn Hisham 1/293,294]

Abu Talib Assembles Bani Hashim and Bani al-Muttalib
Abu Talib still had a deep sensation of fear over his nephew. He deliberated on the previous series of incidents including the barter affair of 'Amarah bin Al-Waleed, Abu Jahl's rock, 'Uqbah's attempt to choke the Prophet [pbuh], and finally 'Umar's (before conversion) intention to kill Muhammad [pbuh]. The wise man understood that all of these unequivocally smacked of a serious plot being hatched to disregard his status as a custodian of the Prophet [pbuh], and kill the latter publicly. [Ibn Hisham 1/269; Mukhtasar Seerat Ar-Rasool p.106]

Abu Talib was right. The polytheists had laid a carefully-studied plan to kill the Prophet [pbuh], and banded together to put their plan into effect. He, therefore, assembled his kinsfolk of Bani Hashim and Bani Al-Muttalib, sons of 'Abd Munaf and exhorted them to immunize and defend his nephew. All of them, whether believers or disbelievers, responded positively except his brother Abu Lahab, who sided with the idolaters.

General Social Boycott
Four events of special significance occurred within less than four weeks - the conversion of Hamzah, the conversion of 'Umar, Muhammad's [pbuh] refusal to negotiate any sort of compromise and then the pact drawn up between Banu Muttalib and Banu Hashim to immunize Muhammad [pbuh] and shield him against any treacherous attempt to kill him. The polytheists were baffled and at a loss as to what course they would follow to rid themselves

of this obstinate and relentless obstacle that had appeared to shatter to pieces their whole tradition of life. They had already been aware that if they killed Muhammad [pbuh] their blood would surely flow profusely in the valleys of Mecca and they would certainly be exterminated. Taking this dreadful prospect into consideration, they grudgingly resorted to a different iniquitous course that would not imply murder.

A Pact of Injustice and Aggression

The pagans of Mecca held a meeting in a place called Wadi Al-Muhassab, and formed a confederation hostile to both Bani Hashim and Bani Al-Muttalib. They decided not to have any business dealings with them nor any sort of inter-marriage. Social relations, visits and even verbal contacts with Muhammad [pbuh] and his supporters would discontinue until the Prophet [pbuh] was given up to them to be killed. The articles of their proclamation, which had provided for merciless measures against Bani Hashim, were committed to writing by an idolater, Bagheed bin 'Amir bin Hashim and then suspended in Al-Ka'bah. The Prophet [pbuh] invoked Allah's imprecations upon Bagheed, whose hand was later paralyzed. [Zad Al-Ma'ad 2/46]

Abu Talib wisely and quietly took stock of the situation and decided to withdraw to a valley on the eastern outskirts of Mecca. Banu Hashim and Banu Al-Muttalib, who followed suit, were thus confined within a narrow pass (Shi'b of Abu Talib), from the beginning of Muharram, the seventh year of Muhammad's mission till the tenth year, viz., a period of three years. It was a stifling siege. The supply of food was almost stopped and the people in confinement faced great hardships. The idolaters used to buy whatever food commodities entered Mecca lest they should leak to the people in Ash-Shi'b, who were so overstrained that they had to eat leaves of trees and skins of animals. Cries of little children suffering from hunger used to be heard clearly. Nothing to eat reached them except, on few occasions, some meagre quantities of food were smuggled by some compassionate Meccans. During 'the prohibited months' - when hostilities traditionally ceased, they would leave their confinement and buy food coming from outside Mecca. Even then, the food stuff was unjustly overpriced so that their financial situation would fall short of finding access to it.

Hakeem bin Hizam was once on his way to smuggle some wheat to his aunt Khadijah [R][1] when Abu Jahl intercepted and wanted to debar him. Only when Al-Bukhtari intervened, did Hakeem manage to reach his destination. Abu Talib was so much concerned about the personal safety of his nephew. Whenever people retired to sleep, he would ask the Prophet [pbuh] to lie in his place, but when all the others fell asleep, he would order him to change his place and take another, all of which in an attempt to trick a potential assassin. Despite all odds, Muhammad [pbuh] persisted in his line and his determination and courage never weakened. He continued to go to Al-Ka'bah and to pray publicly. He used every opportunity to preach to outsiders who visited Mecca for business or on pilgrimage during the sacred months and special seasons of assemblies.

This situation ultimately created dissension amongst the various Meccan factions, who were tied with the besieged people by blood relations. After three years of blockade and in Muharram, the tenth year of Muhammad's mission, the pact was broken. A group of five people set out to abrogate the pact and declare all relevant clauses null and void.

Abu Talib meanwhile was sitting in a corner of the Mosque. He came to communicate to them that a Revelation had been sent to his nephew, the Prophet [pbuh] to the effect that ants had eaten away all their proclamation that smacked of injustice and aggression except those parts that bore the Name of Allah. He contended that he would be ready to give Muhammad [pbuh] up to them if his words proved untrue; otherwise, they would have to recant and repeal their boycott. The Meccans agreed to the soundness of his proposition. Al-Mut'im went to see the parchment and there he did discover that it was eaten away by ants and nothing was left save the part bearing (in the Name of Allah).

The proclamation was thus abrogated, and Muhammad [pbuh] and the other people were permitted to leave Ash-Sh'ib and return home. In the context of this trial to which the Muslims were subjected, the polytheists had a golden opportunity to experience a striking sign of Muhammad's Prophethood (the white ants eating away the parchment) but to their miserable lot they desisted and augmented in disbelief:

"But if they see a Sign, they turn away, and say 'This is continuous magic." [Qur'an 54:2] [Bukhari (in several chapters); Zad al-Ma'ad 2/46; Ibn Hisham 1/350]

The Final Phase of the Diplomacy of Negotiation

The Messenger of Allah [pbuh] left his confinement and went on preaching his Faith as usual. Quraish, likewise, repealed the boycott but went on in their atrocities and oppression on the Muslims. Abu Talib, the octogenarian notable, was still keen on shielding his nephew but by that time, and on account of the series of tremendous events and continual pains, he began to develop certain fits of weakness. No sooner had he emerged victorious from the inhuman boycott, than he was caught in a persistent illness and physical enervation. The polytheists of Mecca, seeing this serious situation and fearing that the stain of infamy that the other Arabs could attribute to them in case they took any aggressive action against the Prophet [pbuh] after he had lost his main support, Abu Talib, took a decision to negotiate with the Prophet [pbuh] once more and submit some concessions withheld previously. They then delegated some representatives to see Abu Talib and discuss the issue with him. Ibn Ishaq and others related: "When a serious illness caught Abu Talib, the people of Quraish began to deliberate on the situation and reviewed the main features that characterized that period and which included the conversion of 'Umar and Hamzah to Islam, coupled with the tremendous stir that Muhammad [pbuh] had created amongst all the tribes of Quraish. They then deemed it imperative to see Abu Talib before he died to pressure his nephew to negotiate a compromise on the various disputed points. They were afraid that the other Arabs might attribute to them the charge of opportunism."

The delegation of Quraish comprised 25 men including notables like 'Utbah bin Rabi'a, Shaibah bin Rabi'a, Abu Jahl bin Hisham, Omaiyah bin Khalaf, Abu Sufyan bin Harb. They first paid tribute to him and confirmed their high esteem of his person and position among them. They then shifted to the new give-and-take policy that they claimed they wanted to follow. To substantiate their argument they alleged that they would refrain from intervening in his religion if he did the same.

Abu Talib summoned his nephew and apprised him of the minutes of his meeting with them, and said:

"Well, my nephew, here are the celebrities of your people. They have proposed this meeting to submit a policy of mutual concessions and peaceful coexistence."

The Messenger of Allah [pbuh] turned to them saying:

"I will guide you to the means by which you will gain sovereignty over both the Arabs and non-Arabs."

Abu Jahl asked, "What is that word? The Prophet said:

"I want you to testify that there is no god worthy to be worshipped but Allah, and then divest yourselves of any sort of worship you harbor for any deities other than Allah."

They immediately clapped their hands in ridicule, and said, "How can you expect us to combine all the deities in one God. It is really something incredible." On their way out leaving, they said to one another, "By god this man (Muhammad [pbuh]) will never relent, nor will he offer any concessions. Let us hold fast to the religion of our forefathers, and Allah will in due course adjudicate and settle the dispute between us and him." As regards this incident, Allah revealed the following verses:

"Sâd: [These letters (Sâd, etc.) are one of the miracles of the Qur'an and none but Allah (Alone) knows their meanings]. By the Qur'an full of reminding. Nay, those who disbelieve are in false pride and Apposition. How many a generation We have destroyed before them, and they cried out when there was no longer time for escape! And they (Arab pagans) wonder that a warner (Prophet Muhammad [pbuh]) has come to them from among themselves! And the disbelievers say, 'This (Prophet Muhammad [pbuh]) is a sorcerer, a liar. Has he made the gods (all) into One God (Allah). Verily, this is a curious thing!' And the leaders among them went about (saying): 'Go on, and remain constant to your gods! Verily, this is a thing designed (against you)! We have not heard (the like) of this among the people of these later days. This is nothing but an invention.'" [Qur'an 38:1-7] [Ibn Hisham 1/417-419; Tafheem-ul-Qur'an 4/316; Mukhtasar Seerat Ar-Rasool p.9]

Khadijah Passes away to the Mercy of Allah
Only two months after the death of his uncle, did the Messenger of Allah [pbuh] experience another great personal loss viz., his wife Khadijah passed away in Ramadan of the tenth year of his Prophethood, when she was sixty-five years old, and he was fifty [Talqeeh Fuhoom Ahl-al-Athar p.7; Rahmat-ul-lil'alameen 2/164].

Khadijah, for twenty-five years, shared with him the toils and trials of life, especially in the first ten years of his ministry of Prophethood. He deeply mourned over her death, and once he replied in an honest burst of tender emotions:
"She believed in me when none else did. She embraced Islam when people disbelieved me. And she helped and comforted me in her person and wealth when there was none else to lend me a helping hand. I had children from her only."[Musnad Imam Ahmad 6/118]

The Year of Grief
These two painful events took place within a short lapse of time and added a lot to his grief and suffering. The Meccans now openly declared their campaign of torture and oppression. The Prophet [pbuh] lost all hope of bringing them back to the right path, so he set out for Al-Ta'if seeking a supportive atmosphere. But there too, he was disappointed and he sustained unbearable tortures and maltreatment that far outweighed his miserable situation in his native town.
His Companions were on equal footing subjected to unspeakable torture and unbearable oppression. [Bukhari 1/552; Ibn Hisham 1/372]

The death of Abu Talib rendered the Prophet [pbuh] vulnerable, and the polytheists availed them of that opportunity to give free rein to their hatred and highhandedness and to translate them in terms of oppression and physical tortures. Once an insolent Quraishite intercepted him and sprinkled sand on his head. When he arrived home, a daughter of his washed the sand away and wept. "Do not weep, my daughter. Allah will verily protect your father." The Prophet [pbuh] said. [Ibn Hisham 1/416]

Rapid succession of misfortunes, led the Prophet [pbuh] to call that period, 'the year of grief and mourning'. Thenceforth, that year bore that appellation.

The Third Phase: Calling unto Islam beyond Mecca, to al-Ta'if
In Shawwal [Tareekh-e-Islam 1/122] (in the last of May or in the beginning of June 619 A.D.), ten years after receiving his mission from his Lord, the Prophet [pbuh] set out towards At-Ta'if, about 60 kilometers from Mecca, in the company of his freed slave Zaid bin

Haritha inviting people to Islam. But contrary to his expectations, the general atmosphere was terribly hostile.

Is it true that Allah has sent you as a Messenger?" said one of them.

"Has not Allah found someone else to entrust him with His Message?" said the second.

For ten days he stayed there delivering his message to several people, one after another, but all to no purpose. Stirred up to hasten the departure of the unwelcome visitor, the people hooted him through the alley-ways, pelted him with stones and obliged him to flee from the city pursued by a relentless rabble. Blood flowed down both his legs; and Zaid, endeavoring to shield him, was wounded in the head. The mob did not desist until they had chased him two or three miles across the sandy plains to the foot of the surrounding hills. There, wearied and exhausted, he took refuge in one of the numerous orchards, and rested against the wall of a vineyard. At a time when the whole world seemed to have turned against him, Muhammad [pbuh] turned to his Lord and betook himself to prayer and the following touching words are still preserved as those through which his oppressed soul gave vent to its distress. He was weary and wounded but confident of the help of his Lord:

"O Allah! To You alone I make complaint of my helplessness, the paucity of my resources and my insignificance before mankind. You are the most Merciful of the mercifuls. You are the Lord of the helpless and the weak, O Lord of mine! Into whose hands would You abandon me: into the hands of an unsympathetic distant relative who would sullenly frown at me, or to the enemy who has been given control over my affairs? But if Your wrath does not fall on me, there is nothing for me to worry about."

"I seek protection in the light of Your Countenance, which illuminates the heavens and dispels darkness, and which controls all affairs in this world as well as in the Hereafter. May it never be that I should incur Your wrath, or that You should be wrathful to me. And there is no power nor resource, but Yours alone."

The Prophet with a Christian Servant from Nineveh

Seeing him in this helpless situation, Rabi'a's two sons, wealthy Meccans, were moved on grounds of kinship and compassion, and sent to him one of their Christian servants with a tray of grapes. The Prophet [pbuh] accepted the fruit with pious invocation: "In the

Name of the Allah." The Christian servant 'Addas was greatly impressed by these words and said: "These are words which people in this land do not generally use." The Prophet [pbuh] inquired of him whence he came and what religion he professed. 'Addas replied: "I am a Christian by faith and come from Nineveh." The Prophet [pbuh] then said: "You belong to the city of the righteous Jonah, son of Matta." 'Addas asked him anxiously if he knew anything about Jonah. The Prophet [pbuh] significantly remarked: "He is my brother. He was a Prophet and so am I." Thereupon 'Addas paid homage to Muhammad [pbuh] and kissed his hands. His masters admonished him at this act but he replied: "None on the earth is better than he is. He has revealed to me a truth which only a Prophet can do." They again reprimanded him and said: "We forewarn you against the consequences of abandoning the faith of your forefathers. The religion which you profess is far better than the one you feel inclined to."

The Prophet Forgives
Heart-broken and depressed, Muhammad [pbuh] set out on the way back to Mecca. When he reached Qarn Al-Manazil, Allah, the Almighty sent him Gabriel together with the angel of mountains. The latter asked the Prophet [pbuh] for permission to bury Mecca between Al-Akhshabain
The Prophet said in reply:
"That I would rather have someone from their loins who will worship Allah, the All-Mighty with no associate." [Bukhari 1/458; Muslim 2/109]

Back to Mecca
The Messenger of Allah [pbuh] then came back to wakefulness and his heart was set at rest in the light of that invisible Divinely provided aid. Zaid bin Harithah, his companion, addressing the Prophet [pbuh] said, "How dare you step into Mecca after they (Quraish) have expatriated you?"
The Prophet [pbuh] answered: "Hearken Zaid, Allah will surely provide relief and He will verily support His religion and Prophet."

When he was a short distance from Mecca, he retired to Hira' Cave. Whence he dispatched a man from Khuza'ah tribe to Al-Akhnas bin Shuraiq seeking his protection. The latter answered that he was Quraish's ally and in no position to offer protection. He dispatched the messenger to Suhail bin 'Amr, but to no avail, either. Al-Mut'im bin 'Adi, a notable in Mecca, however, volunteered to respond to the Prophet's appeal for shelter. He asked his people to prepare themselves fully armed and then asked Muhammad [pbuh] to enter into the town and directly into the Holy Sanctuary. The Prophet [pbuh] observed a two-Rak'a prayer and left for his house guarded by the heavily-armed vigilant 'Adi's.

Islam being introduced to Arabian Tribes and Individuals
In Dhul Qa'dah, the tenth year of Prophethood, i.e. July 619, the Prophet [pbuh], returned to Mecca to resume his activities. The time for pilgrimage to Mecca was approaching so he hastened to introduce people both tribes and individuals to Islam and call upon them to embrace it, just as it was his practice since the fourth year of his Prophethood.
The Prophet [pbuh] was not dismayed at all. He persisted in his mission for the fulfillment of which he had been commissioned to strive despite all odds. He did not confine his efforts to the tribes but also conducted contacts with individuals from some of whom he was able to receive a favorable response. Moreover, later in the same season, some of them did believe in his Prophethood and entered the fold of Islam. One of them was Abu Dhar Al-Ghifari and Tufail bin 'Amr Ad-Dausi.

Hope Inspiring Breezes from the Madinese
It was during the pilgrimage season, in the eleventh year of Prophethood, that the Islamic Call found the righteous seeds through which it would grow up to constitute tall trees whose leaves would foster the new faith and shelter the new vulnerable converts from the blows of injustices and high-handness of Quraish. It was the Prophet's wise practice to meet the delegates of the Arabian tribes by night so that the hostile Meccans would not debar him from achieving his objectives. [Tareekh-e-Islam p.129] In the company of his two truthful Companions 'Ali and Abu Bakr, he had an interesting talk regarding Islam with Bani Dhuhal, but the latter suspended their conversion. [Mukhtasar Seerat Ar-Rasool p.150]

In pursuit of the same objective, the Prophet and his Companions passed by 'Aqabat Mina where they heard people talking. They went at their heels until they encountered six men from Yathrib, all of whom from Khazraj tribe: As'ad bin Zurarah, 'Awf bin Harith,

Rafi' bin Malik, Qutbah bin 'Amir, 'Uqbah bin 'Amir and Jabir bin 'Abdullah. The last two being from Aws and the former four from Khazraj.

The Madinese always heard the Jews say that a Prophet was about to rise, for the time for a new dispensation had arrived. Him they would follow and then smite their enemies as the children of 'Ad and Iram had been smitten. [Rahmat-al-lil'alameen 1/84; Ibn Hisham 1/429; Zad Al-Ma'ad 2/50]

"Of what tribe are you?" asked the Prophet.
"Of the tribe of Khazraj," they replied.
"Are you the allies of the Jews?" The Prophet enquired.
They said: "Yes."
"Then why not sit down for a little and I will speak to you."

The offer was readily accepted for the fame of Muhammad [pbuh] had spread to Madina and the strangers were curious to see more of the man who had created a stir in the whole area. The Prophet [pbuh] presented to them an expose of Islam, explained its implications, and the responsibilities that fell upon the men who accepted it. When the Prophet [pbuh] concluded his talk, they exchanged among themselves ideas to the following effect: "Know surely, this is the Prophet with whom the Jews are ever threatening us; wherefore let us make haste and be the first to join him."

They, therefore, embraced Islam, and said to the Prophet, "We have left our community for no tribe is so divided by hatred and rancor as they are. Allah may cement our ties through you. So let us go and invite them to this religion of yours; and if Allah unites them in it, no man will be dearer than you."

The handful of Madinese converts remained steady to the cause and they preached the Islam with full zeal and devotion with the result that they succeeded in winning adherents for Islam from amongst their fellow citizens and hardly was there a house in Madina not talking curiously and enthusiastically about the Messenger of Allah [pbuh]. [Ibn Hisham 1/428-430]

17. Al-Isra' and Al-Mi'raj

(The Miraculous Night Journey from Mecca to the Farthest Mosque in Jerusalem, and the Ascent through the Spheres of Heavens)

This happened between 16-12 months prior to migration to Madina. The following is an epitome of the details of that miraculous event narrated on the authority of Ibn al-Qayyim. [Zad al-Ma'ad 2/49; Tareekh-e-Islam 1/124; Rahmat-al-lil'alameen 1/76]

The Messenger of Allah [pbuh] was carried in body from the Sacred Mosque in Mecca to the Distant Mosque in Jerusalem on a horse called Al-Buraq in the company of Gabriel, the archangel. There he alighted, tethered the horse to a ring in the gate of the Mosque and led the Prophets in prayer. After that Gabriel took him to the heavens on the same horse. When they reached the first heaven Gabriel asked the guardian angel to open the door of heaven. It was opened and he saw Adam, the progenitor of mankind. The Prophet [pbuh] saluted him and the other welcomed him and expressed his faith in Muhammad's Prophethood. He saw the souls of martyrs on his right and those of the wretched on his left.

Gabriel then ascended with the Prophet to the second heaven, asked for opening the gate and there he saw and saluted John, son of Zachariya (Yahya bin Zakariya) and Jesus, son of Mary. They returned the salutation, welcomed him and expressed their faith in his Prophethood. Then they reached the third heaven where they saw Joseph (Yusuf) and saluted him. The latter welcomed the Prophet and expressed faith in his Prophethood. The Prophet, in the company of Gabriel, then reached the fourth heaven where he met the Prophet Enoch (Idris) and saluted him. Prophet Enoch returned the salutation and expressed faith in his Prophethood. Then he was carried to the fifth heaven where he met the Prophet Aaron (Harun) and saluted him. The latter returned the salutation and expressed faith in his Prophethood. In the sixth heaven he met Moses (Musa) and saluted him. The latter returned the salutation and expressed faith in his Prophethood. Muhammad [pbuh] on leaving saw that Moses began to weep. He asked about the reason. Moses answered that he was weeping because he witnessed a man sent after him as a Messenger (Muhammad) who was able to lead more of his people to the Paradise than he himself did. Then Prophet Muhammad [pbuh] reached the seventh heaven and met Abraham (Ibrahim) and saluted him. The latter returned the salutation and expressed faith in his Prophethood. Then he was carried to Sidrat-al-Muntaha (the remotest lote tree) and was shown Al-Bait-al-Ma'mûr [(the much frequented house) which is like the Ka'bah (Sacred House) encompassed daily by seventy thousand angels, so that the angels who once encompassed it would not have their turn again till the Resurrection]. He was then presented to the Divine Presence and experienced the thrill of witnessing the Divine Glory and Manifestation at the closest possible propinquity. There the Lord revealed unto His servant that which He revealed, and ordained fifty daily prayers for him. On his return, he spoke to Moses that his followers had been enjoined to pray fifty times a day. Moses addressing the Prophet [pbuh] said: "Your followers cannot perform so many prayers. Go back to your Lord and ask for a remission in number." The Prophet [pbuh] turned to Gabriel as if holding counsel with him. Gabriel nodded, "Yes, if you desire," and ascended with him to the Presence of Allah. The All-Mighty Allah, Glory is to Him, made a reduction of ten prayers. He then descended and reported that to Moses, who again urged him to request for a further reduction. Muhammad [pbuh] once more begged his Lord to reduce the number still further. He went again and again in the Presence of Allah at the suggestion of Moses for reduction in the number of prayers till these were reduced to five only. Moses again asked him to implore for more reduction, but he said: "I feel ashamed now of repeatedly asking my Lord for reduction. I accept and resign to His Will." When Muhammad [pbuh] went farther, a Caller was heard saying: "I have imposed My Ordinance and alleviated the burden of My servants."

There is however some difference as regards the issue whether the Prophet saw Allah with his physical eye or not. Some interpreters say that seeing Allah with his naked eyes was not confirmed. Ibn 'Abbas, on the other hand, says that the word Ru'ya as used in the Noble Qur'an signifies the observation with the help of the eye. In Surat An-Najm (Chapter -The Star) we read:

"Then he approached and came closer." [Qur'an 53:8]

Here (he) refers to archangel Gabriel, and this context is completely different from that in the Prophetic tradition of Isra' and Mi'raj, where 'the approach' relates to that of the Lord, Glory is to Him.

The First 'Aqabah Pledge

We have already spoken about six Madinese who embraced Islam in the pilgrimage season in the eleventh year of Prophethood. They promised to communicate the Message of Islam to their townsfolk.

1. The following year, on the occasion of the pilgrimage, there came a group of twelve disciples ready to acknowledge Muhammad as their Prophet. The group of men comprised five of the six who had met the Prophet [pbuh] the year before.

They avowed their faith in Muhammad [pbuh] as a Prophet and swore:

"We will not worship any one but one Allah; we will not steal; neither will we commit adultery, nor kill our children; we will not utter slander, intentionally forging falsehood and we will not disobey you in any just matter."

When they had taken the pledge, Muhammad [pbuh] said:

"He who carries it out, Allah will reward him; and who neglects anything and is afflicted in this world, it may prove redemption for him in the Hereafter; and if the sin remains hidden from the eyes of the men and no grief comes to him, then his affair is with Allah. He may forgive him or He may not." [Bukhari 1/550; 2/727; 2/1003]

The Muslim Envoy in Madina

After the Pledge (in the form of an oath had been taken) the Prophet [pbuh] sent to Yathrib (Madina) Mus'ab bin 'Umair, the first Muslim 'ambassador' to teach the people there the doctrines of Islam, give them practical guidance and make attempts at propagating the Islam among those who still professed polytheism. So prepared was the ground, and so zealous the propagation that the Islam spread rapidly from house to house and from tribe to tribe. There were various cheerful and promising aspects of success that characterized Mus'ab's task.

Mus'ab stayed in Madina carrying out his mission diligently and successfully until all the houses of Al-Ansar (the future Helpers) had Muslims elements, men and women. One family only stood obdurate to the Islamic Da'wah (Call). They were under the influence of the poet Qais bin Al-Aslat, who managed to hold them at bay and screen off the Call of Islam from their ears until the year 5 A.H.

Shortly before the approach of the following pilgrimage season, i.e. the thirteenth year of Prophethood, Mus'ab bin 'Umair returned to Mecca carrying to the Prophet [pbuh] glad tidings about the new fertile soil of Islam in Madina, and its environment rich in the prospects of good, and the power and immunity that that city was bound to provide to the cause of Islam. [Ibn Hisham 1/435; Zad Al-Ma'ad 2/51]

The Second 'Aqabah Pledge
The next year, thirteenth of Prophethood, June 622 A.D., during the pilgrimage season, over seventy converts from Madina came in the trail of their polytheist people to perform the rituals of pilgrimage in Mecca. The oft-repeated question amongst them was "Isn't it high time we protect Muhammad instead of leaving him forsaken, deserted and stumbling in the hillocks of Mecca?"
Shortly after arrival, they conducted clandestine contacts with the Prophet [pbuh] and agreed to meet him secretly at night in mid Tashreeq Days (the 11th, 12th and 13th days of Dhul Hijja) in a hillock at Al-'Aqabah, the last year's meeting place.
One of the leaders of the Ansar (Helpers), Ka'b bin Malik Al-Ansari, gave an account of the historic meeting which changed the whole course of the struggle between Islam and paganism, he said:
We set out for pilgrimage and struck a rendezvous in mid Tashreeq Days. We were accompanied by a celebrity and a notable of ours called 'Abdullah bin 'Amr bin Haram, who was still a polytheist. We disclosed to him our intention of meeting Muhammad [pbuh] and exhorted him to join our ranks and give up polytheism lest he should serve as wood for Hell in the Hereafter. He promptly embraced Islam and witnessed the serious meeting at Al-'Aqabah.
That very night we slept with our people in our camps. After a third of the night had elapsed, we began to leave stealthily and met in a hillock nearby. We were seventy-three men and two women Nusaibah bint Ka'b from the Najjars and Asma' bint 'Amr from Bani Salamah. We waited for the Messenger of Allah [pbuh] until he came in the company of his uncle Al-'Abbas bin 'Abdul Muttalib who (though himself not a Muslim), adjured us not to draw his nephew away from the protection of his own kindred unless we were fully prepared to defend him even at the risk of our lives. He was the first to speak:

"O you people of the Khazraj - the Arabs used to call the Ansar (Helpers) Khazraj, whether from Khazraj or Aws - you all know the position that Muhammad holds among us. We have protected him from our people as much as we could. He is honored and respected among his people. He refuses to join any party except you. So if you think you can carry out what you promise while inviting him to your town, and if you can defend him against the enemies, then assume the burden that you have taken. But if you are going to surrender him and betray him after having taken him away with you, you had better leave him now because he is respected and well defended in his own place." [Ibn Hisham 1/440-442]

Ka'b replied: "We have heard your words, and now O Messenger of Allah, it is for you to speak and take from us any pledge that you want regarding your Lord and yourself."

It was a definite stance showing full determination, courage and deep faith to shoulder the daunting responsibility and bear its serious consequences.
The Messenger of Allah then preached the Faith, and the pledge was taken.

Al-Imam Ahmad, on the authority of Jabir, gave the following details:
The Ansar (Helpers) asked the Messenger of Allah about the principles over which they would take a pledge. The Prophet answered:
1. To listen and obey in all sets of circumstances.
2. To spend in plenty as well as in scarcity.
3. To enjoin good and forbid evil.
4. In Allah's service, you will fear the censure of none.
5. To defend me in case I seek your help, and debar me from anything you debar yourself, your spouses and children from. And if you observe those precepts, Paradise is in store for you. [Mukhtasar Seerat Ar-Rasool p.155; Ibn Hisham 1/454]

The Prophet [pbuh] then asked the group to appoint twelve deputies to preach Islam to their people in Madina, to shoulder the responsibility of implementing the articles of this pledge and to guide the respective men of their own tribes in matters relating to the propagation of Islam. The deputies elected were nine from al-Khazraj and three others were from al-Aws.

That is the story of the Second 'Aqabah Pledge, later known as the Great 'Aqabah Pledge, took place in an atmosphere of love, allegiance and mutual support between Madinese believers and weak Meccan Muslims.

18. The Migration or Hijra

The Vanguard of Migration
After the endorsement of the Second 'Aqabah Pledge and the establishment of a petite Muslim state in a vast desert surging with disbelief and ignorance - the most serious gain in terms of Islam -, the Prophet [pbuh] gave his leave for the Muslims to migrate to Madina, the nascent Muslim state.

Migration to Madina, in terms of personal interests, was no more than material waste and sacrifice of wealth, all in return for personal safety only. Even here, the migrant could not expect full security; he was liable to be robbed or even killed either at the beginning or end of his departure. The future was foggy, pregnant with various unpredictable sorts of sorrows and crises.

Bearing all this in mind, the Muslims began to migrate, while the polytheists spared no effort in hindering and debarring them, knowing beforehand that such a move implied unimaginable threats and unthinkable destructive dangers to their whole society:

1. The first one to migrate was Abu Salamah, a year before the Great 'Aqabah Pledge. When he had made up his mind to leave Mecca, his in-laws, in a desperate attempt to raise obstacles, detained his wife and snatched his son and dislocated his hand. Umm Salamah, after the departure of her husband and the loss of her son spent a year by herself weeping and lamenting. A relative of hers eventually had pity on her and exhorted the others to release her son and let her join her husband. She then set out on a journey of 500 kilometers with no help whatsoever. At a spot called At-Tan'im, 'Uthman bin Talhah came across her and offered to give her a ride to Madina. She, along with her son, joined Abu Salamah in the village of Quba', a suburb of Madina. [Ibn Hisham 1/468]

2. Another instance of the atrocities of the polytheist Meccans, as regards migration, is Suhaib. This man expressed his wish to migrate and of course this was a source of indignation to the disbelievers. They began to insult him claiming that he had come into Mecca as a worthless tramp, but their town was gracious enough and thanks to them he managed to make a lot of money and become wealthy. They gave orders that he would not leave. Seeing this, he offered to give away all his wealth to them. They eventually agreed to release him on that condition. The Prophet heard this

story and commented on it saying: "Suhaib is the winner, after all." [Ibn Hisham 1/477]

3. Then, there was the story of 'Umar bin Al-Khattab, 'Ayyash bin Abi Rabi'a and Hisham bin Al-'Asi, who agreed to meet at a certain place one morning in order to leave for Madina; 'Umar and 'Ayyash came but Hisham was detained by the Meccans.

Shortly afterwards Abu Jahl, and his brother Al-Harith came to Madina to see their third brother 'Ayyash. They cunningly tried to touch the most sensitive area in man, i.e. his relation with his mother. They addressed him claiming that his mother had sworn she would never comb her hair, nor shade herself off the sun unless she had seen him. 'Ayyash took pity on his mother, but 'Umar was intelligent enough to understand that they wanted to entice 'Ayyash away from Islam so he cautioned him against their tricks, and added "your mother would comb her hair if lice pestered her, and would shade herself off if the sun of Mecca got too hot for her." These words notwithstanding, 'Ayyash was determined to go and see his mother, so 'Umar gave him his manageable docile camel advising him to stick to its back because it would provide rescue for him if he perceived anything suspicious on their part. The party of three then set forth towards Mecca. As soon as they covered part of the distance, Abu Jahl complained about his camel and requested 'Ayyash to allow him to ride behind him on his camel. When they knelt down to the level of the ground, the two polytheists fell upon 'Ayyash and tied him. They rode on into Mecca shouting at people to follow their example with respect to 'fools'. [Ibn Hisham 1/474; Bukhari 1/558]

These are just three self-explanatory models of the Meccans' reaction towards anyone intending to migrate. Nevertheless, the believers still managed to escape in successive groups and so rapidly that within two months of the Second 'Aqabah Pledge, entire quarters of Mecca were deserted. Almost all the followers of Muhammad had migrated to their new abode, except Abu Bakr, 'Ali, the Prophet [pbuh] himself, and those helpless noble souls who had been detained in confinement or were unable to escape. The Prophet [pbuh], together with Abu Bakr and 'Ali, had made all the necessary preparations for migration but was waiting for leave from his Lord. [Zad al-Ma'ad 2/52]

It is noteworthy that most of the Muslims who had migrated to Abyssinia (Ethiopia) came back to Madina to join the rest of the Muslims there.

The situation was no doubt critical in Mecca but Muhammad [pbuh] was not at all perturbed. Abu Bakr was, however, urging the Prophet to depart from that town. He was also eagerly waiting for an opportunity to accompany Muhammad [pbuh] on this eventful journey. But the Prophet told him that the time had not yet come; the Lord had not given him the command to migrate. In anticipation of the Command of Allah, Abu Bakr had made preparations for the journey. He had purchased two swift camels and had fed them properly for four months so that they could successively stand the ordeals of the long desert journey. [Bukhari 1/553]

In An-Nadwah (Council) House: The Parliament of Quraish

The polytheists were paralyzed by the carefully planned and speedy movement of Muhammad's followers towards their new abode in Madina. They were caught in unprecedented anxiety and got deeply worried over their whole pagan and economic entity. They already experienced Muhammad [pbuh] as an influential leader; and his followers as determined, decent and always ready to sacrifice all they had for the sake of the Messenger of Allah [pbuh]. Al-Aws and Al-Khazraj tribes, the would-be-hosts of the Meccan Muslims, were also known in Arabia for their might and power in war, and judicious and sensible approach in peace. They were also averse to rancor and prejudice for they themselves had had bitter days of inter-tribal warfare. Madina, itself, the prospective headquarters of the ever-growing Islamic Call, enjoyed the most serious strategic position. It commanded the commercial routes leading to Mecca whose people used to deal in about a quarter of a million gold dinar-worth commodities every year. Security of the caravan routes was crucial for the perpetuity of prosperous economic life. All those factors borne in mind, the polytheists felt they were in the grip of a serious threat. They, therefore, began to seek the most effective method that could avert this imminent danger. They convened a meeting on Thursday, 26th Safar, the year fourteen of Prophethood / 12th September 622 A.D [For details see Rahmat-al-lil'alameen 1/95-102], i.e. two and a half months after the Great 'Aqabah Pledge. On that day, "the Parliament of Mecca" held the most serious meeting ever, with one item on the agenda: How to take effective measures with a view to stopping that tidal wave.

Delegates representing all the Quraishite tribes attended the meeting.

There was a lengthy debate and several proposals were put forward. Expulsion from Mecca was proposed and debated in turn but finally turned down on grounds that his sweet and heart-touching words could entice the other Arabs to attack them in their own city. Imprisonment for life was also debated but also refused for fear that his followers might increase in number, overpower them and release him by force. At this point, the arch-criminal of Mecca, Abu Jahl bin Hisham suggested that they assassinate him. But assassination by one man would have exposed him and his family to the vengeance of blood. The difficulty was at last solved by Abu Jahl himself, who suggested that a band of young men, one from each tribe, should strike Muhammad simultaneously with their swords so that the blood-money would be spread over them all and therefore could not be exacted, and his people would seek a mind-based recourse for settlement. The sinful proposal was unanimously accepted, and the representatives broke up the meeting and went back home with full determination for immediate implementation. [Ibn Hisham 1/480-482]

Migration of the Prophet [pbuh]
When the iniquitous decision had been made, Gabriel was sent down to Muhammad [pbuh] to reveal to him Quraish's plot and give him his Lord's Permission to leave Mecca. He fixed to him the time of migration and asked him not to sleep that night in his usual bed. At noon, the Prophet [pbuh] went to see his Companion Abu Bakr and arranged with him everything for the intended migration. Abu Bakr was surprised to see the Prophet [pbuh] masked coming to visit him at that unusual time, but he soon learned that Allah's Command had arrived, and he proposed that they should migrate together, to which the Prophet [pbuh] gave his consent. [Bukhari 1/553]

To make the necessary preparations for the implementation of their devilish plan, the chiefs of Mecca had chosen eleven men all were on the alert. As night advanced, they posted assassins around the Prophet's house. Thus they kept vigil all night long, waiting to kill him the moment he left his house early in the morning, peeping now and then through a hole in the door to make sure that he was still lying in his bed. Abu Jahl, the great enemy of Islam, used to walk about haughtily and arrogantly jeering at Muhammad's words, saying to the people around him: "Muhammad claims that if you follow him, he will appoint you rulers over the Arabs and non-Arabs and in the Hereafter your reward will be Gardens similar to those in Jordan, otherwise, he will slaughter you and after death you will be burnt in fire."[Ibn Hisham 1/483] He was too confident of the success of his devilish plan. Allah, the All-Mighty, however, in Whose Hands lie the sovereignty of the heavens and earth, does what He desires; He renders succour and can never be overpowered. He did exactly what He later said to His Prophet:

"And (remember) when the disbelievers plotted against you (O Muhammad [pbuh]) to imprison you, or to kill you, or to get you out (from your home, i.e. Mecca); they were plotting and Allah too was planning, and Allah is the Best of the planners." [Qur'an 8:30]

At that critical time the plans of Quraish utterly failed despite the tight siege they laid to the Prophet's house, the Prophet [pbuh] and 'Ali were inside the house. The Prophet [pbuh] told 'Ali to sleep in his bed and cover himself with his green mantle and assured him full security under Allah's protection and told him that no harm would come to him. The Prophet [pbuh] then came out of the room and cast a handful of dust at the assassins and managed to work his way through them reciting verses of the Noble Qur'an:

"And We have put a barrier before them, and a barrier behind them, and We have covered them up, so that they cannot see." [Qur'an 36:9]

He proceeded direct to the house of Abu Bakr who, immediately accompanied him and both set out southwards, clambered up the lofty peak of Mountain Thawr, and decided to take refuge in a cave. [Ibn Hisham 1/483; Zad al-Ma'ad 2/52]

The assassins who laid siege to the house were waiting for the zero hour when someone came and informed them that the Prophet [pbuh] had already left. They rushed in and to their utter surprise, found that the person lying in the Prophet's bed was 'Ali not Muhammad [pbuh]. This created a stir in the whole town. The

Prophet [pbuh] had thus left his house on Safar 27th, the fourteenth year of Prophethood, i.e. 12/13 September 622 A.D. [Rahmat-al-lil'alameen 1/95]

Knowing already that Quraish would mobilize all its potentials to find him, he played a clever trick on them and instead of taking the road to Madina in north side of Mecca as the polytheist would expect, he walked along a road least expected lying south of Mecca and leading to Yemen. He walked for 5 miles until he reached a rough rocky mountain called Thawr. There his shoes were worn out, some said he used to walk tiptoe in order not to leave a trail behind him. Abu Bakr carried him up the mountain to a cave called after the name of the mountain, Cave Thawr. Abu Bakr first entered to explore the cave and be sure that it was safe, closed all holes with pieces torn off from his clothes, cleaned it and then asked the Prophet [pbuh] to step in. The Prophet [pbuh] went in and immediately laid his head in Abu Bakr's lap and fell asleep. Suddenly Abu Bakr's foot was stung by a poisonous insect. It hurt so much that his tears fell on the Prophet's face. The Prophet [pbuh] immediately applied his saliva on Abu Bakr's foot and the pain went off on the spot. They confined themselves to this cave for three nights, Friday, Saturday and Sunday. 'Abdullah, the son of Abu Bakr would go to see them after dusk, stay the night there, apprise them of the latest situation in Mecca, and then leave in the early morning to mix with the Meccans as usual and not to draw the least attention to his clandestine activities. 'Amir bin Fuhairah, while in the company of other shepherds of Mecca tending his master Abu Bakr's flock, used to stole away unobserved every evening with a few goats to the cave and furnished its inmates with a plentiful supply of milk. [Bukhari 1/553; Ibn Hisham 1/486]

Quraish, on the other hand, were quite baffled and exasperated when the news of the escape of the two companions was confirmed. They brought 'Ali to Al-Ka'bah, beat him brutally and confined him there for an hour attempting desperately to make him divulge the secret of the disappearance of the two 'fugitives', but to no avail. They then went to see Asma', Abu Bakr's daughter, but here also their attempts went in vain. While at her door Abu Jahl slapped the girl so severely that her earring broke up. [Rahmat-al-lil'alameen 1/96; Ibn Hisham 1/487]

The notables of Mecca convened an emergency session to determine the future course of action and explore all areas that could help arrest the two men. They decided to block all avenues leading out of Mecca and imposed heavy armed surveillance over all potential exits. A price of 100 camels was set upon the head of each one. [Bukhari 1/554] Horsemen, infantry and tracers of tracks scoured the country. Once they even reached the mouth of the cave where the Prophet [pbuh] and Abu Bakr were hiding. When he saw the enemy at a very close distance, Abu Bakr whispered to the Prophet [pbuh]:

"What, if they were to look through the crevice and detect us?" The Prophet [pbuh] in his God-inspired calm replied:

"Silence Abu Bakr! What do you think of those two with whom the Third is Allah?" [Bukhari 1/516; Mukhtasar Seerat Ar-Rasool p.168]

It was a Divine miracle; the chasers were only a few steps from the cave. For three days Muhammad [pbuh] and Abu Bakr lived in the cave and Quraish continued their frantic efforts to get hold of them.

Someone called 'Abdullah bin Uraiquit, who had as yet not embraced Islam, but was trusted by Abu Bakr, and had been hired by him as a guide, reached the cave after three nights according to a plan bringing with him Abu Bakr's two camels. His report satisfied the noble 'fugitives' that the search had slackened. The opportunity to depart was come. Here Abu Bakr offered the Prophet [pbuh] the swift animal to ride on. The latter agreed provided that he would pay its price. They took with them the food provisions that Asma', daughter of Abu Bakr, brought and tied in a bundle of her waistband, after tearing it into two parts, hence the appellation attached to her: "Asma' of the two waistbands." The Prophet [pbuh], Abu Bakr and 'Amir bin Fuhairah departed, and their guide 'Abdullah bin Uraiquit led them on hardly ever trodden ways along the coastal route. That was in Rabi' Al-Awwal, 1st year A.H., i.e. September 622 A.D. The little caravan traveled through many villages on their way to Quba'. In this context, it is relevant to introduce some interesting incidents that featured their wearying journey:

1. One day they could find no shelter from the scorching heat so Abu Bakr cast a glance and found a little shade beside a rock. He cleaned the ground, spread his mantle for the Prophet [pbuh] to lie on and himself went off in search of food. He came across a shepherd, a bedouin boy, who was also seeking a shelter. Abu Bakr asked him for some milk and took it to the Prophet [pbuh], cooled it with some water and waited till the Prophet [pbuh] woke up and quenched his thirst. [Bukhari 1/510]

2. Whoever asked Abu Bakr about the identity of his honorable companion; he would reply that he was a man who guided him on his way. The questioner would think that Muhammad [pbuh] was a guide, in terms of roads, whereas Abu Bakr used to mean guide to the way of righteousness. [Bukhari 1/556]

3. Quraish, as we have already mentioned, had declared that whoever would seize Muhammad [pbuh] would receive a hundred camels as reward. This had spurred many persons to try their luck. Among those who were on the lookout for the Prophet [pbuh] and his companion in order to win the reward was Suraqah, the son of Malik. He, on receiving information that a party of four, had been spotted on a certain route, decided to pursue it secretly so that he alone should be the winner of the reward. He mounted a swift horse and went in hot pursuit of them. On the way the horse stumbled and he fell on the ground. On drawing a lot so as to divine whether he should continue the chase or not, as the Arabs used to do in such circumstances, he found the omens unpropitious. But the lust for material wealth blinded him altogether and he resumed the chase. Once more he met with the same fate but paid no heed to it. Again he jumped onto the saddle and galloped at a break-neck speed till he came quite close to the Prophet [pbuh]. Abu Bakr's heart agitated and he kept looking back while the Prophet [pbuh] remained steadfast and continued reciting verses of the Qur'an.
The repeated stumbling of Suraqah's horse and his falling off awakened him to the situation, and he realized that it was a constant warning of Allah for his evil design which he contemplated against the Prophet [pbuh]. He approached the traveling group with a penitent heart and begged of the Prophet [pbuh] forgiveness in all humility. He addressed the Prophet [pbuh] and his companion, saying:

"Your people (the Quraishites) have promised a generous reward to anyone who captures you."

He added that he offered them provision but they declined his offer. They only asked him to screen off their departure and blind the polytheists to their hiding place. Then the Prophet [pbuh] forgave him and confirmed it with a token written by 'Amir bin Fuhairah on a piece of parchment. Suraqah hurried back to Mecca and tried to foil the attempts of those who were in pursuit of Muhammad [pbuh] and his noble companions. The sworn enemy was converted into an honest believer. [Bukhari 1/516, 1/554; Zad Al-Ma'ad 2/53]

4. The party continued its journey until it reached to solitary tents belonging to a woman called Umm Ma'bad Al-Khuza'iyah. She was a gracious lady who sat at her tent-door with a mat spread out for any chance traveler that might pass by the way. Fatigued and thirsty, the Prophet [pbuh] and his companions wanted to refresh themselves with food and some milk. The lady told them that the flock was out in the pasture and the goat standing nearby was almost dry. It was a rainless year. The Prophet [pbuh], with her permission, touched its udders, reciting over them the Name of Allah, and to their great joy, there flowed plenty of milk out of them. The Prophet [pbuh] first offered that to the lady of the house, and he shared what was left with the members of the party. Before he left, he milked the goat, filled the container and gave it to Umm Ma'bad. Later on, her husband arrived with slender goats hardly having any milk in their udders. He was astonished to see milk in the house. His wife told him that a blessed man passed by the way, and then she gave details about his physical appearance and manner of talk. Here Abu Ma'bad realized on the spot that the man was the one whom Quraish were searching for and asked her to give full description of him. She gave a wonderful account of his physique and manners, to which we will go in detail later in the process of talking about his attributes and merits.

Abu Ma'bad, after listening to his wife's account, expressed a sincere wish to accompany the Prophet [pbuh] whenever that was possible, and reiterated his admiration in verses of poetry that echoed all over Mecca to such an extent that the people therein thought it was a jinn inculcating words in their ears. Asma', daughter of Abu Bakr, on hearing those lines, got to know that the two companions were heading for Madina. [Zad al-Ma'ad 2/54] The short poem opened with thanks giving to Allah having given them (the Ma'bads) the chance to host the Prophet [pbuh] for a while. It then gave an account of the bliss that would settle in the heart of the Prophet's companion whosoever he was; it closed with an invitation to all mankind to come and see by themselves Umm Ma'bad, her goat and the container of milk that would all testify to the truthfulness of the Prophet [pbuh].

5. On his way to Madina, the Prophet [pbuh] met Abu Buraidah, one of those driven by their lust for the reward of Quraish. No sooner did he face the Prophet [pbuh] and talk with him, than he embraced Islam along with seventy of his men. He took off his turban, tied it round his lance and took it as a banner bearing witness that the angel of security and peace had come to imbue the whole world with justice and fairness. [Rahmat-al-lil'alameen 1/101]

6. The two Emigrants resumed their journey. It was during this time that they met Az-Zubair at the head of a caravan returning from Syria. There was warm greeting and Az-Zubair presented to them two white garments which they thankfully accepted. [Bukhari 1/554]

Arriving Madina
On Monday, 8th Rabi' al-Awwal, the fourteenth year of Prophethood, i.e. September 23rd. 622, the Messenger of Allah arrived at Quba'. [Rahmat-ul-lil'alameen 1/102]
As soon as the news of Muhammad's arrival began to spread, crowds came flocking out of Madina. They would come every morning and wait eagerly for his appearance until forced by the unbearable heat of the midday sun to return. One day they had gone as usual, and after a long wait and watch they retired to the city when a Jew, catching a glimpse of three travelers clad in white winding their way to Madina, shouted from the top of a hillock: "O you people of Arabia! Your grandfather has come! He, whom you have been eagerly waiting for, has come!" The Muslims immediately rushed holding their weapons, (to defend him). [Bukhari 1/555] The joyful news soon spread through the city and people marched forward to greet their noble guest.

Ibn al-Qayyim said: "The shouts of 'Allahu Akbar' (Allah is Great) resounded in Banu 'Amr bin 'Auf. Muhammad's [pbuh] elation correspondingly increased, but with rare sense of timing and propriety, called a halt. Serenity enveloped him and the revelation was sent down: [Zad al-Ma'ad 2/54]
"... then verily, Allah is his Maula (Lord, Master or Protector), and Gabriel, and the righteous among the believers, - and furthermore, the angels - are his helpers." [Al-Qur'an 66:4][Zad Al-Ma'ad 2/54; Ibn Hisham 1/493]
'Urwah bin Az-Zubair said: They received the Messenger of Allah [pbuh], and went with them to the right. There Banu 'Amr bin 'Awf hosted him. That was on Monday, Rabi' Al-Awwal. He sat down silent, and al-Ansar (the Helpers), who had not had the opportunity to see him before, came in to greet him: It is said that the sun became too hot so Abu Bakr stood up to shade him from the hot sun rays. [Bukhari 1/555] It was really an unprecedented day in Madina.
Muhammad [pbuh] stayed in Quba'. Here he spent four days: Monday, Tuesday, Wednesday and Thursday. It was during this period that the foundation of Quba' Mosque was laid on the basis of pure piety. 'Ali hung back in Mecca for three days to return the trusts, on behalf of the Prophet [pbuh], to their respective owners. After that he started his emigration journey to catch up with him at Quba'. [Zad al-Ma'ad 2/54; Ibn Hisham 1/493]
On Friday morning, the Prophet [pbuh], sent for Bani An-Najjar, his maternal uncles, to come and escort him and Abu Bakr to Madina. He rode towards the new headquarters amidst the cordial greetings of his Madinese followers who had lined his path. He halted at a place in the vale of Banu Salim and there he performed his Friday prayer with a hundred others [Bukhari 1/555]. Meanwhile the tribes and families of Madina, the new name for Yathrib and a short form of 'The Messenger's Madina (City)', came streaming forth, and vied with one another in inviting the noble visitor to their homes. The girls of the Madinese used to chant beautiful verses of welcome rich in all meanings of obedience and dutifulness to the new Messenger.
Though not wealthy, every Ansar (Helper) was wholeheartedly eager and anxious to receive the Messenger in his house. It was indeed a triumphal procession. Around the camel of Muhammad [pbuh] and his immediate followers, rode the chiefs of the city in their best raiment and in glittering armour, everyone saying:

"Alight here O Messenger of Allah, abide by us." Muhammad [pbuh] used to answer everyone courteously and kindly: "This camel is commanded by Allah, wherever it stops, that will be my abode."

The camel moved onward with slackened rein, reached the site of the Prophetic Mosque and knelt down. He did not dismount until it rose up again, went on forward, turned back and then returned to kneel down in the very former spot. Here, he alighted in a quarter inhabited by Banu Najjar, a tribe related to the Prophet [pbuh] from the maternal side. In fact, it was his wish to honor his maternal uncles and live among them. The fortunate host, Abu Ayyub Al-Ansari, stepped forward with unbounded joy for the Divine blessing appropriated to him, welcomed the Noble Guest and solicited him to enter his house. [Zad al-Ma'ad 2/55]

A few days later, there arrived the Prophet's spouse Sawdah, his two daughters Fatimah and Umm Kulthum, Usama bin Zaid, Umm Aiman, 'Abdullah - son of Abu Bakr with Abu Bakr's house-hold including 'Aishah. Zainab was not able to emigrate and stayed with her husband Abi Al-'As till Badr Battle. [Bukhari 1/556]

'Aisha said: "When the Messenger of Allah [pbuh] arrived in Madina, both Abu Bakr and Bilal fell ill. I used to attend to their needs. When the fever took firm grip of Abu Bakr he used to recite verses of poetry that smacked of near death; Bilal, when the fit of fever alleviated, would also recite verses of poetry that pointed to clear homesickness." 'Aishah added:

"I briefed the Prophet [pbuh] on their grave situation, and he replied: O Allah, we entreat You to establish in our hearts a strong love for Madina equal to that we used to have for Mecca, or even more. O Allah, bless and increase the wealth of Madina and we beseech You to transmute its rotten mud into wholesome edible fat." [Bukhari 1/588]

19. The Establishment of the Islamic State

Life in Madina
The Madinese era could be divided into three phases:

1. The first phase was characterized by too much trouble and discord, and too many obstacles from within coupled by a hostile wave from without aiming at total extermination of the rising faith. It ended with Al-Hudaibiyah Peace Treaty in Dhul Qa'da 6 A.H.

2. The second phase featured a truce with the pagan leadership and ended in the conquest of Mecca in Ramadan 8 A.H. It also witnessed the Prophet [pbuh] inviting kings beyond Arabia to enter the fold of Islam.

3. In the third phase, people came to embrace Islam in hosts. Tribes and other folks arrived in Madina to pay homage to the Prophet [pbuh]. It ended at the death of the Prophet [pbuh] in Rabi' Al-Awwal 11 A.H.

The First Phase: The Status Quo in Madina at the Time of Emigration
Emigration to Madina could never be attributable to attempts to escape from jeers and oppression only, but it also constituted a sort of cooperation with the aim of erecting the pillars of a new society in a secure place. Hence it was incumbent upon every capable Muslim to contribute to building this new homeland, immunizing it and holding up its prop. As a leader and spiritual guide, there was no doubt the Noble Messenger [pbuh], in whose hands exclusively all affairs would be resolved.
In Madina, the Prophet [pbuh] had to deal with three distinctively different categories of people with different respective problems:

1. His Companions, the noble and Allah fearing elite.
2. Polytheists still detached from the Islam and were purely
   Madinese tribes.
3. The Jews.

1. As for his Companions, the conditions of life in Madina were totally different from those they experienced in Mecca. There, in Mecca, they used to strive for one corporate target, but physically,

they were scattered, overpowered and forsaken. They were helpless in terms of pursuing their new course of orientation. Their means, socially and materially, fell short of establishing a new Muslim community. In parallel lines, the Meccan Chapters of the Noble Qur'an were confined to delineating the Islamic precepts, enacting legislations pertaining to the believers individually and enjoining good and piety and forbidding evils and vices.

In Madina, things were otherwise; here all the affairs of their life rested in their hands. Now, they were at ease and could quite confidently handle the challenges of civilization, construction, means of living, economics, politics, government administration, war and peace, codification of the questions of the allowed and prohibited, worship, ethics and all the relevant issues. In a nutshell, they were in Madina at full liberty to erect the pillars of a new Muslim community not only utterly different from that pre-Islamic code of life, but also distinctive in its features in the world at large. It was a society that could stand for the Islamic Call for whose sake the Muslims had been put to unspeakable tortures for 10 years. No doubt, the construction of a society that runs in line with this type of ethics cannot be accomplished overnight, within a month or a year. It requires a long time to build during which legislation and legalization will run gradually in a complementary process with mind cultivation, training and education. Allah, the All-Knowing, of course undertook legislation and His Prophet Muhammad [pbuh], implementation and orientation:

"He it is Who sent among the unlettered ones a Messenger (Muhammad [pbuh]) from among themselves, reciting to them His Verses, purifying them (from the filth of disbelief and polytheism), and teaching them the Book (this Qur'an, Islamic laws and Islamic Jurisprudence) and Al-Hikmah (As-Sunna: legal ways, orders, acts of worship, etc. of the Prophet Muhammad [pbuh].)." [Qur'an 62:2]

The Prophet's Companions, rushed enthusiastically to assimilate these Qur'anic rules and fill their hearts joyfully with them:

"And when His Verses (this Qur'an) are recited unto them, they (i.e. the Verses) increase their Faith." [Qur'an 8:2]

With respect to the Muslims, this task constituted the greatest challenge for the Messenger of Allah [pbuh]. In fact, this very purpose lay at the heart of the Islamic Call and Muhammad's mission; it was never an incidental issue though there were the matters that required urgent addressing.

The Muslims in Madina consisted virtually of two parties:

The first one already settled down in their abode, land and wealth, fully at ease, but seeds of discord amongst them were deeply seated and chronic enmity continually evoked; they were al-Ansar (the Helpers).

The second party was al-Muhajirun (the Emigrants), homeless, jobless and penniless. Their number was not small, on the contrary, it was increasing day by day after the Prophet [pbuh] had given them the green light to leave for Madina whose economic structure, originally not that prosperous one, began to show signs of imbalance aggravated by the economic boycott that the anti-Islamic groups imposed and consequently imports diminished and living conditions worsened.

2. The Jews (the Hebrews), who had migrated to Al-Hijaz from Syria following the Byzantine and Assyrian persecution campaigns, were the third category existent on the demographic scene in Madina. In their new abode they assumed the Arabian stamp in dress, language and manner of life and there were instances of intermarriage with the local Arabs, however they retained their ethnic particularism and detached themselves from amalgamation with the immediate environment. They even used to pride in their Jewish-Israeli origin, and spurn the Arabs around designating them as illiterate meaning brutal, naïve and backward. They desired the wealth of their neighbors to be made lawful to them and they could thus appropriate it the way they liked.

"... because they say: "There is no blame on us to betray and take the properties of the illiterates (Arabs)" [Qur'an 3:75]

They excelled at the arts of earning money and trading. They in fact monopolized trading in cereals, dates, wine, clothes, export and import. For the services they offered to the Arabs, the latter paid heavily. Usury was a common practice amongst them, lending the Arab notables great sums to be squandered on mercenary poets, and in vanity avenues, and in return seizing their fertile land given as surety.

Three famous tribes of Jews constituted the demographic presence in Yathrib (now Madina):

Banu Qainuqua', allies of al-Khazraj tribe,
Banu An-Nadir and
Banu Quraidah who allied al-Aws and inhabited the suburbs of Madina.

Islam came to bring about a spirit of rapport, to terminate the state of enmity and hatred, and to establish a social regime based on denunciation of the prohibited and promotion of the allowed. Adherence to these canons of life implied paving the way for an Arab unity that could work to the prejudice of the Jews and their interests at both the social and economic levels; the Arab tribes would then try to restore their wealth and land misappropriated by the Jews through usurious practices.
The Jews of course deeply considered all these things ever since they had known that the Islamic Call would try to settle in Yathrib, and it was no surprise to discover that they harbored the most enmity and hatred to Islam and the Messenger [pbuh] even though they did not have the courage to uncover their feelings in the beginning.

The following incident could attest clearly to that abominable antipathy that the Jews harbored towards the new political and religious changes that came to stamp the life of Madina. Ibn Ishaq, on the authority of the Mother of believers Safiyah narrated: Safiyah, daughter of Huyayi bin Akhtab said: I was the closest child to my father and my uncle Abi Yasir's heart. Whenever they saw me with a child of theirs, they should pamper me so tenderly to the exclusion of anyone else. However, with the advent of the Messenger of Allah [pbuh] and setting in Quba' with Bani 'Amr bin 'Awf, my father, Huyayi bin Akhtab and my uncle Abu Yasir bin Akhtab went to see him and did not return until sunset when they came back walking lazily and fully dejected. I, as usually, hurried to meet them smiling, but they would not turn to me for the grief that caught them. I heard my uncle Abu Yasir say to Ubai and Huyayi: "Is it really he (i.e. Muhammad [pbuh])?" The former said: "It is he, I swear by Allah!" "Did you really recognize him?" they asked. He answered: "Yes, and my heart is burning with enmity towards him"[Ibn Hisham 1/518, 519]

The Story of a Jewish Rabbi Accepting Islam

An interesting story that took place on the first day, the Prophet [pbuh] stepped in Madina, could be quoted to illustrate the mental disturbance and deep anxiety that beset the Jews. 'Abdullah bin Salam, the most learned rabbi among the Jews came to see the Prophet [pbuh] when he arrived, and asked him certain questions to ascertain his real Prophethood. No sooner did he hear the Prophet's answers than he embraced Islam, but added that if his people knew of his acceptance of Islam they would advance false arguments against me. The Prophet [pbuh] sent for some Jews and asked them about 'Abdullah bin Salam, they testified to his scholarly aptitude and virtuous standing. Here it was divulged to them that he had embraced Islam and on the spot, they imparted categorically opposite testimonies and described him as the most evil of all evils. In another narration 'Abdullah bin Salam said, "O Jews! Be Allah fearing. By Allah, the only One, you know that he is the Messenger of Allah sent to people with the Truth." They replied, "You are lying." That was the Prophet's first experience with the Jews. [Bukhari 1/459]

Muslims in Madina

That was the demo-political picture within Madina. Five hundred kilometers away in Mecca, there still lay another source of detrimental threat, the archenemy of Islam, Quraish. For ten years, while at the mercy of Quraish, the Muslims were subjected to all sorts of terrorism, boycott, harassment and starvation coupled by a large-scale painstaking psychological war and aggressive organized propaganda. When they had emigrated to Madina, their land, wealth and property were seized, wives detained and the socially humble in rank brutally tortured. Quraish also schemed and made attempts on the life of the first figure of the Call, Muhammad [pbuh]. Due to their acknowledged temporal leadership and religious supremacy among the pagan Arabs, given the custodianship of the Sacred Sanctuary, the Quraishites spared no effort in enticing the Arabians against Madina and boycotting the Madinese socially and economically. To quote Muhammad Al-Ghazali: "A state of war virtually existed between the Meccan tyrants and the Muslims in their abode. It is foolish to blame the Muslims for the horrible consequences that were bound to ensue in the light of that long-standing feud."[Fiqh As-Seerah p.162]

The Muslims in Madina were completely eligible then to confiscate the wealth of those tyrants, mete out for them exemplary punishment and bring twofold retaliation on them in order to deter them from committing any folly against the Muslims and their sanctities.

That was a resume of the major problems that the Prophet Muhammad [pbuh] had to face, and the complicated issues he was supposed to resolve.

In full acknowledgment, we could safely say that he quite honestly shouldered the responsibilities of Messengership, and cleverly discharged the liabilities of both temporal and religious leadership in Madina. He accorded to everyone his due portion whether of mercy or punishment, with the former usually seasoning the latter in the overall process of establishing Islam on firm grounds among its faithful adherents.

19.1. A New Society being Built and a New Islamic Calendar

We have already mentioned that the Messenger of Allah [pbuh] arrived in Madina on Friday, 12th Rabi' al-Awwal 1 A.H., i.e. September 27th. 622 A.D. and took the downstairs of Abi Ayyub's house as a temporary residence.

The first task to which the Prophet [pbuh] attended on his arrival in Madina was the construction of a Mosque, in the very site where his camel knelt down. The land, which belonged to two orphans, was purchased. The Prophet [pbuh] himself contributed to building the Mosque by carrying adobe bricks and stones while reciting verses:

"O Allah! no bliss is there but that of the Hereafter, I beseech you to forgive the Emigrants and Helpers."

The Qiblah (the direction in which the Muslims turn their faces in prayer) was constructed to face Jerusalem; two beams were also erected to hold the ceiling up. It was square in form, each side measuring approximately 100 yards, facing towards the north and having three gates on each of the remaining sides. Nearby, rooms reserved for the Prophet's household were built of stones and adobe bricks with ceilings of palm leaves. [Bukhari 1/71,555,560; Zad Al-Ma'ad 2/56] To the north of the Mosque a place was reserved for the Muslims who had neither family nor home. The Adhan (summoning the Muslims to the Mosque by the Call for prayer) was initiated at this early stage of post-migration era. The Mosque was not merely a locus to perform prayers, but rather an Islamic league

where the Muslim's were instructed in Islam and its doctrines. It served as an assembly place where the conflicting pre-Islamic trends used to come to terms; it was the headquarter wherein all the affairs of the Muslims were administered, and consultative and executive councils held.
The Mosque being thus constructed, the Prophet [pbuh] next turned his attention to cementing the ties of mutual brotherhood amongst the Muslims of Madina, Al-Ansar (the Helpers) and al-Muhajirun (the Emigrants). It was indeed unique in the history of the world. A gathering of 90 men, half of whom Emigrants and the others Helpers assembled in the house of Anas bin Malik where the Prophet [pbuh] gave the spirit of brotherhood his official blessing. When either of the two persons who had been paired as brothers, passed away, his property was inherited by his brother-in-faith. This practice continued till the following verse was revealed at the time of the battle of Badr, and the regular rule of inheritance was allowed to take its usual course:
"But kindred by blood are nearer to one another regarding inheritance." [Zad al-Ma'ad 2/56]

"Brotherhood-in-faith" to quote Muhammad Al-Ghazali, "was holding subordinate every distinction of race and kindred and supporting the Islamic precept: none is superior to the other except on the basis of piety and God-fearing. [Fiqh As-Seerah p140,141]"
The Prophet [pbuh] attached to that brotherhood a valid contract; it was not just meaningless words but rather a valid practice relating to blood and wealth rather than a passing whim taking the form of accidental greeting.
The atmosphere of brotherhood and fellow-feeling created a spirit of selflessness infused deeply in the hearts of his followers, and produced very healthy results. For example, Sa'd bin Ar-Rabi', a Helper, said to his fellow brother 'Abdur Rahman bin 'Awf, "I am the richest man amongst the Helpers. I am glad to share my property half and half with you. I have two wives, I am ready to divorce one and after the expiry of her 'Iddah, (the prescribed period for a woman divorcee to stay within her house unmarried) you may marry her." But 'Abdur Rahman bin 'Awf was not prepared to accept anything: neither property nor home. So he blessed his brother and said: "Kindly direct me to the market so that I may make my fortune with my own hands." And he did prosper and got married very shortly by his own labor. [Bukhari 1/553]

The Helpers were extremely generous to their brethren-in-faith. Abu Hurairah reported that they once approached the Prophet [pbuh] with the request that their orchards of palm trees should be distributed equally between the Muslims of Madina and their brethren from Mecca. But the Prophet [pbuh] was reluctant to put this heavy burden upon them. It was, however, decided that the Emigrants would work in the orchards along with the Helpers and the yield would be divided equally amongst them. [Bukhari 1/312]
Such examples point directly to the spirit of sacrifice, altruism and cordiality on the part of the Helpers, and also to the feeling of appreciation, gratitude and self-respect that the Emigrants held dear to their hearts. They took only what helped them eke a reasonable living. In short, this policy of mutual brotherhood was so wise and timely that many obstinate problems were resolved wonderfully and reasonably.

19.2. A Charter of Islamic Alliance
Just as the Prophet [pbuh] had established a code of brotherhood amongst the believers, so too he was keen on establishing friendly relations between the Muslims and non-Muslim tribes of Arabia. He established a sort of treaty aiming at ruling out all pre-Islamic rancour and inter-tribal feuds. He was so meticulous not to leave any area in the charter that would allow pre-Islamic traditions to sneak in or violate the new environment he wanted to establish. Herein, we look over some of its provisions.
In the Name of Allah, the Most Beneficent, the Most Merciful. This is a document from Muhammad, the Messenger of Allah, concerning Emigrants and Helpers and those who followed and strove with them.

1. They are one nation to the exclusion of other people.

2. The Emigrants of Quraish unite together and shall pay blood money among themselves, and shall ransom honorably their prisoners. Every tribe of the Helpers unite together, as they were at first, and every section among them will pay a ransom for acquitting its relative prisoners.

3. Believers shall not leave anyone destitute among them by not paying his redemption money or blood money in kind.

4. Whoever is rebellious or whoever seeks to spread enmity and sedition, the hand of every God-fearing Muslim shall be against him, even if he be his son.

5. A believer shall not kill another believer, nor shall support a disbeliever against a believer.

6. The protection of Allah is one (and is equally) extended to the humblest of the believers.

7. The believers are supported by each other.

8. Whosoever of the Jews follows us shall have aid and succour; they shall not be injured, nor any enemy be aided against them.

9. The peace of the believers is indivisible. No separate peace shall be made when believers are fighting in the way of Allah. Conditions must be fair and equitable to all.

10. It shall not be lawful for a believer, who holds by what is in this document and believes in Allah and the Day of Judgment, to help a criminal nor give him refuge. Those who give him refuge and render him help shall have the curse and anger of Allah on the Day of Resurrection. Their indemnity is not accepted.

11. Whenever you differ about a matter, it must be referred to Allah and to Muhammad. [Ibn Hisham 1/502,503]

12. Killing a believer deliberately with no good reason entails killing the killer unless the sponsor deems it otherwise.

It was solely by his wisdom and dexterity, that the Prophet [pbuh] erected the pillars of the new society. This phenomenon no doubt left its mark on the virtuous Muslims. He used to bring them up in the light of the Islamic education, he sanctified their selves, enjoined them to observe righteousness and praiseworthy manners and was keen on infusing into them the ethics of amity, glory, honor, worship and first and foremost obedience to Allah and His Messenger.

19.3. The Prophet Establishing Peace and Virtues

The following is a cluster of the virtues he used to inculcate in the minds of his followers:

A man asked the Messenger of Allah [pbuh] which of the merits is superior in Islam. He (the Prophet [pbuh]) remarked:

"That you provide food and extend greetings to one whom you know or do not know."[Bukhari 1/6,9]

'Abdullah bin Salam said: When the Prophet [pbuh] arrived in Madina, I went to see him and I immediately recognized through his features that he would never be a liar. The first things he (the Prophet [pbuh]) said was:

"Extend peace greetings amongst yourselves, provide food to the needy, maintain uterine relations, observe prayer at night while people are asleep, then you will peacefully enter the Garden (Paradise)."[Narrated by At-Tirmidhi; Mishkat Al-Masabih 1/168]

The Prophet said:
"None amongst you believes (truly) till one likes for his brother that which he loves for himself. [Bukhari 1/6]"

And said:
"He will not enter Paradise, he whose neighbor is not secure from his wrongful conduct. [Narrated by Muslim; Mishkat Al-Masabih 2/422]"

And said:
"To remove something harmful from the road is charity. [Mishkat Al-Masabih 1/12]"

And said:
"A Muslim is the brother of a Muslim; he neither oppresses him nor does he fail him. Whosoever removes a worldly grief from a believer, Allah will remove from him one of the grief of the Day of Judgment. Whosoever shields a Muslim, Allah will shield him on the Day of Resurrection. [Mishkat Al-Masabih 2/422; Sahih Al-Bukhari; Sahih Muslim]"

The Prophet also said:
"Charity erases sins just as water extinguishes fire. [Mishkat Al-Masabih 1/12]"

And said:
"He is not a perfect believer, who goes to bed full and knows that his neighbor is hungry. [ibid 2/424]"

And said:
"Show mercy to people on earth so that Allah will have mercy on you in heaven. [Sunan Abu Da'ud 2/235]"

And said:
"Try to avert fire even by half a date (in charity) if not by tendering a good word. [Bukhari 2/190]"

And said:
"Clothing an under-clad Muslim, entitles you to a garment from the Paradise; feeding a hungry Muslim will make you eligible (by Allah's Will) for the fruit of the Paradise, and if you provide water to a thirsty Muslim, Allah will provide you with a drink from 'the Sealed Nectar'. [Mishkat Al-Masabih 1/169]"

He used as well to exhort the believers to spend in charity reminding them of relevant virtues for which the hearts yearn.

He said:
"The bonds of brotherhood between two Muslims are like parts of a house, one part strengthens and holds the other. [Bukhari 2/890]"

And said:
"Do not have malice against a Muslim; do not be envious of other Muslims; do not go against a Muslim and forsake him. O the slaves of Allah! Be like brothers with each other. It is not violable for a Muslim to desert his brother for over three days. [Bukhari 2/896]"

The Prophet [pbuh] used as well to promote that habit of abstention from asking the others for help unless one is totally helpless. He used to talk to his companions a lot about the merits, virtues and Divine reward implied in observing the prescribed worships and rituals. He would always bring forth corroborated proofs in order to

link them physically and spiritually to the Revelation sent to him, hence he would apprise them of their duties and responsibilities in terms of the consequences of the Call of Islam, and at the same time emphasize the exigencies of comprehension and contemplation.
That was his practice of maximizing their morale and imbuing them with the noble values and ideals so that they could become models of virtue to be copied by subsequent generations.

Those were the attributes and qualities on whose basis the Prophet [pbuh] wanted to build a new and most honorable society. On these grounds, he strove to resolve the longstanding problems, and later gave mankind the chance to breathe a sigh of relief after a long wearying journey in dark and gloomy avenues. Such lofty morale lay at the very basis of creating a new society with integrated components immune to all fluctuations of time, and powerful enough to change the whole course of humanity.

19.4. A Cooperation and Non-Aggression Pact with the Jews
Soon after emigrating to Madina and making sure that the pillars of the new Islamic community were well established on strong bases of administrative, political and ideological unity, the Prophet [pbuh] commenced to establish regular and clearly-defined relations with non-Muslims. All of these efforts were exerted solely to provide peace, security, and prosperity to all mankind at large, and to bring about a spirit of rapport and harmony within his region, in particular.
Geographically, the closest people to Madina were the Jews. The Prophet decided to ratify a treaty with them with clauses that provided full freedom in faith and wealth.
The treaty came within the context of another one of a larger framework relating to inter-Muslim relationships. The most important provisions of the treaty are the following:

1. The Jews of Bani 'Awf are one community with the believers. The Jews will profess their religion, and the Muslims theirs.

2. The Jews shall be responsible for their expenditure, and the Muslims for theirs.

3. If attacked by a third party, each shall come to the assistance of the other.

4. Each party shall hold counsel with the other. Mutual relation shall be founded on righteousness; sin is totally excluded.

5. Neither shall commit sins to the prejudice of the other.

6. The wronged party shall be aided.

7. The Jews shall contribute to the cost of war so long as they are fighting alongside the believers.

8. Madina shall remain sacred and inviolable for all that join this treaty.

9. Should any disagreement arise between the signatories to this treaty, then Allah, the All-High and His Messenger shall settle the dispute.

10. The signatories to this treaty shall boycott Quraish commercially; they shall also abstain from extending any support to them.

11. Each shall contribute to defending Madina, in case of a foreign attack, in its respective area.

12. This treaty shall not hinder either party from seeking lawful revenge. [Ibn Hisham 1/503,504]

Madina and its suburbs, after the ratification of this treaty, turned into a coalition state, with Madina proper as capital and Muhammad [pbuh] as 'president'; authorities lay mainly in the hand of the Muslims, and consequently it was a real capital of Islam. To expand the zone of peace and security the Prophet [pbuh] started to enter into similar treaties with other tribes living around 'his state'.

19.5. The Battle with Quraish
The Quraishites, mortified at the escape of the Prophet [pbuh] along with his devoted companions, and jealous of his growing power in Madina, kept a stringent watch over the Muslims left behind and persecuted them in every possible way. They also initiated clandestine contacts with 'Abdullah bin Ubay bin Salul, chief of Madinese polytheists, and president designate of the tribes 'Aws

and Khazraj before the Prophet's emigration. They sent him a strongly-worded ultimatum ordering him to fight or expel the Prophet, otherwise they would launch a widespread military campaign that would exterminate his people and proscribe his women. [Narrated by Abu Da'ud]

His pride wounded and kingship no longer his, 'Abdullah bin Ubay bin Salul, a priori responded positively to his Quraishite co-polytheists. He mobilized his supporters to counteract the Muslims. The Prophet [pbuh] on hearing about this unholy alliance, summoned 'Abdullah and admonished him to be more sensible and thoughtful and cautioned his men against being snared in malicious tricks. [Narrated by Abu Da'ud] The men, on grounds of cowardice, or reason, gave up the idea. Their chief, however, seemingly complied, but at heart, he remained a wicked unpredictable accomplice with Quraish and the envious Jews. Skirmishes and provocations started to pave the way for a major confrontation between the Muslims and polytheists. Sa'd bin Mu'adh, an outstanding Helper, announced his intention to observe 'Umrah (lesser pilgrimage) and headed for Mecca. There Omaiya bin Khalaf provided tutelage for him to observe the ritual circumambulation. Abu Jahl, an archenemy of Islam saw him in the Sacred Sanctuary and threatened he would have killed him if he had not been in the company of Omaiya. Sa'd, fearlessly and defiantly, challenged him to committing any folly at the risk of cutting their caravans off. [Bukhari 2/563]

Provocative actions continued and Quraish sent the Muslims a note threatening to put them to death in their own homeland. Those were not mere words, for the Prophet [pbuh] received information from reliable sources attesting to real intrigues and plots being hatched by the enemies of Islam. Precautionary measures were taken and a state of alertness was called for, including the positioning of security guards around the house of the Prophet [pbuh] and strategic junctures. 'Aisha [R] reported that Allah's Messenger [pbuh] lay down on bed during one night on his arrival in Madina and said: Were there a pious person from amongst my Companions who should keep a watch for me during the night?

She ('Aisha) said: We were in this state when we heard the clanging noise of arms. He (the Prophet [pbuh]) said:

Who is it?

He said: This is Sa'd bin Abi Waqqas. Allah's Messenger [pbuh] said to him:

What brings you here? Thereupon he said:
I harbored fear (lest any harm should come to) Allah's Messenger [pbuh], so I came to serve as your sentinel. Allah's Messenger [pbuh] invoked blessings upon him and then he slept. [Muslim 2/280; Bukhari 1/404]
This state of close vigilance continued ceaselessly until the Words of Allah were revealed saying:
"Allah will protect you from mankind." [Qur'an 5:67]
Here, the Prophet [pbuh] glanced from the dome of his house asking his people to go away, and making it clear that Allah would take the charge of protecting him. [At-Tirmidhi 2/130]

The Prophet's life was not the only target of the wicked schemes, but rather the lives and the whole entity of the Muslims. When the Madinese provided the Prophet [pbuh] and his Companions with safe refuge, the desert bedouins began to look at them all in the same perspective, and outlawed all the Muslims.
At this precarious juncture with Quraish, intent on pursuing their aggressive and devilish plans, Allah, the All-High, gave the Muslims the permission to take arms against the disbelievers:

"Permission to fight is given to those (i.e. believers against those disbelievers), who are fighting them, (and) because they (believers) have been wronged, and surely Allah is Able to give them (believers) victory." [Qur'an 22:39]

This verse was revealed in a larger context of Divine instructions to eradicate all aspects of falsehood, and hold in honor the symbols and rites of Allah:

"Those (Muslim rulers) who, if We give them power in the land, (they) order for Iqamat-as-Salât: [i.e. to perform Salat (prayer) - the five compulsory, congregational prayers (the males in Mosques)], to pay the Zakat (obligatory charity), and they enjoin Al-Ma'ruf (i.e. Islamic Monotheism and all that Islam orders one to do), and forbid Al-Munkar (i.e. disbelief, polytheism and all that Islam has forbidden) [i.e. they make the Qur'an as the Law of their country in all the spheres of life]." [Qur'an 22:41]

Doubtlessly, the permission to fight was revealed in Madina after emigration, not in Mecca, still the exact date where of is in doubt.

The permission to fight was already there, but in the light of the status quo, it was wise for the Muslims to bring the commercial routes leading to Mecca under their control. The Muslims at the behest of their Lord, were ordered to go to war in Sha'ban 2 A.H:

"And fight, in the way of Allah those who fight you; but transgress not the limits. Truly, Allah likes not the transgressors. And kill them wherever you find them, and turn them out from where they have turned you out. And Al-Fitnah (polytheism or calamity) is worse than killing. And fight not with them at Al-Masjid-Al-Harâm (the Sanctuary at Mecca), unless they (first) fight you there. But if they attack you, then kill them. Such is the recompense of the disbelievers. But if they cease, then Allah is Oft-Forgiving, Most Merciful. And fight them until there is no more Fitnah (disbelief and worshipping of others along with Allah) and (all and every kind of) worship is for Allah (Alone). But if they cease, let there be no transgression except against Az-Zalimûn (polytheists, and wrong-doers, etc.)" [Qur'an 2:190-193]

Shortly afterwards, Allah began to dispraise the hypocrites, the weak at heart and cowardly elements:

"But when a decisive Sura (explaining and ordering things) is sent down, and fighting (Jihad - the holy fighting) is mentioned (i.e. ordained) therein, you will see those in whose hearts is a disease (of hypocrisy) looking at you with a look of one fainting to death. " [Qur'an 47:20]

Another event of great significance featured the same month Sha'ban 2 A.H., i.e. February 624 A.D., which was a Divine injunction ordering that al-Qiblah be changed from Jerusalem to the Sacred Mosque in Mecca.

The Battle of Badr
The First Decisive Battle in the History of Islam. The Muslim army was made up of 300-317 men. They were not well-equipped nor adequately prepared. They had only two horses, 70 camels, and one for two or three men to ride alternatively. The pagan Meccans army was 1000 soldiers, approached Badr.

When the two parties approached closer and were visible to each other, the Prophet [pbuh] began supplicating Allah:

"O Allah! The conceited and haughty Quraishites are already here defying You and belying Your Messenger. O Allah! I am waiting for Your victory which You have promised me. I beseech You Allah to defeat them (the enemies)." He also gave strict orders that his men would not start fighting until he gave them his final word. He recommended that they use their arrows sparingly [Sahih Al-Bukhari 2/568] and never resort to sword unless the enemies came too close. [Abu Da'ud 2/13]

When the fierce engagement grew too hot he again began to supplicate his Lord saying:

"O Allah! Should this group (of Muslims) be defeated today, You will no longer be worshipped."

He continued to call out to his Lord, stretching forth his hands and facing al-Qiblah, until his cloak fell off his shoulders. Then Abu Bakr came, picked up the cloak, and put it back on his shoulders and said: "O Prophet of Allah, you have cried out enough to your Lord. He will surely fulfill what He has promised you."
Immediate was the response from Allah: the Noble Qur'an observes:

"Verily, I am with you, so keep firm those who have believed. I will cast terror into the hearts of those who have disbelieved." [Qur'an 8:12]

Allah, the All-Mighty, also inspired another message to His Messenger, saying:

"I will help you with a thousand of the angels each behind the other (following one another) in succession." [Qur'an 8:9]

The Prophet [pbuh], in his trellis, dozed off a little and then raised his head joyfully crying:

"O Abu Bakr, glad tidings are there for you: Allah's victory has approached, by Allah, I can see Gabriel on his mare in the thick of a sandstorm."

He then jumped out crying:

"Their multitude will be put to flight, and they will show their backs." [Qur'an 54:45]

At the instance of Gabriel, the Prophet [pbuh] took a handful of gravel, cast it at the enemy and said: "Confusion seize their faces!" As he flung the dust, a violent sandstorm blew like furnace blast into the eyes of the enemies. With respect to this, Allah says:
"And you (i.e. Muhammad [pbuh]) threw not when you did throw but Allah threw." [Qur'an 8:17]

Only then did he give clear orders to launch a counter-attack. He was commanding the army, inspiring confidence among his men and exhorting them to fight manfully for the sake of their Lord, reciting the Words of Allah:
"And be quick for forgiveness from your Lord, and for Paradise as wide as are the heavens and the earth." [Qur'an 3:133]

The Muslims won the battle and the Prophet [pbuh] exhorted the Muslims to treat the prisoners so well to such an extent that the captors used to give the captives their bread (the more valued part of the meal) and keep the dates for themselves.

19.6. Prisoners of War Constituted a Problem Awaiting Resolution

The ransom for the prisoners ranged between 4000 and 1000 Dirhams in accordance with the captive's financial situation. Another form of ransom assumed an educational dimension; most of the Meccans, unlike the Madinese, were literate and so each prisoner who could not afford the ransom was entrusted with ten children to teach them the art of writing and reading. Once the child had been proficient enough, the instructor would be set free. Another clan of prisoners was released unransomed on grounds of being hard up. Zainab, the daughter of the Prophet [pbuh], paid the ransom of her husband abul-'As with a necklace. The Muslims released her prisoner and returned the necklace in deference to the

Prophet [pbuh] but on condition that Abul-'As allow Zainab to migrate to Madina, which he actually did.

The battle of Badr was the first armed encounter between the Muslims and Quraish. It was in fact a decisive battle that gained the Muslims a historic victory acknowledged by all the Arabs, and dealt a heavy blow to the religious and economic interests of the polytheists.

19.7. An Attempt on the Life of the Prophet [pbuh]
The impact of defeat at Badr was so great that the Meccans began to burn with indignation and resentment over their horrible losses. To resolve this situation two polytheists volunteered to quench their thirst and muffle the source of that humiliation i.e. the Prophet [pbuh].
'Umair bin Wahab Al-Jumahi, a polytheist, and an archenemy Safwan bin Omaiyah sat together privately lamenting their loss and remembering their dead and captives. 'Umair expressed a fervent desire to kill the Prophet [pbuh] and release his captured son in Madina, if it was not for the yoke of debts he was under and the large family he had to support. Safwan, also had his good reasons to see the Prophet [pbuh] killed, so he offered to discharge 'Umair's debts and support his family if he went on with his plan.
'Umair agreed and asked Safwan to be reticent on the whole scheme. He left for Madina, having with him a sword to which he applied some kind of lethal poison. 'Umar bin Al-Khattab saw him at the door of the Mosque and understood that he had come with evil intentions. He immediately went into the Mosque and informed the Prophet [pbuh]. He was let in looped by the sling of his sword and in greeting he said "good morning", to which the Prophet [pbuh] replied that Allah had been Gracious and taught them the greeting of the dwellers of the Paradise: "peace be upon you!" To a question raised by the Prophet [pbuh], about his object, 'Umair said that he had come to see that his captured son was well treated. As for the sword, which the Prophet [pbuh] asked him about, he cursed it and said that it gained them nothing. On exhorting him to tell his real goal, he remained obdurate and did not divulge the secret meeting with Safwan. Here the Prophet [pbuh] got impatient and he himself revealed to 'Umair his secret mission. 'Umair was taken by surprise, and incredible astonishment seized him, and immediately bore witness to the Messengership of Muhammad [pbuh]. He then

began to entertain Allah's praise for having been guided to the 'Straight Path'. The Prophet [pbuh] was pleased and asked his Companions to teach 'Umair the principles of Islam, recite to him the Noble Qur'an and release his son from captivity.

Safwan, meanwhile, was still entertaining false illusions as to the approaching redemption of honor, and burying the memory of Badr into oblivion. He was impatiently awaiting 'Umair's news but to his great surprise, he was told that the man had embraced Islam and changed into a devoted believer. 'Umair later came back to Mecca where he started to call people unto Islam and he did actually manage to convert a lot of Meccans into Islam.[Ibn Hisham 1/661-663]

The Jews breaking the Treaty
We have already spoken about the treaty that the Prophet [pbuh] signed with the Jews. He was very careful to abide by it to the letter and the Muslims did not show the least violation of any of its provisions.

Shas bin Qais, an elderly Jew, a greatly envious man of the Muslims, passed by a group of Muhammad [pbuh]'s followers of Aws and Khazraj. He perceived a prevalent spirit of reconciliation and an atmosphere of rapport and amity enveloping the whole group; an unusual scene categorically in conflict with the animosity and hatred that characterized their pre-Islam behavior. He, therefore, sent a youth of his to sit among them, remind them of Bu'ath war between them and recite some of their verses which they used to compose satirizing each other; all of this with the intention of sowing the seeds of discord and disagreement and undermining the new Islamically-orientated inter-tribal relations. The youth did in fact succeed and the two parties at no time recalled the old days and pre-Islam tribal fanaticism sprang to the front to bring about a state of war.

The Prophet [pbuh] was reported of this account, and immediately, at the head of some emigrants, set out to see to the situation. He began to rebuke them but in the manner of the great instructor and the tolerant spirit of the understanding guide:

"O, Muslims! Do you still advance pre-Islamic arguments after I have been sent to you (as a Messenger). Remember that it is not rightful for you to turn backward after Allah has guided you to the

Straight Path, delivered you from disbelief and created amity between you."

The Muslims readily realized that it was a satanic whim and a plot hatched by the enemies. They directly embraced each other and went back home quite satisfied and in full obedience to the Messenger of Allah [pbuh]. [Ibn Hisham 1/555, 556]

The Qainuqa' Jews breach the Covenant

The Jews started a series of provocative and harmful deeds publicly. The tribe of Banu Qainuqa', who lived in quarters within Madina named after them. As for jobs, they took up goldsmithery, blacksmithing and crafts of making household instruments, that is why war weaponry was available in large quantities in their houses. They counted 700 warriors, and were the most daring amongst the Jewish community in Arabia, and now the first to breach the covenant of cooperation and non-aggression which they had already countersigned with the Prophet [pbuh]. Their behavior grew too impolite and unbearable. They started a process of trouble-making, jeering at the Muslims, hurting those who frequented their bazaars, and even intimidating their women. Such things began to aggravate the general situation, so the Prophet [pbuh] gathered them in assemblage, admonished and called them to be rational, sensible and guided and cautioned against further transgression. Nevertheless they remained obdurate and paid no heed to his warning, and said: "Don't be deluded on account of defeating some Quraishites inexperienced in the art of war. If you were to engage us in fight, you will realize that we are genuine war experts." In this regard, the Words of Allah were revealed saying:

"Say (O Muhammad [pbuh]) to those who disbelieve: 'You will be defeated and gathered together to Hell, and worst indeed is that place to rest.' There has already been a Sign for you (O Jews) in the two armies that met (in combat - i.e. the battle of Badr): One was fighting in the cause of Allah, and as for the other (they) were disbelievers. They (the believers) saw them (the disbelievers) with their own eyes twice their number (although they were thrice their number). And Allah supports with His Victory whom He pleases. Verily, in this is a lesson for those who understand." [Qur'an 3:12,13] [Sunan Abu Da'ud with Aunul-Ma'bood 3/115; Ibn Hisham 1/552]

The answer of Banu Qainuqa' amounted, as seen, to war declaration. The Prophet [pbuh] suppressed his anger and advised the Muslims to be patient and forbearing and wait for what time might reveal.

A Group of Jews Insulting a Muslim Woman Sexually
The Jews went too far in their transgression. One day a Jewish goldsmith provoked a Muslim woman to take off her Hijab and uncover her face, the Muslim woman refused to respond. A Jewish friend of the goldsmith was present at the time, so he tied the edge of the garment of the Muslim woman to her back so when she stood up her genitals become uncovered. A Muslim man happened to be there and witnessed the sexual abuse and harassment, then he killed the man; the Jews retaliated by killing that Muslim. The man's family called the Muslims for help and war started. [Ibn Hisham 2/47,48]

On Saturday, Shawwal 15th, 2 A.H., the Prophet [pbuh] marched out with his soldiers, Hamzah bin 'Abdul Muttalib, carrying the standard of the Muslims and laid siege to the Jews' forts for 15 days. They were obliged to defer to the Messenger's judgment on their lives, wealth, women and children. At this point, 'Abdullah bin Ubai bin Salul started his hypocritical role and began to intercede for them persistently on grounds of former alliance between those Jews and His tribe Khazraj. Muhammad [pbuh] dealt with this man as being a Muslim -- He had faked conversion into Islam for only one month, by that time -- and so he granted him his request; for Islam accepts people at their face value.

Ka'b bin al-Ashraf Attacking the Prophet and a Muslim Women
Ka'b bin Al-Ashraf was the most resentful Jew at Islam and the Muslims, the keenest on inflicting harm on the Messenger of Allah [pbuh] and the most zealous advocate of waging war against him. He was a wealthy man known for his handsomeness, and a poet living in luxury in his fort south east of Madina at the rear of Banu Nadeer's habitations. On hearing the news of Badr, he got terribly exasperated and swore that he would prefer death to life if the news was true. When this was confirmed he wrote poems satirizing Muhammad [pbuh], eulogizing Quraish and enticing them against the Prophet [pbuh]. He then rode to Mecca where he started to

trigger the fire of war, and kindle rancour against the Muslims in Madina. When Abu Sufyan asked him which religion he was more inclined to, the religion of the Meccans or that of Muhammad [pbuh] and his companions, he replied that the pagans were better guided. With respect to this situation, Allah revealed His Words:

"Have you not seen those who were given a portion of the Scripture? They believe in Jibt and Taghût, and say to the disbelievers that they are better guided as regards the way than the believers (Muslims)." [Qur'an 4:51]

He then returned to Madina to start a fresh campaign of slanderous propaganda that took the form of obscene songs and amatory sonnets with a view to defaming the Muslim women. For this kind of attacking the Muslim community he was killed by a Muslim.

19.8. The Prophet Continuous Work for Love and Peace
The Prophet [pbuh] continued his work and struggle to establish the society of Madina on the basis of love, virtues, and peace until Allah –The Exalted- gave him the opportunity to enter his home town: Mecca at the year 8^{Th} A.H. In spite of the aggression of the Quraishi people of Mecca, the prophet [pbuh] entered it peacefully with no shed of blood. The Muslim emigrants who left their houses, their businesses, and their families and relatives, were able to go back to Mecca and enjoy the reunion and perform religious duties such as Hajj in Mecca. After two years the prophet was able to perform his last Hajj in which he delivered on of his most famous speech.

19.9. Hajjat al-Wada' (Last Ceremony):
This is the Prophet's last speech. It was given in his last Hajj, shortly before his death. It defines very well rights and duties.

(The last Ceremony)

[1] "O People, lend me an attentive ear, for I don't know whether, after this year, I shall ever be amongst you again. Therefore listen to what I am saying to you carefully and take these words to those who could not be present here today. [2] O People, just as you regard this month, this day, this city as Sacred, so: Regard the life and property of every Muslim as a sacred trust. Return the goods entrusted to you to their rightful owners. Hurt no one so that no one may hurt you. Remember that you will indeed meet your Lord, and that He will indeed reckon your deeds.

[3] Allah has forbidden you to take usury (Interest), therefore all interest obligation shall henceforth be waived...[4] Beware of Satan, for your safety of your religion. He has lost all hope that he will ever be able to lead you astray in big things, so beware of following him in small things.

[5] O People, it is true that you have certain rights with regard to your women, but they also have right over you. If they abide by your right then to them belongs the right to be fed and clothed in kindness. Do treat your women well and be kind to them for they are your partners and committed helpers. And it is your right that they do not make friends with any one of whom you do not approve, as well as never to commit adultery.

[6] O People, listen to me in earnest, worship Allah, say your five daily prayers (Salah), fast during the month of Ramadhan, and give your wealth in Zakat. Perform Hajj if you can afford to. [7] You know that every Muslim is the brother of another Muslim. You are all equal. Nobody has superiority over other except by piety and good action.

[8] Remember, one day you will appear before Allah and answer for your deeds. So beware, do not astray from the path of righteousness after I am gone. [9] O People, no prophet or apostle will come after me and no new faith will be born. Reason well, therefore, O People, and understand my words which I convey to you.

[10] I leave behind me two things, the Qur'an and my example, the Sunnah and if you follow these you will never go astray.

[11] All those who listen to me shall pass on my words to others and those to others again; and may the last ones understand my words better than those who listen to me directly. Be my witness oh Allah that I have conveyed your message to your people."

20. The Death of the Prophet Muhammad (pbuh)

Symptoms of Farewell
When the Call to Islam grew complete and the new faith dominated the whole situation. The Messenger of Allah [pbuh] started to develop certain symptoms that bespoke of leave-taking. They could be perceived through his statements and deeds:
In Ramadan in the tenth year of Al-Hijra he secluded himself for twenty days in contrast to ten, previously.
The archangel Gabriel reviewed the Qur'an twice with him. His words in the Farewell Pilgrimage (i.e. *Al-Wida'*):

"I do not know whether I will ever meet you at this place once again after this current year."

The revelation of *An-Nasr* Chapter. So when it was sent down on him, he realized that it was the parting time and that *Sura* was an announcement of his approaching death.

On the early days of Safar in the eleventh year of Al-Hijra, the Prophet [pbuh] went out to Uhud and observed a farewell prayer to the martyrs. It looked like saying goodbye to both the dead and the living alike. He then ascended the pulpit and addressed the people saying:

"I am to precede you and I have been made witness upon you. By Allah, you will meet me at the 'Fountain' very soon. I have been given the keys of worldly treasures. By Allah, I do not fear for you that you will turn polytheists after me. But I do fear that acquisition of worldly riches should entice you to strike one another's neck." [Sahih Al-Bukhari 2/585]

One day, at midnight he went to Al-Baqee' cemetery, and implored Allah to forgive the martyrs of Islam. He said: "Peace be upon you tomb-dwellers! May that morning that dawns upon you be more relieving than that which dawn upon the living. Afflictions are approaching them like cloudy lumps of a dark night — the last of which follows the first. The last one is bearing more evil than the first." He comforted them saying: "We will follow you."

The Start of the Disease
On Monday the twenty-ninth of Safar in the eleventh year of Al-Hijra, he participated in funeral rites in Al-Baqee'. On the way back he had a headache, his temperature rose so high that the heat effect could be felt over his headband.

He led the Muslims in prayer for eleven days though he was sick. The total number of his sick days was either thirteen or fourteen.

Five Days before Death
On Wednesday, five days before he died the Prophet's temperature rose so high signaling the severeness of his disease. He fainted and suffered from pain. "Pour out on me seven *Qirab* (water skin pots) of various water wells so that I may go out to meet people and talk to them." So they seated him in a container (usually used for washing) and poured out water on him till he said: "That is enough. That is enough."

Then he felt well enough to enter the Mosque. He entered it band-headed, sat on the pulpit and made a speech to the people who were gathering together around him. He said:

"Do not make my tomb a worshipped idol." [Muatta' Imam Malik p.65]

Then he offered himself and invited the people to repay any injuries he might have inflicted on them, saying:

"He whom I have ever lashed his back, I offer him my back so that he may avenge himself on me. He whom I have ever blasphemed his honor, here I am offering my honor so that he may avenge himself."

Then he descended, and performed the noon prayer. Again he returned to the pulpit and sat on it. He resumed his first speech about enmity and some other things.

A man then said: "You owe me three Dirhams." The Prophet [pbuh] said: "Fadl, pay him the money." He went on saying:

"Allah, the Great, has given a slave of His the opportunity to make a choice between whatever he desires of Allah's provisions in this world, and what He keeps for him in the world, but he has opted for the latter."

Abu Sa'îd Al-Khudri said: "Upon hearing that, Abu Bakr cried and said: 'We sacrifice our fathers and mothers for your sake.' We wondered why Abu Bakr said such a thing. People said: 'Look at that old man! The Messenger of Allah [pbuh] says about a slave of Allah who was granted the right between the best fortunes of this world and the bounty of Allah in the Hereafter, but he says: We sacrifice our fathers and mothers for your sake!' It was later on that we realized what he had aimed at. The Messenger of Allah [pbuh] was the slave informed to choose. We also acknowledged that Abu Bakr was the most learned among us." [Mishkat Al-Masabih 2/546] Then the Messenger of Allah [pbuh] said:

"The fellow I feel most secure in his company is Abu Bakr. If I were to make friendship with any other one than Allah, I would have Abu Bakr a bosom friend of mine. For him I feel affection and brotherhood of Islam. No gate shall be kept open in the Mosque except that of Abu Bakr's." [Sahih Al-Bukhari 1/22, 429, 449, 2/638; Mishkat Al-Masabih 2/548]

Four Days before his Death

In spite of the strain of disease and suffering from pain, the Prophet [pbuh] used to lead all the prayers till that Thursday — four days before he died. On that day he led the sunset prayer and recited surat al-Mursalat.

In the evening he grew so sick that he could not overcome the strain of disease or go out to enter the Mosque. 'Aishah said: The Prophet [pbuh] asked:

"Have the people performed the prayer?"
"No. They haven't. They are waiting for you."
"Put some water in the washing pot." Said he.
We did what he ordered. So he washed and wanted to stand up, but he fainted. When he came round he asked again "Have the people prayed?" Then the same sequence of events took place again and again for the second and the third times from the time he washed to the time he fainted after his attempts to stand up. Therefore he sent to Abu Bakr to lead the prayer himself. Abu Bakr then led the prayer during those days. [Sahih Al-Bukhari 1/99] They were seventeen prayers in the lifetime of Muhammad [pbuh].

A Day or Two Prior to Death
On Saturday or on Sunday, the Prophet [pbuh] felt that he was well enough to perform the prayer; so he went out leaning on two men in order to perform the noon prayer. Abu Bakr, who was then about to lead the prayer withdrew when he saw him coming; but the Prophet [pbuh] made him a gesture to stay where he was and said: "Seat me next to him." They seated him on the left hand side of Abu Bakr. The Prophet [pbuh] led the prayer, and Abu Bakr followed him and raised his voice at every *'Allahu Akbar'* (i.e. Allah is the Greatest) the Prophet [pbuh] said, so that the people may hear clearly. [Sahih Al-Bukhari 1/98,99]

A Day before His Death
On Sunday, a day before he died, the Prophet [pbuh] set his slaves free, paid as a charity the seven Dinars he owned and gave his weapons as a present to the Muslims. So when night fell 'Aishah had to borrow some oil from her neighbor to light her oil-lantern.
Even his armour was mortgaged as a security with a Jew for thirty *Sa'* (a cubic measure) of barley.

The Last Day Alive
In a narration by Anas bin Malik, he said: "While the Muslims were performing the dawn prayer on Monday — led by Abu Bakr, they were surprised to see the Messenger of Allah [pbuh] raising the curtain of 'Aisha's room. He looked at them while they were praying aligned properly and smiled cheerfully. Seeing him, Abu Bakr withdrew to join the lines and give way to him to lead the prayer. For he thought that the Prophet [pbuh] wanted to go out and pray." Anas said: "The Muslims, who were praying, were so delighted that they were almost too enraptured at their prayers. The Messenger of Allah [pbuh] made them a gesture to continue their prayer, went into the room and drew down the curtain." [ibid 2/640]

The Messenger of Allah [pbuh] did not live for the next prayer time.
When it was daytime, the Prophet [pbuh] called Fatimah and told her something in a secret voice that made her cry. Then he whispered to her something else which made her laugh. 'Aishah enquired from her after the Prophet's death, as to this weeping and laughing to which Fatimah replied: "The first time he disclosed to me that he would not recover from his illness and I wept. Then he

told me that I would be the first of his family to join him, so I laughed." [Sahih Al-Bukhari 2/638] He gave Fatimah glad tidings that she would become the lady of all women of the world. [Rahmat-ul-lil'alameen 1/282] Fatimah witnessed the great pain that afflicted her father. So she said: "What great pain my father is in!" To these words, the Prophet [pbuh] remarked:

"He will not suffer any more when today is over." [Sahih Al-Bukhari 2/641]

He asked that Al-Hasan and Al-Husain be brought to him. He kissed them and recommended that they be looked after. He asked to see his wives. They were brought to him. He preached them and told them to remember Allah. Pain grew so much severe that the trace of poison he had at Khaibar came to light. It was so sore that he said to 'Aishah: "I still feel the painful effect of that food I tasted at Khaibar. I feel as if death is approaching." [ibid 2/637] He ordered the people to perform the prayers and be attentive to slaves. He repeated it several times.

The Prophet [pbuh] Breathes his Last

When the pangs of death started, 'Aishah leant him against her. She used to say: One of Allah's bounties upon me is that the Messenger of Allah [pbuh] died in my house, while I am still alive. He died between my chest and neck while he was leaning against me. Allah has mixed his saliva with mine at his death. For 'Abdur Rahman — the son of Abu Bakr — came in with a *Siwak* (i.e. the root of a desert plant used for brushing teeth) in his hand, while I was leaning the Messenger of Allah [pbuh] against me. I noticed that he was looking at the *Siwak*, so I asked him — for I knew that he wanted it — "Would you like me to take it for you?" He nodded in agreement. I took it and gave it to him. As it was too hard for him, I asked him "Shall I soften it for you?" He nodded in agreement. So I softened it with my saliva and he passed it (on his teeth).

In another version it is said: "So he brushed (*Istanna*) his teeth as nice as he could." There was a water container (*Rakwa*) available at his hand with some water in. He put his hand in it and wiped his face with it and said:

"There is no god but Allah. Death is full of agonies." [Sahih Al-Bukhari 2/640]

As soon as he had finished his *Siwak* brushing, he raised his hand or his finger up, looked upwards to the ceiling and moved his lips. So 'Aishah listened to him. She heard him say: "With those on whom You have bestowed Your Grace with the Prophets and the Truthful ones (*As-Siddeeqeen*), the martyrs and the good doers. O Allah, forgive me and have mercy upon me and join me to the Companionship on high." [ibid 2/638-641] Then at intervals he uttered these words: "The most exalted Companionship on high. To Allah we turn and to Him we turn back for help and last abode." This event took place at high morning time on Monday, the twelfth of Rabi' Al-Awwal, in the eleventh year of Al-Hijra. He was sixty-three years and four days old when he died.

The Companions' Concern over the Prophet's Death
The great (loss) news was soon known by everybody in Madina. Dark grief spread on all areas and horizons of Madina. Anas said:

"I have never witnessed a day better or brighter than that day on which the Messenger of Allah [pbuh] came to us; and I have never witnessed a more awful or darker day than that one on which the Messenger of Allah [pbuh] died on." [Mishkat-ul-Masabih 2/547]

'Umar's Attitude
'Umar, who was so stunned that he almost lost consciousness and stood before people addressing them: "Some of the hypocrites claim that the Messenger of Allah [pbuh] died. The Messenger of Allah [pbuh] did not die, but went to his Lord in the same way as Moses bin 'Imran did. He stayed away for forty nights, but finally came back though they said he had been dead. By Allah, the Messenger of Allah [pbuh] will come back and he will cut off the hands and legs of those who claim his death." [Ibn Hisham 2/655]

Abu Bakr's Attitude
Abu Bakr left his house at As-Sunh and came forth to the Mosque on a mare-back. At the Mosque, he dismounted and entered. He talked to nobody but went on till he entered 'Aisha's abode, and went directly to where the Messenger of Allah [pbuh] was. The Prophet [pbuh] was covered with a Yemeni mantle. He uncovered his face and tended down, kissed him and cried. Then he said: "I sacrifice my father and mother for your sake. Allah, verily, will not

cause you to die twice. You have just experienced the death that Allah had ordained."
Then he went out and found 'Umar talking to people. He said: "'Umar, be seated." 'Umar refused to do so. People parted 'Umar and came towards Abu Bakr, who started a speech saying:

"And now, he who worships Muhammad [pbuh]. Muhammad is dead now. But he who worships Allah, He is Ever Living and He never dies. Allah says:

"Muhammad (pbuh) is no more than a Messenger, and indeed (many) Messengers have passed away before him. If he dies or is killed, will you then turn back on your heels (as disbelievers)? And he who turns back on his heels, not the least harm will he do to Allah, and Allah will give reward to those who are grateful.'" [Qur'an 3:144]

Ibn 'Abbas said: "By Allah, it sounded as if people had never heard such a Qur'anic verse till Abu Bakr recited it as a reminder. So people started reciting it till there was no man who did not recite it."
Ibn Al-Musaiyab said that 'Umar had said: "By Allah, as soon as I heard Abu Bakr say it, I fell down to the ground. I felt as if my legs had been unable to carry me so I collapsed when I heard him say it. Only then did I realize that Muhammad [pbuh] had really died." [Sahih Al-Bukhari 2/640,641]

Burial and Farewell Preparations to his Honorable Body

Dispute about who would succeed him [pbuh] broke out even before having the Messenger of Allah's body prepared for burial. Lots of arguments, discussions, dialogues took place between the Helpers and Emigrants in the roofed passage (portico) of Bani Sa'ida. Finally they acknowledged Abu Bakr [R] as a caliph. They spent the whole Monday there till it was night. People were so busy with their arguments that it was late night — just about dawn of Tuesday — yet his blessed body was still lying on his bed covered with an inked-garment. He was locked in the room.
On Tuesday, his body was washed with his clothes on. He was washed by Al-'Abbas, 'Ali, Al-Fadl and Qathm — the two sons of Al-'Abbas, as well as Shaqran — the Messenger's freed slave, Osamah bin Zaid and Aws bin Khauli. Al-'Abbas, Al-Fadl and

Qathm turned his body round, whereas Osamah and Shaqran poured out water. 'Ali washed him and Aws leant him against his chest.
They shrouded him in three white Sahooli cotton cloth which had neither a headcloth [Sahih Al-Bukhari 1/169; Sahih Muslim 1/306] nor a casing and inserted him in.

A sort of disagreement arose with regard to a burial place. Abu Bakr said: "I heard the Messenger of Allah [pbuh] say: 'A dead Prophet is buried where he dies.' So Abu Talhah lifted the bed on which he died, dug underneath and cut the ground to make the tomb.
People entered the room ten by ten. They prayed for the Prophet [pbuh]. The first to pray for him were people of his clan. Then the Emigrants, then the Helpers. Women prayed for him after men. The young were the last to pray.

This process took Tuesday long and Wednesday night (i.e. the night which precedes Wednesday morning). 'Aishah said: "We did not know that the Prophet [pbuh] was being buried till we heard the sound of tools digging the ground at the depth of Wednesday night." [Mukhtasar Seerat Ar-Rasool p.471; Ibn Hisham 2/649-665; Talqeeh Fuhoom Ahl Al-Athar p.38, 39; Rahmat-ul-lil'alameen 1/277-286]

21. The Prophet (pbuh), Attributes and Manners

Here we list a brief summary of the versions about Prophet Muhammad's beauty and perfection.

Beauty of Creation
After the Messenger of Allah [pbuh], passed by her tent on his journey of migration, **Umm Ma'bad** described him to her husband saying:

"He was innocently bright and had broad countenance. His manners were fine. Neither was his belly bulging out nor was his head deprived of hair. He had black attractive eyes finely arched by continuous eyebrows. His hair glossy and black, inclined to curl, he wore long. His voice was extremely commanding. His head was large, well formed and set on a slender neck. His expression was pensive and contemplative, serene and sublime. The stranger was fascinated from the distance, but no sooner he became intimate with him than this fascination was changed into attachment and respect. His expression was very sweet and distinct. His speech was well set and free from the use of superfluous words, as if it were a rosary of beads. His stature was neither too high nor too small to look repulsive. He was a twig amongst the two, singularly bright and fresh. He was always surrounded by his Companions. Whenever he uttered something, the listeners would hear him with rapt attention and whenever he issued any command, they vied with each other in carrying it out. He was a master and a commander. His utterances were marked by truth and sincerity, free from all kinds of falsehoods and lies."[Zad Al-Ma'ad 2/45]

Abu Huraira said:
"I have never seen a thing nicer than the Messenger of Allah [pbuh]. It seems as if the sunlight were moving within his face. I have never seen one who is faster in pace than the Messenger of Allah [pbuh]. It seemed as if the earth had folded itself up to shorten the distance for him. For we used to wear ourselves out while he was at full ease." [ibid 2/518]

The Perfection of Soul and Nobility
The Prophet [pbuh] was an accurate, unpretending straightforward speaker. His stamina, endurance and forgiveness — out of a

commanding position — his patience and standing what he detested — these were all talents, attributes and qualities Allah Himself had brought him on. Even wise men have their flaws, but the Messenger of Allah [pbuh], unlike everybody, the more he was hurt or injured, the more clement and patient he became. The more insolence an ignorant anybody exercised against him the more enduring he became.

'Aisha said:
"The Messenger of Allah [pbuh], whenever he is given the opportunity to choose between two affairs, he always chooses the easiest and the most convenient. But if he is certain that it is sinful, he will be as far as he could from it.

He has never avenged himself; but when the sanctity of Allah is violated he would. That would be for Allah's not for himself.

He is the last one to get angry and the first to be satisfied.

His hospitality and generosity were matchless.

His gifts and endowments manifest a man who does not fear poverty." [Sahih Al-Bukhari 1/503]

Ibn'Abbas said:
"The Prophet [pbuh] was the most generous. He is usually most generous of all times in Ramadan, the times at which the angel Gabriel comes to see him. Gabriel used to visit him every night of Ramadan and review the Qur'an with him. Verily the Messenger of Allah [pbuh] is more generous at giving bounty or charity than the blowing wind."

Jabir said:
"The Prophet [pbuh] would never deny anything he was asked for." [Sahih Al-Bukhari 1/503]
His courage and his might are distinguishable. He was the most courageous. He witnessed awkward and difficult times and stoodfast at them. More than once brave men and daring ones fled away leaving him alone; yet he stood with full composure facing the enemy without turning his back. All brave men must have experienced fleeing once or have been driven off the battlefield at a

round at a time except the Prophet [pbuh]. 'Ali said: "Whenever the fight grew fierce and the eyes of fighters went red, we used to resort to the Prophet [pbuh] for succour. He was always the closest to the enemy." [As-Shifa 1/89]

His Humbleness and Social Character
Whoever served him should be served by him too. 'Ugh' (an utterance of complaint) is a word that had never been said by him to his servant; nor was his servant blamed for doing a thing or leaving it undone.
Loving the poor and the needy and entertaining them or participating in their funerals were things the Prophet [pbuh] always observed. He never contempted or disgraced a poor man for his poverty.

Once he was traveling with his Companions and when it was time to have food prepared, he asked them to slaughter a she-sheep. A man said: I will slaughter it, another one said:
I will skin it out. A third said:
I will cook it. So the Messenger of Allah [pbuh] said:
I will collect wood for fire.
They said: "No. We will suffice you that work."
"I know that you can do it for me, but I hate to be privileged. Allah hates to see a slave of his privileged to others." So he went and collected firewood. [Khulasat As-Siyar p.22]

His magnanimity, broad mindedness his tolerance could embrace all people and entitled him to be regarded as father for them all. In justice, all of them were almost equal. Nobody was better than another except on the criterion of Allah fearing. A favored one, to him, was the most Allah fearing. His assembly was a meeting of clemency, timidness, patience and honesty. Voices were not raised in rows or riots. Inviolable things were never violable. Fearing Allah and worship were their means to sympathy and compassion. They used to esteem the old and have mercy on the young. They assisted the needy and entertained strangers.
Those were the attributes and qualities that the Prophet [pbuh] enjoyed which made the hearts, of the people close to him, draw near to him and love him. Those traits made him so popular that the restraint and enmity of his people grew less and they started to embrace Islam in large crowds.

22. The Miracles of Prophet Muhammad
Peace be upon him

Al-Qur'an: The Living Miracle
The Prophet (pbuh) said: "Every Prophet was given miracles because of which people believed, but what I have been given is Divine Inspiration which Allah has revealed to me, so I hope my followers will outnumber the followers of other Prophets on the Day of Resurrection. (Bukhari)

Historic Miracle: Hijra
Ibn 'Abbas said: "One night Quraish consulted together in Mecca. Some said they should tie him up (i.e. the Prophet) in the morning; others said they should rather kill him; and others said they should rather expel him. Allah informed His prophet (pbuh) about that, so 'Ali spent that night on the Prophet's bed, and the Prophet (pbuh) went out till he came to the cave. The polytheists spent the night keeping guard on 'Ali thinking he was the Prophet, and in the morning they rushed on him, but when they saw 'Ali, Allah –the exalted- had turned away their guile. They asked, "Where is this companion of yours?" and he replied. "I do not know." They tracked him, but when they reached the mountain his tracks became confused, so they went up the mountain and passed by the cave. They saw a spider's web at the entrance and said, "If he had entered here there would not have been a spider's web at the entrance." He stayed in it for three nights. (Ahmad)

The splitting of the Moon
Narrated Anas that the people of Mecca requested Allah's Messenger (pbuh) to show them a miracle and he showed them the splitting of the moon. (Bukhari)

The Date Palm Cried for Him
Narrated Jabir: The Prophet used to stand by a tree or a date-palm on Friday. Then the Ansari woman or man said, "O Allah's Messenger, Shall we make a pulpit for you?" He replied, "If you wish." So they made a pulpit for him and when it was Friday, he proceeded towards the pulpit (for delivering the sermon). The date-palm cried like a child! The Prophet (pbuh) descended (the pulpit) and embraced it while it continued moaning like a child being quietened. The Prophet (pbuh) said, "It was crying for (missing)

what it used to hear of religious knowledge given near to it." (Bukhari)

Water Flowed from his Fingers
Narrated Jabir bin 'Abdullah: I was with the Prophet (pbuh) and the time for 'Asr prayer became due. We had no water with us except a little which was put in a vessel and was brought to the Prophet (pbuh). He put his hand into it and spread out his fingers and then said, "Come along! Hurry up! All those who want to perform ablution. The Blessing is from Allah." I saw the water gushing out from his fingers. So the people performed the ablution and drank, and I tried to drink more of that water (beyond my thirst and capacity), for I knew that it was a blessing. The sub-narrator said: I asked Jabir, "How many persons were you then?" He replied, "We were one thousand four hundred men." (Bukhari)

His Baraka (Blessing) in the Dates
Narrated Jabir: My father died in debt. So I came to the Prophet (pbuh) and said: "My father died and left unpaid debts and I have nothing except the yield of date-palms; and their yield for many years will not cover his debts. So please come with me, so that the creditors may not misbehave with me." The Prophet (pbuh) went around one of the heaps of dates and invoked Allah and then did the same with another heap and sat on it and said, "Measure (for them)". He paid them their rights and what remained was as much as had been paid to them. (Bukhari)

His Baraka (Blessing) in the Food
Anas reports: "In a walima-feast given by the Holy Prophet (pbuh) my mother prepared malidah (pounded bread mixed with ghee and sugar) and offered it in a bowl to him. He asked me to call such and such persons and anyone who might meet me on the way. I went out and whoever came across me I kept sending him to the Prophet (pbuh) until the whole house and the place where the Companions of the Suffa resided were crowded. Then the Prophet (pbuh) said: "Make batches of ten persons and go on eating." When all the guests had eaten heartily he ordered the bowl to be picked up." Hadrat Anas exclaims: "I cannot say whether the bowl was fuller before or after all the guests had partaken from it!" (Tirmidhi)

His Baraka (Blessing) in the Milk

Abu Huraira relates: "By Allah, except whom there is no God, during the days of the Prophet (pbuh) I used to press my stomach against the ground due to extreme hunger, or I used to tie a stone over it. One day I was sitting by the side of a public thoroughfare when the Prophet (pbuh) passed by me. On seeing me he smiled and recognized from my face my condition (that I was hungry). He called "Abahir" (meaning Abu Huraira) and I responded: 'I am here, O Messenger of Allah'. He said: 'Come along with me' and he walked on; I followed him.

On reaching home he sought permission of the inmates, and entered, and also permitted me to enter in the house. He found a cup full of milk, and asked the inmates 'From where has this milk come? They said: 'It is a present for you from some gentleman or lady.' He called me 'Abahir' and I responded: 'I am here, O Messenger of Allah'. He said: Go and call my Suffa Companions.' These companions were the guests of the Muslims, who had no house, no property, no friends or relatives with whom they could live. As such they were guests of all Muslims. Whenever the Prophet (pbuh) received something as charity he used to send it to them and would not retain anything out if it for himself (as charity was forbidden for him and his family). However, whenever he received something as a gift he would send for them and shared it with them.

But on this occasion I did not like his invitation to them, and thought: 'How would this milk suffice so many? I deserve this more than others, as by drinking it I might gain some energy. When these companions of the Suffa would come, the Prophet (pbuh) will ask me to serve the milk to them. When they start drinking I do not think that anything would be left for me out of this milk. But what could I have done, I could not dare avoid the orders of Allah –the Exalted- and His Messenger (pbuh).

Accordingly I went out and called them; they came and solicited permission to come in, which was granted and they came in and took their seats. The Prophet (pbuh) called me 'Abahir' and I replied: 'I am here, O Messenger of Allah.' He said: 'Take hold of the cup of milk and give it to them.' I took the cup and passed it to one man who would drink and when he felt satisfied, he would return it to me, and I would give it to the next person who likewise drank the milk to his fill. I went on doing this till the cup reached the Prophet (pbuh). By that time all had drunk the milk to their satisfaction.

The Prophet (pbuh) took the cup in his hand, looked towards me, smiled and said: 'Abahir?' I said 'I am here, O Messenger of Allah.' He said, "Now only two persons, myself and you are left!" I said: "Of course, O Messenger of Allah, you are right." Then he said: "Sit and drink." I sat down and started drinking the milk. The Prophet (pbuh) said: "Take more." I took a bit more and he continued saying; 'Drink a little more', till I said: By Allah! Who has commissioned you with the truth , now I have no more room in my stomach.' He said: 'Then let me have it.' So I passed on the cup to him. He thanked Allah –the Exalted- and with the name of Allah –the Exalted- drank the milk which was left in the cup. (Bukhari)

PART FOUR

ISLAM, IMAN, IHSAN

23. Hadith Gebreel: The Prophetic Tradition of Gabriel

On the authority of 'Umar (may Allah be pleased with him), who said:

One day while we were sitting with the Messenger of Allah (may the blessings and peace of Allah be upon him) there appear before us a man whose clothes were exceedingly white and whose hair was exceedingly black; no signs of journeying were to be seen on him and none of us knew him. He walked up and sat down by the Prophet (may the blessings and peace of Allah be upon him). Resting his knees against his and placing the palms of his hands on his thighs, he said:

O Muhammad, tell me about **Islam**.

The Messenger of Allah (may the blessings and peace of Allah be upon him) said:

Islam is to testify that there is no god but Allah and Muhammad is the Messenger of Allah, to perform the prayers, to pay the zakat, to fast in Ramadan and to make the pilgrimage to the House if you are able to do so.

He said:
You have spoken rightly, and we were amazed at him asking him and saying that he had spoken rightly. He said:

Then tell me about **Iman**.

He said:
It is to believe in Allah, His angels, His books, His messengers, and the Last Day, and to believe in divine destiny, both the good and the evil thereof.

He said: You have spoken rightly.

He said:
Then tell me about **Ihsan**.
He [the Prophet (pbuh)] said:
It is to worship Allah as though you are seeing Him, and while you see Him not yet truly He sees you.

He said:
Then tell me about the **Hour**.

He [the Prophet (pbuh)] said:
The one questioned about it knows no better than the questioner.

He said:
Then tell me about **its signs**.

He [the Prophet] said:
That the slave-girl will give birth to her mistress and that you will see the barefooted, naked, destitute herdsmen competing in constructing lofty buildings.

Then he took himself off and I stayed for a time.

Then he [the Prophet (pbuh)] said:
O 'Umar, do you know who the questioner was?

I said:
Allah and His Messenger know best.

He [the Prophet (pbuh)] said:
It was Gabriel, who came to you to teach you your religion.

(It was related by Muslim)

24. ISLAM: Pillars and Rituals

Is Islam a Religion or is the Religion Islam?

Allah –the Exalted- said:

"The religion before Allah is Islam (submission to His Will)" (Qur'an, 3:19)

The Qur'an teaches that *the* religion is Islam and it does not teach that Islam is *a* religion, in other words the Qur'an teaches that the entire religion of man on earth is nothing more than a total submission of the will of man to the will of the Creator. Submission is the form of total devotion, the Arabic words *Islam* and *Aslama* means to turn oneself over to,[29] in this sense to turn the non eternal to the eternal: to the Creator, to turn the finite to the infinite, to turn the less knowledgeable to the absolute knowledge of Allah, and to obey Him.

How do Muslims Submit to Allah?

Since Islam is a structured religion, submission and obedience should not be blindly practiced and should not be determined according to an individual approach or personal reflection, instead it is universally set and must be practiced in the same way by all Muslims. Islamic religion does not allow some people to hold themselves superior to others based on race, color, ethnicity, intellectuality, money, or any other thing.

Obedience to Allah must be practiced in certain ways, which are the ways set by Allah in a manner that is achievable by all. The practice of all Muslims is unified through the activities of worship. When the Prophet Muhammad (pbuh) answered Angel Gabriel in the above Hadith, he defined Islam as follows:

"Islam is to testify that there is no god but Allah and Muhammad is the Messenger of Allah, to perform the prayers, to pay the zakat, to fast in Ramadan and to make the pilgrimage to the House if you are able to do so."

---

[29] Al-Razi (1989): p. 273.

These are the five Pillars of Islam, which we will discuss in this order:

1. Shahada: to testify that there is no god but Allah and Muhammad is the Messenger of Allah.
2. Salat: Prayer
3. Zakat: Obligatory Charity
4. Sawm: Fasting during the Month of Ramadan
5. Hajj: Pilgrimage to Mecca

24.1. Shahada
Shahada is to testify or to bear witness that there is no deity worthy of worship except Allah, and Muhammad is the Messenger of Allah. It takes this form:

"I bear witness that there is no deity worthy of worship but Allah, and I bear witness that Muhammad (pbuh) is the Messenger of Allah"

This Shahada has two parts:

One is about the unity of Allah; that Allah the exalted is one, the Creator of everything, the Source of everything, and the Cause of everything. Everything else is only a creation of Allah and their existence depends on Him, thus, Allah is the only necessary being and the only Reality and everything else is not only possible, but possible by Him, therefore, they are not worthy of worship and Allah is the only deity that is worthy of such submission. This emphasis on the ultimate reality of Allah is called *tawheed* in the Arabic language.

Tawheed (that there is only One God) is very essential to Islamic creed or *'Aqida*. The opposite of Tawheed is called *Shirk*, which means associating other gods or powers with Allah, which is absolutely prohibited in Islam because it nullifies the belief in Allah as The Only God and Ultimate Reality. By shirk a person shifts the submission from One God to many, which is contradictory to the meaning of Islam itself. By shirk a person becomes an infidel (*Kafer*). Thus, associating any thing with Allah is *Kufr* or infidelity. Shirk is the worst of sins and is unforgivable, Allah –the Exalted– said:

"Indeed, Allah does not forgive association with Him, but he forgives what is less than that for whom He wills. And he who associates others with Allah has certainly fabricated a tremendous sin." (Qur'an, 4:48)

The punishment of associating a partner with Allah is hell fire, Allah –the Exalted- said:

"Indeed, he who associates others with Allah – Allah has forbidden him Paradise, and his refuge is the Fire. And there are not for the wrongdoers any helpers." (Qur'an, 5:72)

For these reasons faith should be established properly from the beginning so that we know to whom we are devoting our life, and it becomes necessary to testify that there is no deity worthy of worship but Allah, the Lord of heaven and earth.

The second part of Shahada is to testify that Muhammad (pbuh) is the messenger of Allah. This is very necessary because the messenger is the one who delivers the message of Allah to humans. Thus, knowing the religion and the revelation of Allah is only possible through him. Muhammad is the one who received this revelation and delivered it to people. Allah –the Exalted- sent Muhammad as the last prophet and the seal of prophets and prophethood. Allah supported him, as He supported other prophets before, with many miracles, the most famous of them is the Qur'an itself with which he challenged the Arabs while Muhammad himself was illiterate. These miracles will be mentioned later in the text.

24.2. Salat (Prayer)
Salat is the second pillar in Islam. It is derived, in the Arabic language, from the word *silah*, which means connection. Thus, salat is the religious activity that establishes a connection between the creation and the Creator, between man and his Lord. Humans are more than a physical body, they are also a spiritual entity. They desire love and spirituality as much as they desire food and sexuality. Nothing satisfies in us this need for love and spirituality more than Allah the light (Noor) and source of light, the Merciful and the source of mercy, and the source of love and beauty. The

spiritual part in us desires connection with Allah the ultimate source of spirituality and Salat is offering this connection.

Salat is over emphasized in Islam as an obligatory act (Wajeb or Fardh). The Prophet Muhammad (pbuh) described salat, comparing it with the other pillars of Islam, as the "center pole" and the establishment of which is an establishment of the religion, and destruction of which leads to the destruction of the religion itself. It is similar to a tent with a main pole in the middle; the collapse of the center pole is the collapse or destruction of the whole tent.

Salat is purification of the soul; the Prophet (pbuh) made an analogy between the purification of the soul and the cleanliness of the body as both necessary for a balanced human existence. In as much as water necessary for material cleanliness, prayer is presented as a spiritual river in which a believer dive five times a day. As Abu Hurairah, may Allah be pleased with him, reported: I heard the Messenger of Allah (may peace be upon him) say:

"Just see, can anything of his filthiness remain on (the body of) any one of you if there were a river at his door in which he washed himself five times daily?
They said: Nothing of his filthiness will remain (on his body).
He said: That is like the five Prayers by which Allah obliterates sins" (agreed upon)

In regards to obligation, salat or prayer is divided in Islam into two kinds:

1. Obligatory prayer (Salat al-Fardh)
2. Non-obligatory prayer or recommended (Salt al-Sunan or Nawafl)

We will discuss each kind briefly.

Obligatory Salat
This salat is an obligatory action that one is rewarded for doing and punished for not doing. The source of its obligation is the Qur'an itself. Allah –the Exalted- said:

"perform regular prayers: for such prayers are decreed upon the Believers at specified times." (Qur'an, 4:103)

However, the details and description of doing prayer is derived from the Sunnah, or the acts of the Prophet Muhammad (pbuh). All Muslims - male and female - regardless of where they are, and regardless of their different status, essentially pray in the same way, which is the way in which the Prophet Muhammad performed salat more than 1400 years ago.

Obligatory Prayers are Five:
There are specific time frames in which these prayers must be performed in order to meet the obligation of Salat.

Salat al-Fajr or the morning prayer, its time starts from after dawn and ends before sunrise.

Salat al-Duhr or noon prayer, starts after midday when the sun starts to decline.

Salat al-'Asr or the mid-afternoon prayer, begins from mid-afternoon and ends at sunset.

Salat al-Maghrib or the sunset prayer, is said from sunset until the red glow of the sun disappears in the west.

Salat al-'Isha' or the night prayer, can be said from the full darkness of the night until midnight.

These five obligatory prayers are wisely set to establish spiritual connection with Allah and to break the worldly involvement of every day activity through the journey of gaining sustenance. A Muslim starts the day by prayer and connection with Allah - the source of everything. During the day and being busy with work, and before he or she get into the indulgences of the material, a call for noon prayer comes asking him or her to break the connection with the material world and reestablish the spiritual connection with Allah - the source of substance. This prayer keeps a person not only in the pursuit of spirituality, but also supplies him or her with a moment of reevaluation of their deeds and a realization that comes to measure their lives by the teaching of Allah - to whom we will return and be held accountable. After the noon prayer people can resume their worldly work, but before they are deeply involved in the material world another call for mid-afternoon prayer comes. It is time to enhance spirituality, after this people can resume their activities. Toward the end of the day, around sunset time, the call for Maghrib prayer comes. After this people might enjoy their social life with family or friends, then another call for night prayer comes to remind them that a prayer in congregation is even a more beautiful social activity, and by this prayer Muslims end their day. They begin the day by praying to Allah and praising Him and they end their day in similar devotion. These five obligatory prayers are recommended to be performed in congregation. Congregational prayer is carries 27 times more reward than individual prayer. The Prophet, (pbuh) said:

"The merit of congregational Prayer surpasses that of individual Prayer by twenty-seven degrees." (agreed upon)

Of course salat should be performed with awareness, humbleness, and consciousness. The prophet (pbuh) said:

" Though he performs the whole Prayer, a man may be credited with no more than one sixth or one tenth of it. A man gets credit only for that part of his Prayer of which he is conscious." (Abu Da'ood and Al-Nasa'i)

How Muslims Call for Salat (prayer)?
The call for prayer is called Adhan. In each neighborhood there is a mosque, big or small, in which Muslims pray in congregation. The mosque has a dome and a minaret or tower. The person who calls for prayer (Mu'adhen) is a designated man with a strong and beautiful voice. At the time of prayer he goes to the minaret and calls for prayer. In modern times they use microphones with speakers and call from inside without the need to go outside. Adhan or the call for salat is always performed in the following way:

Allah is greater   Allah is greater
Allah is greater   Allah is greater

I bear witness that there is no god but Allah

I bear witness that there is no god but Allah

I bear witness that Muhammad is the messenger of Allah

I bear witness that Muhammad is the messenger of Allah

Come to the Salat
Come to the Salat

Come to the Salvation
Come to the Salvation

Allah is greater
Allah is greater

There is no god but Allah

The Adhan for all prayers is the same except the Adhan for salat al-Fajr; in which a sentence saying: "The salat is better than sleep" is added after "Come to salvation".

What the Adhan, or the call for salat, says is that Allah has greater meaning, that Allah is greater than anything that we might be busy with. He is greater than any material engagement, thus, everyone who hears the call for prayer should leave work or business and begin preparing for prayer. They should head toward the mosque for congregational prayer if possible. If it is impossible to go to the mosque, then prayer should be performed individually or in a group of local people or friends.

Two Things about Adhan
In regard to Adhan we should notice two things:

First, that Adhan is to be performed by mere human voice.
Second, if there is no designated Mu'adhen, then any Muslim who knows how to perform Adhan can perform Adhan. After knowledge, a good and beautiful voice is preferable.

How do Muslims Call for Prayer in a Non-Islamic Country?
In countries in which religious freedom is granted with no discrimination, Adhan or the call for salat should be performed outside or with speakers in as much as other people practice their religious freedom by ringing bells or any other form.
If there is no such freedom granted to practice religion publicly, the Adhan is performed inside the mosque, and people go to perform congregational prayer according to the timetable of that city or town.

Who was the First Person to Call for Prayer?
The first person to call for was Bilal al-Habashi; a black Muslim from Abyssinia who lived in Mecca and accepted Islam early and was tortured by non-Muslims, but he held fast to the religion. When Muslims migrated to Madina the prophet (pbuh) chose Bilal to be the first Mu'adhdhen. Bilal –may Allah be pleased with him- had a beautiful voice.
By hearing the Adhan Muslims should head toward the mosque to pray the obligatory prayers. But what is a mosque?

What is a Mosque?
It is a building or a place inside which the congregational prayers are held. If the building is big and holds many people, as in major towns and cities then it is called Jame', if it is smaller than Jame', then it is called Masjed (or Mosque = place of prostration), if it is smaller than a masjed, such as a room inside university building or work place, then it is called Musalla. The word Mosque is derived from the Arabic word Masjed.

If salat is to be performed at home or in an office the place should be clean and pure. Most Muslims take extra care of the cleanliness of their homes in order to keep it pure and suitable for prayer.

Are there any Conditions for Salat or Prayer?

Salat in Islam is a ritual act, the performance of which must meet the following conditions and requirements:

Time (al-Waqt): is the first of these conditions. Praying any of the five obligatory prayers before their proper time is unacceptable and must be repeated when its proper time comes.

Purity (al-Tahara): is the second condition. Purity is achieved by cleaning the body before prayer with water[30], in order to remove any impurities. There are two categories of purity or tahara in Islam:

1. Ghusl to remove the major impurity (janaba) that occurs because of sexual intercourse, menstruation, emission of semen, wet dreams, and childbirth. To remove this impurity a Muslim should perform Ghusl starting with the niyyah or intention to take a ritual bath, then washing the whole body, including the hair, by water making sure that every part gets wet, in order to be ready for prayer, then they should perform Wudu'.

2. Wudu' (Ablution) in order to remove the minor impurity that occurs after sleep, going to the toilet, breaking wind. This impurity must be removed before performing any prayer. Wudu' is basically for purity and cleaning the body by having the intention first to do this ritual ablution, starting by mentioning the name of Allah, then washing with water these parts: the hands three times, the mouth three times, the nose three times, the face three times, the forearms, which is till the elbow, three times starting with the right hand, the head once, the ears once, each foot three times starting with the right.

Included with purity of course are the purity of the clothes and the area of prayer. If water is not available or its use inflicts harm on

---

[30] Water, according to Islamic jurisprudence, is a pure substance and a purifying substance. It is the source of Tahara unless it is mixed with other substances that change its characteristics. Adding vinegar or rose water to water to the degree that is no longer pure water then it is not suitable for Tahara or purity.

the person, then tayammum or using clean sand as way of purification is permissible.

Covering The Body: is the third condition. This means to wear decent clothes and cover the body. Men are to cover the body from the navel to the knees, and females cover all their body except the hands and the face.

Qiblah: finding the Qiblah, or facing Ka'ba, is the fourth condition. A Muslim should stand in prayer position turning their face toward Ka'ba in Mecca.

Iqama: iqama is the fifth condition. Which is repeating the Adhan and adding after "come to salvation" this sentence twice: "Qad Qamat as-Salat" (salat is being established). It is also possible to reduce the number of the spoken sentences in adhan to half in Iqama; anything said four times will be said twice, and anything said twice will be said once.

Intention: the intention of doing this specific prayer is the sixth condition. One should have this intention in their heart.

How to Pray?
We will take morning prayer, which is two Rak'a, as an example. **Notice** that a Rak'a is one unit of salat or prayer.[31]

"**A.** After the utterance of the Adhan the person summons the intent of prayer in his heart and raises both hands to the level of his shoulders (Fig. 1), saying: "Allahu Akbar (Allah is greater)". He does this to arouse consciousness in himself that Allah is greater than all. Now that he has resolved on starting his confidential talk to God, he pays attention to nothing else. With this, he lowers his hands, putting his right hand over the left one (Fig. 2)

B. Then he recites the Invocation of Commencement: "I hereby turn myself wholly to the Maker of heavens and the earth, in true faith and submission, and I am not of the polytheists. All my prayers and ceremonial rites, all my life and death are dedicated to

---

[31] Describing one prayer is not difficult and is available in many books; however, I decided to use the description given by Tabbarah in his book (1993) pp. 121-125, with some modification as needed.

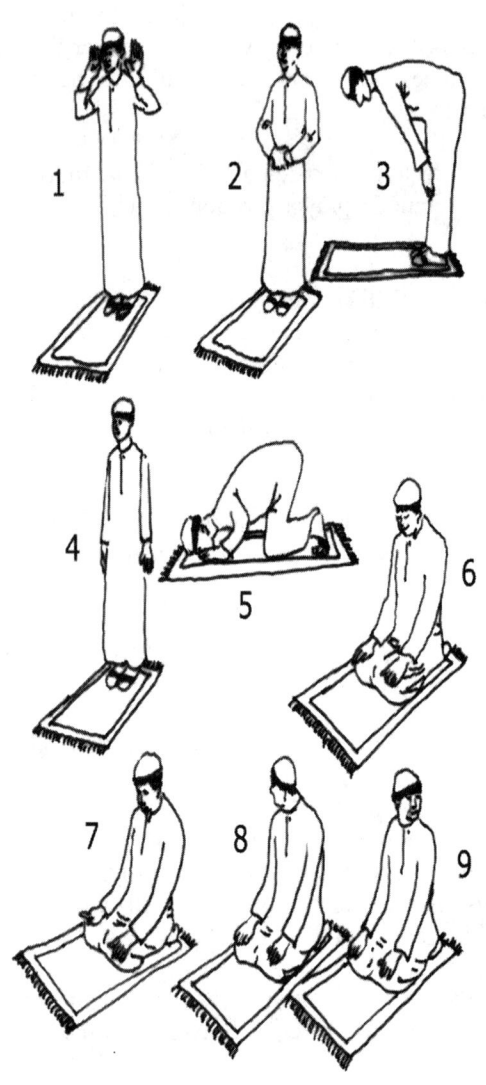

the Lord of the Worlds. None shares Him His Deity. Thus have I been commanded to proclaim, and I am indeed of those who bow in submission to the Will of Allah." The worshipper utters these words to arouse in him the awareness of God's Glory, and to guide himself to sincerity and faithfulness in action.

C. Following the Invocation of Commencement, the person recites al-Fatiha (The Opening Chapter of The Qur'an):

"In the name of God, Most Gracious, Most Merciful. Praise be to God, the Cherisher and Sustainer of the Worlds; Most Gracious, Most Merciful; Master of the Day of Judgment. Thee do we worship, and Thine Aid we seek. Show us the Straight Way, the Way of those on whom Thou hast bestowed Thy Grace, those whose (portion) is not wrath, and who go not astray".

D. Having recited al-Fatiha and meditated on its meanings, the worshipper then says, "Amen"

E. The worshipper then bends forward in the first Rukoo' (Fig. 3), saying: "Allahu Akbar" He places the palms of his hands on his knees, saying:
"Glory to my Lord, the Most Great" three times. Repeating this statement more than three times is recommendable if the worshipper is not the leader of the prayer.

F. Then he stands erect in a qiyam (Fig. 4) to express further praise and gratitude to the Lord Who bestowed guidance on him, and says: "God listens to all those who praise him". Then he adds, "All praise is due to Thee, O Lord"

G. Realizing that Allah's graces are innumerable and that he cannot offer the praise due to them, he prostrates himself (Fig. 5) to glorify his Lord with "Allahu Akbar" on his lips. He touches the ground with the toes of both feet, both knees, both hands and the forehead. Thus finding that he has assumed a posture of humbleness, he whispers: "Glory to my Lord, the Most High" three times.

H. He raises his head, saying: "Allahu Akbar" and assumes a sitting position (jalsa) (Fig. 6). He entreats forgiveness from God, saying: "I entreat Thy Forgiveness and Mercy, O Lord"

I. Then he makes another prostration (Fig. 5), saying: "Allahu Akbar." When his forehead rests on the ground (as in step G above), he whispers: "Glory to my Lord, the Most High" three times.

J. After this, he stands up erect, saying: "Allahu Akbar" and repeats the same round of steps C, D, E, F, G, H and I.

It is noteworthy here that the repeated utterance of "Allahu Akbar" in steps A, E, F, G and I habituates Muslims on honor and nobility, without submitting themselves to any creature, since Allah is greater and mightier than all proud and arrogant people.

K. Having performed the second Rak'a, and immediately after the final prostration (step 1), the worshipper exclaims: "Blessed greetings and good prayers are due to Allah! Peace be unto thee, O Prophet! along with Allah's Mercy and Blessing! Peace be unto us and unto the righteous bondsmen of the Lord! I bear witness that there is no god but He, and that Muhammad is His Messenger.

In this way, the Muslim expresses the most refined praise to Allah before he closes his prayer. This suggests that true salutation and exaltation are due only to Allah, and the prayers we perform are offered to none else than the Lord of the Worlds. And here Allah commands us to address our salutations to His Messenger as well, as a reference to his good memory and a recognition of his favor.
In the worshipper's exclamation "Peace be unto us and Unto the righteous bondsmen of the Lord" there is an indication of the graceful bearings of Islam ("peace", being the root from which Islam is derived). It is a religion that calls for peace and commands its followers to exercise it in their daily prayers. Peace shall be the motto to be repeated every day.

Raising the index finger of his right hand (Fig. 7), and uttering, "I bear witness that there is no god but He, and that Muhammad is His Messenger" the worshipper establishes again his covenant of faith with God, and his adherence to the Message of Muhammad.
L. After the Call of Tashahhud, the worshipper pleads for Allah's Mercy on the Prophet and his People, saying:

"O Allah Exalt Muhammad and the true followers of Muhammad as Thou didst exalt Abraham and the true followers of Abraham: surely Thou art praised and glorified! O Allah Bless Muhammad and the true followers of Muhammad as Thou didst bless Abraham and the true followers of Abraham: Surely Thou art praised and glorified!"

M. The worshipper then makes whatever good pleas he wishes in his life and the Hereafter.

N. Finally he concludes his prayer by turning his face to the right (Fig. 8), saying: "Peace be on you, and Allah's Mercy!" Then he turns to the left (fig. 9) and repeats the same statement.

Having performed his prayer, the person can go back to his normal daily affairs with a new heart bearing a sense of peace and mercy.

For noon and afternoon prayer there are four ruk'as, in maghreb prayer there are three ruk'a, and in night prayers there are four. The performance of these prayer follows the same steps of the morning prayer from A-k, then after the performance of the second Rak'a, the worshipper stands up erect. He/she starts the third and the fourth. In the third and the forth the worshiper recites the Fatiha only. With the last Rak'a he/she must end the prayer as in L, M, and N.

Notice: while in the posture of Fig. 2, in the first two Rak'as of his prayers, the worshipper recites al-Fatiha with some Qur'anic verses. In the same posture of the remaining Rak'as, he recites al-Fatiha alone.

In this posture also, the worshipper's recitation is audible in the first two Rak'as of the Morning, Evening and Night prayers; in the Noon and Afternoon prayers, the worshipper's recitation is done only at heart throughout the Rak'as.

Salat al-Jumu'a (Friday Prayer) as an Obligatory Prayer
Friday prayer is required of all Muslims who are male and mature. Women have the option to attend or not to attend. Also the sick or the unable are exempt. Friday prayer must be performed in congregation every Friday at the time of the Noon prayer. It

replaces the Noon prayer and it reduces it from four Rak'as to two Rak'as. Friday prayer consists of two parts:

1. Khutba or ceremony that is given by the Imam or the religious leader. This khutba is equal to the half of the noon prayer.
2. Two Rak'as, which makes the other half of the noon prayer.

Allah –the Exalted- said:

"O you who believe! When the call is proclaimed to prayer on Friday (the Day of Assembly), proceed earnestly to the Remembrance of Allah, and leave off business (and traffic): that is best for you if you but knew!" (Qur'an, 62:9)

"There is leniency in cases of an excuse, like heavy rain, biting cold and burning heat. Similarly it is not an obligation for the State employees whose absence from work causes public harm, like those in charge of wireless communications, radar engineers, and those who guide airplanes at the airport. As for those who miss the performance of the Friday prayer in congregation at the mosque, they have to perform four Rak'ahs instead, as if it were a daily Noon prayer."[32]

---

[32] Tabbarah (1993): p. 125.

There are many other non-obligatory prayer and I will talk about tahajud as an example.[33]

Tahajjud
After these prayers and during the night till fajr prayer Muslims also encouraged to pray in the form of even number of two Rak'as called shaf', then conclude by an odd or single Rak'a called Witr. Total numbers of this prayer could be 3-11 or more. It is recommended that Muslims perform this prayer, which is called Tahajjud or Qiyam al-layel, in the last third of the night, which is after 3 o'clock in the morning. This time is a blessed time as it is a very quiet time in the deep silence, and during the sleep of every thing the voice of the worshipper breaks the clouds of laziness by the voice of worship and obedience.

Internal States Conducive to Perfecting the Life in Prayer
Imam al-Ghazali (1058-1111) discussed thoroughly the spiritual dimensions of Salat emphasizing the qualities that perfect the Muslim's life through prayer. He said:

"These qualities can be expressed in many ways, but they are well summed up in six words, namely: awareness; understanding; reverence; awe; hope; shame.

AWARENESS
By conscious awareness we mean that state in which one's mind and feelings are in no way distracted from what one is doing and saying. Perception is united with action and speech. Thoughts do

---

[33] The Non-obligatory prayers (Sunan or Nawafl):
Two Rak'as before Fajr prayer is a Sunnah that is emphasized by the continuous acts of the Prophet Muhammad (pbuh) it becomes Mu'akkada. This is why Abu Hanifa considers it a Wajeb and not a mandoob.
Four Rak'as before Noon prayer and four after is a Sunnah.
Four Rak'as before the midd afternoon prayer is also a Sunnah.
Two Rak'as after Maghreb prayer is a Sunnah too.
Four Rak'as after Ishaa' prayer is a Sunnah too.

There are also other non-obligatory Prayers for special occasions such as Salat al-'Eid, Salat al-Janaza, Salat al-Haja, Salat al-Estikhara, and Salat al-Estisqa'.

not wander. When the mind remains attentive to what one is doing, when one is whole-heartedly involved, and when nothing makes one heedless, that is when one has achieved conscious awareness.

UNDERSTANDING
Understanding the meaning of one's words is something that goes beyond awareness, for one may be conscious of making an utterance, yet not be aware of the meaning of that utterance. What we mean by understanding, therefore, is an awareness that also includes comprehension of the meaning of one's utterance. People differ In this respect, not sharing a common understanding of the Qur'an and the glorifications.

How many subtleties of meaning we come to understand in the course of ritual Prayer! Things that had never occurred to us before...It is in this context that prayer becomes a deterrent to indecency and mischief, for the understanding it brings is a positive obstacle to vice.

REVERENCE
As for reverence, this is something beyond both awareness and understanding. A man may address his servant in full awareness of his speech, and understanding the meaning of his words, yet without reverence, for reverence is an additional element.

AWE
As for awe, it is over and above reverence. In fact, it represents a kind of fear that grows out of the latter. Without experiencing fear, one will not stand in awe. There is an ordinary fear of things we find repugnant, like scorpions or bad temper, but this is not called awe. What we call awe is the kind of fear we have of a mighty king. Awe is the kind of fear induced by a sense of majesty.

HOPE
As for hope, this is unquestionably something else again. There are many who revere some king or other, and who are in awe of him or afraid of his power, yet do not hope to be rewarded by him. In our Prayers, however, we must hope for the reward of God, Great and Glorious is He, just as we fear His punishment for our faults.

SHAME
As for shame, it is something additional to all the rest, for it is based on the realization of one's deficiencies and the apprehension of sin. It is quite possible to conceive of reverence, fear and hope, without this element of shame."[34]

24.3. Zakat (Almsgiving or Obligatory Charity)
Zakat is one of the five pillars of Islam. It is obligatory and its binding obligation is derived from the Qur'an and Sunnah. Allah- the Exalted- says:

"And be steadfast in prayer; practice regular charity." (Qur'an, 2:43)

The Prophet (pbuh) mentioned it in the Hadith of Gabriel quoted above.

Zakat is derived from the Arabic root zakaa زكى meaning purified. Zakat is purification of one's wealth and possessions by paying a percentage of 2.5% of the wealth, possessions, or profit every year if it fulfills the following conditions:

"A. The property on which the duty of charity applies should be fully owned.
There is no dues of charity apply to property in mortmain (waqf), or a property whose owner has no freedom to dispose of it such as mortgaged property.

B . The property on which the duty of charity is due should come to a certain minimum which the Revelation specifies in every kind of property. In this condition, a property whose value is below this minimum has no dues of charity,

C. This minimum of property should stay in the full possession of its owner for a complete lunar year, and accordingly, when the ownership of the property goes to another person after half a year, for instance, no dues of charity apply to it.

---

[34] Al-Ghazali (2000): Inner Dimensions of Islamic Worship, pp. 38-39.

D. The property to which the dues of charity apply should exceed the basic needs and debts - if any - of its owner. Hence, no dues of charity apply to the property that is enough only to meet the expenses of its owner and of those he supports, or if his debts are too heavy for him to bear.

E. With respect to movable property, the dues of charity are collected once every year, and charity dues that apply to agricultural products are paid every time the earth yields its produce.

F. The dues of charity that apply to the property of infants, and insane people, are also paid when the property in question mounts to the minimum, and it is the legal guardian or trustee who pays the required dues. In charity, there is no difference between a male or female, a prisoner or free man.

G. The revenues of charity have nothing to do with the budget of the government, because a separate department should be in charge of these revenues. In a big country, the collection and distribution of the revenues of charity are left to the administration of the local governments.

Kinds of Charity Dues
The Revelation determines five kinds of charity dues:

Dues on gold and silver
Dues on merchandise
Dues on agricultural products
Dues on livestock
Dues on minerals and treasures

No dues of charity apply to kinds of property other than these five; like the property of houses; private clothing; house furniture; animals used for riding; vehicles limited to individual usage; arms, rarities, articles of make-up, jewelry precious diamonds; or machinery employed in industry, agriculture, or in producing books. If any of these, however, is used as an item of trade, the duty of charity then applies to it."[35]

To whom Zakat should be Given?
Allah –the Exalted- mentioned in the Qur'an kinds of people who deserve the money of obligatory charity as follow:

"Alms are for the poor and the needy, and those employed to administer the [funds]; for those whose hearts have been [recently] reconciled [to the truth]; and for freeing captives [slaves], and for those in debt; and for the cause of Allah; and for the [stranded] traveler – [thus is it] ordained by Allah, and Allah is full of knowledge and wisdom." (Qur'an, 9:60)

We can list them according to the Qur'an:
1. The Poor
2. The Needy
3. Collectors of Funds
4. New Believers
5. Those who Free Captives
6. Those in Debt
7. Those working for the Cause of Allah
8. The Stranded Traveler

24.4. Sawm (Fasting)
The Arabic word "Sawm", in the religious sense, means the abstinence from food, drink, and sexual intercourse. This obligatory act of fasting is once a year during the month of Ramadam, and must be performed on a daily basis from dawn until sunset. The obligation of fasting and its principles is mentioned in the Qur'an:

"O you who believed, decreed upon you is Fasting as it was decreed upon those before you that you may become righteous. [Fasting for] a limited number of days. So whoever among you is ill or on a journey – then an equal number of days [are to be made up]. And upon those who are able [to fast, but with hardship] – a ransom [a substitute] of feeding a poor person [each day]. And whoever volunteers good it is better for him.

---
[35] Tabbarah (1993): pp 143-147.

But to fast is best for you, if you only knew."(Qur'an, 2:183-184)

Although fasting is to abstain from food, drink and sexual intercourse, however it must be achieved in a way that satisfies the goal of it and thus it is not only the fasting of the stomach or sexual organs, it must be an act of worship in which the whole body is involved; the limbs and the five senses. Thus the hand should not be involved in any act of disobedience, the eyes must do so, the tongue should not involve in any harmful or violent speech, and the rest of the senses must do the same.

Who is Exempt from Fasting?
1. The ill
2. The traveler
3. Women nursing babies
4. Women who are pregnant
5. Women during their monthly period

Every one of the persons in the above categories who break the fast should make up the days and fast outside the month of Ramadan when they can, if they cannot, then they should offer food to feed a poor person instead.

Imam al-Ghazali Divided Fasting into Three Levels:
"Ordinary,
Special, and
Extra-special.

Ordinary Fasting: means abstaining from food, drink and sexual satisfaction.

Special Fasting: means keeping one's ears, eyes, tongue, hands and feet - and all other organs - free from sin.

Extra-special Fasting: means fasting of the heart from unworthy concerns and worldly thoughts, in total disregard of everything but God, Great and Glorious is He. This kind of Fast is broken by thinking of anything other than God, Great and Glorious is He, and the Hereafter; it is broken by thinking of worldly matters, except for those conducive to religious ends, since these constitute provision for the Hereafter and are not of this lower world. Those versed in the spiritual life of the heart have even said that a sin is recorded against one who concerns himself all day with arrangements for breaking his Fast. Such anxiety stems from lack of trust in the bounty of God, Great and Glorious is He, and from lack of certain faith in His promised sustenance,

To this third degree belong the Prophets, the true saints and the intimates of God. It does not lend itself to detailed examination in words, as its true nature is better revealed in action. It consists in utmost dedication to God, Great and Glorious is He, to the neglect of everything other than God, Exalted is He."[36]

Al-Ghazali went further to emphasize the inward spiritual act of fasting as follow:

"Importance of Observing Inward Aspects
Now you may say: 'Suppose someone confines himself to curbing his appetite for food and drink and his sexual desire, to the neglect of these inward aspects. According to the experts in jurisprudence his Fast is valid. So what are we to make of this?

You must realize that those versed in the external requirements of the law base their formal stipulations on evidence less cogent than the proofs we have advanced in support of these internal prerequisites, especially those relating to backbiting and the like. However, scholars of external legality are concerned only with such obligations as fall within the capacity of ordinary heedless people, wholly caught up in the affairs of this world.

As for those learned in knowledge of the Hereafter, the meaning they attach to validity is acceptance, and by acceptance they mean attainment of the goal. According to their understanding, the goal of Fasting is the acquisition of one of the qualities of God, Great and Glorious is He, namely steadfastness (samadiya), as well as following the example of the angels by abstaining as far as possible from the desires of the flesh, for they are immune to such passions. The human status is superior to that of the animals, since man is able by the light of reason to tame his lust; yet it is inferior to that

---

[36] Al-Ghazali (2000): p. 75.

of the angels, in that he is subject to carnality and put to the test in combat with its temptations.

Whenever man falls prey to lust, he sinks to the lowest of the low and joins the animal herd. Whenever he curbs his desires, he ascends to the highest of the high and attains the angelic level. The angels are near the presence of God, Great and Glorious is He, so those who follow their example and model themselves on their character will likewise draw near to God, Great and Glorious is He. To resemble one who is near is to be near. This nearness, however, is not spatial but qualitative.

If this is the secret of Fasting among men of profound spiritual understanding, what benefit is to be derived from postponing a meal only to combine two meals after sunset, while indulging in all other passions the whole day long? If there were any good in such conduct, what could the Prophet, on him be peace, have meant by saying: 'How many of those who Fast get nothing from it but hunger and thirst?

This is why Abul Darda' said: 'How fine is the sleep of the wise and their non-Fasting! Don't they just put to shame the Fasting and wakefulness of fools! A mere atom from those possessed of certainty and true piety is better and weightier than seeming mountains of worship by the misguided.' For the same reason one of the scholars said: 'How many who Fast are not keeping Fast, and how many who do not keep Fast are Fasting!'

The Fasting non-Faster is he who keeps his limbs and organs pure of sin while still eating and drinking; the nonFasting Faster is he who goes hungry and thirsty while giving full license to his limbs and organs. Those who understand the significance of Fasting and its secret meaning are aware that he who abstains from food, drink and sexual intercourse, while breaking Fast by involving himself in sin, is like one who performs his ablution by wiping part of his body three times (in compliance with the external legal requirement), yet neglects what is really important, namely the actual washing. Because of this stupidity his ritual Prayer is rejected."[37]

---

[37] Al-Ghazali (2000): pp. 80-81.

24.5. Hajj (Pilgrimage)

Hajj as an obligatory act of worship is the fifth pillar of Islam. It is the journey, at a designated time, to Ka'ba or the Sacred House[38] of Allah in Mecca once in lifetime. It is obligatory on every Muslim male and female who is sane, of age, and able to undertake the journey in health and wealth.

The obligation of the act of worship is established by the two main source of Shari'ah, i.e., the Qur'an and the Sunnah. Allah –the Exalted- said:

"And pilgrimage [Hajj] to the House [Ka'bah] is a duty that mankind owes to Allah, those who can afford the journey." (Qur'an, 3:97)

Hajj has many virtues and benefits; it establishes equality among the different classes of the Islamic community by presenting them all with equal clothing and similar uniform, and thus it also establishes equality between the poor and the rich.

Hajj also has the virtue of exercising the power of the will by taking the journey to Mecca and thus manifesting their love for Allah.

How to Perform Hajj and What are the Basic Rites of Pilgrimage?

In Hajj there are ten acts that need to be performed, four of them are basic rites, and the rest of the acts are Sunnah. These ten acts are:

1. The Ihram at the miqat
2. Circling the Ka'bah (Tawaf)
3. The Run between Safa and Marwah (Sa'y)
4. The Halt at 'Arafat (Wuquf)
5. The Stay at Muzdalifah
6. The Stay at Mina
7. Stoning the Pillars (Ramy Al-Jimar)
8. The Sacrifice in Mina (Yaum Al-Nahr)
9. The Shaving and Hair clipping
10. The Final Tawaf (Tawaf Al-Ifadah)

---

[38] The Sacred House or Ka'ba goes back in history to the time of prophet Ibrahim (pbuh) who erected it with his son Ishmaiel (pbuh).

The four basic are steps **1, 3, 4, and 8**. The following is a brief description of the stapes 1-4.

"1. The Ihram

The first basic rite of pilgrimage is the Ihram which legally means entering upon the state of pilgrimage. The Ihram is performed at a certain place, known as the miqat, beyond which the pilgrim should not proceed unless he is in a special state. The miqat is of two categories: chronical and local, The chronical miqat begins on the first of Shawwal and extends till shortly before the daybreak of Yaum Al-Nahr (the Feast of Sacrifice in Mina), whereas the local miqat differs according to the countries the pilgrims come from. The places appointed en route to Mecca for Ihram are:

- Juhfa for those coming from Egypt, Syria, Lebanon and Morocco
- Dhat 'lrq for those coming from Iraq and the East
- Dhul Hulaifa for those coming from the direction of Medina
- Yalamlam for those coming from the direction of Yemen
- Qarn Al-Manazil for those coming from Najd[39]

When the Moslem reaches one of these places, on his way to Mecca, he has to enter upon the state of Ihram, by taking off his sewed clothes - e.g. shirt, suit, trousers, turban, jubbah and putting on a seamless garment.[40] He is not allowed to use Cent on his garment or body, nor to clip his nails or make love to his wife or even kiss her. He is not to disobey God by committing prohibited acts, or to dispute with his mates and servants. And he should not pursue the landgame.

On considering such prohibitions in the pilgrim's Ihram, one finds three basic purposes:

i. Equality. By forbidding the pilgrim to wear sewed garments and allowing only the simplest of clothing, and by commanding him to

---

[39] Those who come to Mecca by air or by sea do their Ihram near these places or at the airport.
[40] For men this garment consists of two lengths of generally white material, one covering the body from the waist to ankle, the other thrown over the shoulder. For women it is customarily- but not necessariIy - a simple white gown and a headcovering without a veil.

give up adornment by not having a haircut or wearing perfume Islam seeks equality among people. For dress demonstrates rank differences among people, and Islam seeks to wipe out all traces that reveal people's riches, fame, or poverty.

That is why at Mina and 'Arafat, pilgrims wear only their garment of Ihram without any distinction between them: they share a unity of feeling, and appeal to God in total devotional submission entreating His Mercy. Such an equality of dress and feelings entails unity among believers - which is one of the principal goals of Islam.

ii. Peace. To implant peace in people's hearts, Islam prohibits pilgrims in the state of Ihram from doing a number of things, such as quarrels and bad speech. God says: "For Hajj are the months well known. If any one undertakes that duty therein, let there be no obscenity, nor wickedness, nor wrangling in the Hajj. And whatever good ye do, (be sure) God knows it. And take a provision (with you) for the journey, but the best of provisions is right conduct. So fear Me, 0 ye that are wise." (Qur'an: 11: 197)

Likewise, Islam forbids those in Ihram to kill animals, whether lawful for eating or not: God says: -Lawful to you is the pursuit of water-game and its use for food - for the benefit of yourselves and those who travel; but forbidden is the pursuit of land-game, as long as ye are in the Sacred Precincts or in pilgrims garb. And fear God, to Whom ye shall be gathered back" (Qur'an: 5: 96).

Islam also requests believers to repeat phrases of peace when they come into the view of the Sacred House, saying: "O God! Thou art the Author of peace, and from Thee peace doth come. So make us, O God, live in peace. O God, let more honor and veneration be granted to this House, and more honor and veneration to those who come on pilgrimage, or visit, to it." The call for peace is one of the basic purposes of pilgrimage.

iii. Righteousness. Also by forbidding the pilgrim to get in contact with women and worldly pleasures, and indulge in wickedness, Islam directs the pilgrim to free himself of worldly flaws and desires, and fix, instead, righteousness in his heart, and rouses his interest in God's good reward. For, as pointed out above, God says:

"And whatever good you do, (be sure) God knows it. And take a provision (with you) for the journey, but the best of provisions is right conduct. So fear Me, O you that are wise." (Qur'an: 11: 197)

Pilgrimage is a practical training in self-restraint for the purpose of attaining refined ideal human conduct, and getting engrossed in a spiritual life where people's hearts are filled with the love of God and people's throats never tire of keeping up His remembrance. The Prophet instituted this in the form of a Call (the Call of Talbiyah) frequently repeated, first when the pilgrim dons his Ihram and throughout the performance of the other rites of pilgrimage, saying: "Here I am, O God, doubly at Thy Command, here I am! Thou art without associate! Thine are the praise and grace and dominion! Thou art without associates! Here I am."

2. The Run (Sa'y) between Safa and Marwah
The Sa'y is performed by walking briskly seven rounds between the two hillocks of Safa and Marwah, starting first from Safa to Marwah, then coming back from Marwah to Safa, and so on. The move from Safa to Marwah, or from Marwah to Safa, makes one of the seven rounds of Sa'y.

The first person to make the Sa'y between the two hillocks was Hajar, Ismail's mother and Abraham's wife, as she was searching for water for her thirsty infant. God made water gush forth for her and her son Ismail - which was the origin of the Well of Zamzam - as thirst was about to kill both people.

By making the Sa'y between Safa and Marwah, the pilgrim seeks God's refuge to keep harm away from him and forgive his misdeeds, for it was at this place that God rescued Hajar and her son Ismail from harm.

3. The Halt (Wuquf) at 'Arafat
This is one of the basic rites of pilgrimage without which the Hajj becomes invalid, and the pilgrim's presence at 'Arafat should be during a specific period of time - from the noon of the ninth of Dhul Hijjah till the daybreak of Yaum Al-Nahr (Day of Sacrifice).

On this Day, pilgrims come closer to God through supplication and earnest pleas, and on this point it is reported that the Prophet, regarding the virtue of the 'Arafat Plea, once said: "The best Call is that made on the Day of 'Arafa."

Also regarding the reward of Muslims who make their presence there, the Prophet is reported to have said: "No day is better to God than the Day of 'Arafa, on which God descends to the sky and says: Behold how My servants look disheveled, dusty and sunlit. They have come from every quarter, near and far, seeking My Mercy: they have not tasted My Torture, and none will have a better chance to escape the Fire than those who attended the Day of 'Arafa."

At 'Arafat, worshippers devote themselves to God, asking forgiveness, displaying submission, performing prayer.

4. Circling the Ka'bah (Tawaf)

Tawaf is an acknowledgment of worship to God, submission and devotion to Him, as well as a reminder of the unity that keeps Moslems together.

The Tawaf is one of the most important expressions of the believer's affection and strong attachment to God. The devoted person is always in a state of longing and enthusiasm about all that pertains to his beloved. The Ka'bah is God's House: "And sanctify My House for those who compass it round, or stand up, or bow, or prostrate themselves (therein in prayer)" (Qur'an: 22: 26).

The Tawaf is performed by going round the Ka'bah seven times, starting at the Black Stone and keeping the Ka'bah to the left

Worldly Benefits of Pilgrimage

In the view of Islam, worship is performed for its own sake, but this does not deny the fact that it entails certain advantages and worldly benefits. Islam considers that religion and the life of the world complement one another, and to this effect God says: "... that they may witness the benefits (provided) for them" (Qur'an: 22: 27).

Besides its spiritual and devotional aspect, pilgrimage is also an Islamic conference held each year, in which Muslims meet on unity, concord and cooperation; its rites are performed in collectivity combining believers from all over the globe. And every meeting - engulfed in an air of obedience to God and fear of Him - wraps the pilgrims in virtue, bliss and peace.

The collective benefits realized in Hajj are numerous: political, economic and social. The meeting in Hajj of hundreds of thousands of Muslims from all over the world turns the Hart into an Islamic conference, in which the people of authority consult on questions that lead to the welfare of the whole Islamic community, like implementing the terms of the Shari'ah, adherence to righteousness, etc.

Rich Muslims countries have obligations and duties toward poor Muslims countries, and on this point the Prophet says: "There you see believers display mutual mercy and affection like a body: if a limb suffers something, the rest of the body rushes to its attendance and support."

Pilgrimage, as such, is a firm establishment of Islamic brotherhood among Muslims, a call for cooperation among them, and a reminder to the Muslim countries of their duties toward one another."[41]

---

[41] Tabbarah (1993): pp. 164-171.

25. IMAN: Articles of Faith

The articles of Islamic faith usually called the pillars of Iman. They are very important in Islam because they present the Islamic 'Aqeedah (creed) that every Muslim should believe in. The six articles of Iman are:

1. Believing in Allah,
2. His angels,
3. His Books,
4. His Messengers,
5. The Last Day,
6. To believe in divine destiny (al-Qadar), both the good and the evil thereof.

These articles of faith or Iman are mentioned in the Book of Allah and the Sunnah of His Messenger.

In the Sunnah, the Messenger of Allah said, in answer to Gabriel when he asked him about Iman (belief), "Iman is to believe in Allah, His angels, His books, His messengers, and the Last Day, and to believe in divine destiny, both the good and the evil thereof." (Narrated by Muslim).[42]

25.1. Belief in Allah

The belief in Allah is to believe in His existence, that He is One, and to believe in Allah's Names and Attributes.

Allah's existence is affirmed through Fitra (the innate purity that Allah creates in every human being), by the intellect, by the Shari'ah (Islamic Divine Law), and by the senses.

I discussed Fitra and the Oneness of Allah and His divine attributes in part one of this book.

---

[42] In the following explanation of these six articles of Islamic faith or Iman I will rely upon the book called *Explaining The Pillars of Iman*" by Sheikh Muhammad Saleh al-Uthaimeen. My presentation is only a brief summary of these pillars, more details were mentioned in the book.

We will see how Muslim scholars and philosophers used the human intellect and sense data to prove the existence of Allah. I will discuss this part later under the discussion of philosophy.

25.2. Belief in the Angels

The angels are a matter of the unseen. They are created by Allah and they worship Him. Allah created them from light, they are so numerous that only Allah can count their numbers, and He bestowed on them the bounty of obeying Him at all times. He gave them the power to carry and implement His orders: "And those who are near Him (the angels) are not too proud to worship Him, nor are they weary (of His worship). They glorify His praises night and day, (and) they never slacken (to do so)." (Qur'an: 21:19-20).

Belief In The Angels Has Four Parts:
1- Belief in their existence

2- Belief in what we were told of their names, such as Gabriel, and also belief in other angels whom we were not informed of their names.

3 - Belief in what we were told of their attributes. The example to this is the description of Gabriel. The Prophet told us that he saw Gabriel in the shape that Allah created him, having six hundred wings and larger than the horizon.
The angels may change their shapes, by the order of Allah. They may take the shape of men. Allah sent Gabriel to Mariam (Mary) and he came to her in the shape of a man. He was also sent to Prophet Muhammad, while he was sitting down with his companions, in the shape of a man, wearing very white clothes with very dark hair, a stranger to the companions, yet no evidence of traveling was apparent on him. He sat next to the Prophet and laid his knees next to the Prophet's knees and put his hands on the Prophet's thighs. He asked the Prophet about Islam, Iman, Ihsan (excellence in the religion) and the Last Hour and its signs. The Prophet answered him. Then, Gabriel left. The Prophet said to his companions, "This was Gabriel. He came to you to teach you your religion." [Muslim]. Also, Allah sent the angels to Ibrahim (Abraham) and Lut in the shape of men.

4 - Belief in the tasks that they perform, by the order of Allah. They praise Allah and worship him at all times without the slightest boredom or fatigue.

Kinds of Angels and their Special Tasks:
Gabriel is the honorable angel who Allah sends down with revelation to the Prophets and Messengers.
Mikaeel is the angel who controls rain and vegetation, by the order of Allah.
Israfil is the angel who must blow in the Horn when the Hour (Last Day) has started and when it is time to resurrect the dead.
Malik is the keeper and supervisor of Hell.
The angel of death captures the souls at death.
There are angels who supervise fetuses in the wombs. When a fetus is four months old, Allah sends down an angel and orders him to record the fetus's sustenance, maximum age, deeds and if miserable (destined to Hell) or happy (destined to Paradise).
There are angels who record deeds of mankind. They have a record of everyone's deeds. There are two angels for each person, one to the right and the other to the left.
There are other angels who question the dead when they are in their graves. Two angels come to all dead persons and ask each of them about the Lord he worshipped, the religion he followed and the Messenger he obeyed.

25.3. Belief in the Books
Books that Allah sent down to His Messengers as a mercy and guidance for mankind. These Books are designed to lead mankind to what brings them happiness in this life and in the Hereafter.

There are four aspects of believing in the Books

1- To believe that they are truly sent down by Allah.

2- To believe in the Books that mankind were informed of, like the Qur'an, sent down to Muhammad, the Torah, sent down to Moses, the Injil (the Gospel), sent down to Jesus and the Zaboor (the Psalms), sent down to David. We also believe in the other Books, sent down by Allah, even though we do not know their names.

3- To believe in whatever the Books contained, like whatever is contained in the Qur'an and sections of previous Books that have not been corrupted.

4- To implement the Commandments contained in these Books, unless Allah commanded to the contrary through Naskh (overruling). We must accept whatever these Books contained of Commandments, even if we do not know the wisdom behind them. All previous Books were overruled by the Qur'an. Allah said: "And We have sent down to you (O Muhammad) the Book (this Qur'an) in truth, confirming the Scripture that came before it and dominant over it." (Qur'an: 5:48). This means that the Qur'an is dominant over all other Books. Therefore, no Commandment contained in other than the Qur'an can be implemented unless it is in agreement with the Qur'an.

25.4. Belief in the Messengers
The Messengers are sent to deliver a Message. They are the ones to whom Allah has sent down revelation and who convey His Law to mankind. Allah ordered them to deliver these Messages.
The first Messenger to be sent was Noah and the last one was Muhammad. Allah said: "Verily, We have inspired you (O Muhammad) as We inspired Noah and the Prophets after him." (Qur'an: 4:163).

Allah sent Messengers to every nation and provided them with Laws that their nations must follow. Some Messengers were sent to revive a Message of a previous Messenger. Allah said: "And verily, We have sent among every nation a Messenger (proclaiming): 'Worship Allah (alone), and avoid all Taghut (false deities).'" (Qur'an: 16:36), and: "Verily, We did send down the Torah (to Moses), therein was guidance and light, by which the Prophets, who submitted themselves to Allah's will, judged the Jews." (Qur'an: 5:44).

The Messengers are only humans and they do not possess any attributes that qualify them to be gods. Allah described His Messenger, Muhammad, the master of all Messengers and the best of mankind, saying: "Say (O Muhammad): 'possess no power of benefit or hurt to myself except as Allah will. If I had the knowledge of the Unseen, I should have secured for myself an abundance of wealth, and no evil should have touched me. I am but a warner, and a bringer of glad tidings unto people who believe'." (Qur'an: 7:188)

The Messengers are only humans. They get sick and they die, they need to eat and drink and they have other human needs. Abraham described his Lord, saying, as was mentioned in the Qur'an: "And it is He Who feeds me and gives me to drink. And when I am ill, it is He Who cures me; And Who will cause me to die, and then will bring me to life (again)." (Qur'an: 26:79-81).

Allah described the Messengers, while praising them, that they reached the highest human attainable degrees in worshipping Him.

Belief In The Messengers Has Four Parts:

1 - To believe that their Messages are truly from Allah. Whoever disbelieves in one Messenger, will have disbelieved in all Messengers.

2 - To believe in the Messengers whom we were told about, like Noah, Abraham, Moses, Jesus and Muhammad. These are the five strongest Messengers. Allah mentioned them in two versus of the Qur'an: "And (remember) when We took from the Prophets their Covenant, and from you (O Muhammad), and from Noah, Abraham, Moses and Jesus, son of Mary." (Qur'an: 33:7)

Allah –The Exalted- said: "He (Allah) has ordained for you the same Religion (Islam) which He ordained for Noah, and that which We have inspired in you (O Muhammad), and that which We ordained for Abraham, Moses and Jesus, saying you should establish Religion (by implementing the Commandments) and make no divisions in it." (Qur'an: 42:13).

Muslims must also believe in all other Messengers and Prophets whose names were not mentioned to us: "And, indeed We have sent Messengers before you (O Muhammad), of them some We have related to you their story and some We have not related to you their story." (Qur'an: 40:78).

3 - To believe in all what the Messengers have conveyed to us.

4 - To implement the Laws of the Messenger who was sent to us, Muhammad, the final Messenger. Allah sent Muhammad to all mankind.

25.5. Belief in the Last Day

The Last Day is the Day when mankind will be resurrected to be asked about their deeds and receive reward or punishment for them. It is called "the Last Day," because it is the last day, there will be no day after that. Afterwards, people of Paradise will permanently reside and take their places in it, and people of Hell will permanently reside and take their places in it.

The Resurrection is a true event that the Qur'an, the Sunnah and the consensus of Muslims have confirmed. Allah said: "After that, surely you will die. Then (again), surely, you will be resurrected on the Day of Resurrection." (Qur'an: 23:15-16).

To believe in the last day is to believe in the Reckoning. In the Last Day, people will be rewarded or punished for their deeds. Allah said: "Whoever brings a good deed shall have ten times the like thereof to his credit, and whoever brings an evil deed shall have only the recompense of the like thereof, and they will not be wronged." (Qur'an: 6:160)

The Prophet said: "Whoever intends to perform a good deed, and performs it, Allah will record it for him as ten deeds, to seven hundredfold, to many more folds. Whoever intends to commit and evil deed, and commits it, Allah will record it as one evil deed." (al-Bukhari & Muslim).

To believe in the last day is also to believe in Paradise and Hell. They are the final destination for whoever deserves either one of them.

Paradise is the destination of the ultimate happiness and joy that Allah prepared for the believers who believe and obeyed Him and His Messenger. They are the ones who were sincere to Allah and followers of His Messenger. Paradise contains, of Allah's bounties, "What no eye has ever violated, what no ear has ever heard of and what no mind has ever imagined (of joys that Allah hid for the believers)." (al-Bukhari & Muslim).

Allah said: "Verity, those who believe (in Allah) and do righteous, good deeds, they are the best of creatures. Their reward with their Lord is Gardens of Eternity, underneath which rivers flow, they will abide therein forever, Allah Well-Pleased with them, and they with Him. That is for him who fears his Lord." (Qur'an: 98:7-8) and: "No person knows what is kept hidden for them of joy as a reward for what they used to do." (Qur'an: 32:17).

Hell is the destination of torment and punishment that Allah prepared for the unjust disbelievers. They are the ones who disbelieved in Him and disobeyed His Messengers. Hell contains kinds of punishment and torment that no one could ever imagine. Allah said: "And fear the Fire, which is prepared for the disbelievers." (Qur'an: 3:131).

25.6. Belief in al-Qadar
Al-Qadar is Allah's predestination of measurements and sustenance of everything and everyone, according to His Knowledge and Wisdom.

Aspects of Belief in al-Qadar

1. The belief that Allah's Knowledge encompasses everything, every matter, major or minor, and time-frames of everything that happens in this universe. Allah's Knowledge encompasses all of His Actions and actions taken by His slaves.

2. The belief that Allah recorded everything in a Book that He kept with Him, called "Al-Lawh' Al-Mahfoodh" (The Kept Book). He said: "Know you not that Allah knows all that is in heaven and on earth? Verily, it is (all) in the Book (Al-Lawh' Al-Mah'footh). Verily, that is easy for Allah." (Qur'an: 22:70).

3. The belief that nothing, whether related to Allah's Actions or actions taken by His servants, can happen without His permission. He said: "And your Lord creates whatsoever He wills and chooses." (Qur'an: 28:68).
As for actions taken by His creation, Allah said: "Had Allah willed, indeed He would have given them power over you, and they would have fought you." (Qur'an: 4:90)

4. The belief that Allah created all creation, all what they possess of attributes and all their actions.

Believing in al-Qadar, as described above, does not mean that people have no power over the actions they choose to take. Islamic Shari'ah and reality confirm that the person has a will of his own:
As for the Shari'ah, Allah said about one's own will: "So, whosoever wills, let him take a Return to his Lord (by obeying His Commandments)." (Qur'an: 78:39)
As for one's own power over his actions: "Allah burdens not a person beyond his scope. He gets reward for that (good) which he has earned, and he is punished for that (evil) which he has earned." (Qur'an: 2:286).

As for the reality of things, every human knows that he has a power and a will of his own. He uses his power and will to indulge in or avoid actions of his choice. Mankind distinguishes between what they do by their own power and between what they have no power over, like shivering due to illness or extreme cool. However, the power and will of mankind is under the control of Allah's Will and Power: "To whomsoever among you who wills to walk straight. And you will not, unless (it be) that Allah wills, the Lord of the worlds." (Qur'an: 81:28-29). The universe is Allah's property and nothing happens in His Kingdom without His Knowledge and Permission.

Belief in al-Qadar, as explained above, does not provide an excuse for mankind to sin or abandon what they are obligated to do. This excuse can be rejected using the following arguments:

1. Allah said: "Those who took partners (in worship) with Allah will say: 'If Allah had willed, we would not have taken partners (in worship) with Him, nor would our fathers, and we would not have forbidden anything (against His Will).' Likewise bellied those who were before them, till they tasted of Our Wrath. Say: 'Have you any knowledge (proof) that you can produce before us? Verily, you follow nothing but guess and you do nothing but lie'." (Qur'an: 6:148). The disbelievers did not have a valid excuse when they said that what they did was according to al-Qadar. If this excuse was valid, then why will Allah punish them for their sins?

2. Ali Ibn Abi Talib said that the Prophet said, what translated means, "One's final destination, in Hell or Paradise, is already determined for each one of you." A man said, "Should we depend (on this fact), O Messenger of Allah (meaning to abandon working deeds)?" He said, "No. Perform deeds, because everyone will be helped (to go on the path that he chooses and reach his destiny)." Then he read the Ayah: "As for him who gives (in charity) and keeps his duty to Allah and fears Him..." (Qur'an: 92:5). (Al-Bukhari & Muslim, the wordings are by Al-Bukhari,). The Prophet ordered the companions to perform righteous, good deeds and not to depend on al-Qadar.

3. Al-Qadar is a matter of Allah's Knowledge. No one can uncover his own Qadar but after it happens. One's intention to perform a deed precedes the action itself. He does not know what Al-Qadar holds for him. Therefore, al-Qadar is not a valid excuse for sinning and abandoning the Commandments.

4. One always seeks what is convenient for him. No one of sane mind would abandon what brings material benefit to him, saying that Al-Qadar forced him to take this course of action. Therefore, why would one use al-Qadar as an excuse for abandoning what brings benefit to him in matters of religion and not do the same for matters of life?
When one is sick and is given a medicine to take, he will take the medicine even though he does not like its taste. When one is told to go on a diet, he would not eat the food that he likes, in order to satisfy this diet and to stay fit. No one of sane mind would refuse to take medicines or go on medical diets, claiming that this is his Qadar. Therefore, why would one abandon implementing Allah's and His Messenger's Commandments, thus bringing Allah's Wrath on him, claiming that this is his Qadar?

5. If one of those, who abandon the Commandments and indulge in sinning, comes under attack on his honor or possessions, would he accept the excuse of the attacker, if he says that he attacked him because it was his Qadar to attack him, and therefore he is not to be blamed? No, indeed. Therefore, why does this person refuse al-Qadar as an excuse for whoever attacked him, while he depends on al-Qadar as an excuse for abandoning Allah's rights on him?

26. Ihsan: Sufism (Mysticism)

26.1. To "Be" and to "Become"
How to Make a Successful Journey

Bahar is a 36-year-old man, who is sailing from a small island, where he was taken after he was captured. He had established a good life on the island, and enjoyed its pleasure. Bahar realized that he has to go back to his homeland, which is the land of health and happiness. His boat is very small and carries only one person. The ocean is dangerous, and the waves are strong. What do you think that Bahar should carry along in his boat to reach his destination safely?

People who deal with spirituality, especially the Sufis, think that they might have an answer to this problem.

Life is a journey, and regardless of the social aspect of our living, we always reach our destination alone. We die alone. Death is a unique, unrepeatable event. Death is the end of this life. Life in Islam is called 'Dunia'. Dunia means that this life is lower in comparison with the other life, i.e., life after death. In Islam the life in this Dunia is closely related to the life after death. The future of a person in the hereafter is determined, after the mercy of Allah, by their deeds and moral actions in this life. Thus, the journey of life in Islam is an important event, not only because it touches on the philosophical question: "to be or not to be", but also because it is a process of a deep search for self-realization, it is the search for "to become". Life determines the answer to the very existential question about the "process" of what we will be in the hereafter.

The goal of the existence of man on earth is not "being," rather it is "becoming." Islam does not reduce and limit the existence of man to the material phenomena; instead it reflects the very nature of humans being able to transcend their existence, through spirituality, to a higher level of existence, which might be similar to that of angels. While "to be" is not necessarily achieving self-realization, simply because we can "be" something that is not us, or contrary to self. For example, for a girl to "to be" a famous model on a magazine's cover, is a goal that might be very satisfactory, however, after number of years, the girl "becomes" a woman, by then she realizes that the "being" of a model was not real because she is no longer wanted by these agencies, she is no longer capable of "being"; she is growing older, losing her physical appearance, and she cannot gain it back, plastic surgery can help to a certain limit. The "being" of her as a model was a false "being", because it was positioned opposite to the very nature of man and contrary to reality. "Being" a model was positioned in the struggle against time, and we know two things: first that we are temporal beings (we grow older and die), and second, we know that the flowing of time is irresistible and irreversible. In order to win this struggle we have to use the part of our existence that is timeless, that can go beyond time. The soul is timeless and more essential in man, thus any successful journey of "to be" must take the soul seriously in its consideration. To "be" is frozen time, while to become is a process.

The journey has to mach the very nature of the self, and the very nature of the self of man is not the out side physical appearance — there must be an essence for man and the essence of humans is that they are spiritual creatures. As the material part of man seeks realization, the spiritual part seeks fulfillment. The spiritual is more essential than the material, thus there will be no real "to be" without considering the spiritual aspect.

26.2. The Heart
Ihsan is the highest level of spirituality. It represents a state or a station in which the heart of an adherent Muslim is not only firm in its belief in Allah, and not only is his or her heart full of His love, but they are also continuously aware of Allah, as the Prophet defined Ihsan in hadith Gabriel:

"It is to worship Allah as though you are seeing Him, and while you see Him not yet truly He sees you."

Ihsan is a state of spiritual certainty and constant devotion. It was the very practice of the companions of the Prophet, and of those generations who came after them.

In this state of Ihsan the worshipper reduces their attachment to this material world hoping to achieve happiness through spiritual content and the pleasure of Janna in the hereafter. In his journey of life the Sufi realizes that a wonderful destination has been set for those who want to reach it. Thus, the Sufi spares no time in making his boat faster in order to meet the absolute love, absolute beauty, and the source of all good — Allah.

In order to make his boat faster the Sufi obtains the least amount of material things. Dunia (this temporary life) is a means to an eternal life, the life after death. Material things are only a means to help us reach our destination, in as much as water is the medium of this journey. It has been used for sailing so that people can reach their destination. Life itself is like water through which we travel on our journey of existence; between the moment we are born and the moment of death. If the sailor got involved and fell in love with water then the more water he put in his boat the more his boat would sink. This relationship with Dunia was well presented in the saying of Imam Ali: "Put Dunia (this temporal life) in your hand, but not in your heart."

In fact the word "Dunia" in Arabic language means the lower level. So this life is lower compared with the eternal life. This life is a life of change, and short-term pleasure, while the hereafter is the eternal life of perfect felicity.

Reducing attachment to material things is only one step in Ihsan. The second step is how to know the world of ghaib and how to know Allah – the Creator. The faculties of knowledge such as senses and reason are no longer able to know this realm of reality (ghaib), because they are created for recognition of the material world. The Sufis think that there is another faculty of recognition by which we can obtain knowledge of this higher level of reality. This faculty is the heart. The heart, according to the Sufi, is the faculty of spirituality; it is the faculty of knowing Allah. But how can the heart proceed in knowing?

26.3. How to Prepare the Heart?
The Sufi answer: by personal experience, that is not transferable to others. The heart as Imam al-Ghazali said is the place where Allah –the Most High- is concerned. According to the prophetic hadith: that Allah does not look at humans' external images or their bodies, but Allah looks at the heart of people. If the heart enjoys a good spiritual health, then the whole body will be good. The heart, as Imam al-Ghazali said, is like a mirror that reflects images. If the mirror is broken or dirty then it will reflect distorted images. If the mirror is clean then it will reflect good images. Thus, the heart must

be clean and good in order to reflect good spirituality. The interior image according to Imam al-Ghazali is more important than the exterior image.

Then how does one prepare their heart to reflect the spiritual images properly?

First clean the heart and make it a suitable place for the remembrance of Allah. The heart is the only place in human existence that is a receptacle of spiritual images. Thus, it should be filled with spiritual things and not with material things. If we put material things in our heart we will be similar to the sailor who puts more water in his boat. So if we fill our heart with the love of material things we might lose the goal of reaching our destination, we might also suffer because material things are subject to changing and perishing.

Second, to reconstruct and beautify our interior image by practicing good values and staying away from sins by following the teaching of the Qur'an and Sunnah. The prophet (pbuh) said that every time a person sins a black dot will be placed or printed in his or her heart, more sins will be more darkness of the heart, until sins veil the heart and make it unable to reflect the truth.

Third, by eliminating the negative impression and evil from the inner image that are not observable to others, they exist only in the heart such as: bad intentions, jealousy, hate, arrogance, selfishness...etc.

Fourth, by the practice of remembering Allah continuously. This remembrance (Thikr) is very helpful in cleaning and preparing the heart to reflect good spirituality as much as the polishing of a mirror in order to reflect good images.

26.4. Everyone is Unique in Spirituality
After practicing systematically these steps and others according to different teaching of Sufism, the Sufi might experience a state called removal of the veil, meaning the veil of the perception of the heart is no longer preventing the heart from knowing. At this level the Sufi might be able to reach a level of knowledge in which a special illumination might happen to him or her. This experience is

unique to the person, and people vary in their spiritual experience and stations in as much as they vary in other aspects of life.

Contrary to scientific experience, this spiritual experience is inexpressible in language, untranslatable, and untransferable to others. In one word, it is unique. This is why religious experience is a meaningful experience because it gives a serious account to every single human, male or female, it holds every person as special and a unique case. It gives him or her the opportunity to "be", and to "become" something special. While in science the observation or experimentation of the phenomenon is reproducible and repeatable, by everyone in the same manner, in this sense it is redundant.

PART FIVE

ISLAMIC KNOWLEDGE

27. Classification of Sciences

The classification of sciences in Islamic culture is based on the source of knowledge from which we receive these sciences. In his book *The Muqaddemah* Ibn Khaldun (733-808 A.H./1332-1406 A.D.) divided sciences into two major parts:[43]

First: **Revealed Sciences** (al-'Ulum al-Naqliyah): usually learned from and related to revelation and the Shari'ah.

Second: **Rational Sciences** (al-'Ulum al-'Aqliyah): usually developed through the senses and the rational faculties.

27.1. Revealed Sciences:

Sciences related to this type usually revolve around Shari'ah in order to enhance human understanding of its application in daily life.

Since the Qur'an was revealed in the Arabic language and the prophet's tradition is Arabic too, thus learning Arabic language become necessary for understanding The Shari'ah. These sciences are divided into:

1. Sciences of Arabic Language:
   a. Linguistics.
   b. Arabic Grammar.
   c. Bayan (Rhetoric, Eloquence).
   d. Literature.
   e. Calligraphy.
2. 'Ilm al-Tafseer (Qur'anic Interpretation) (exegesis).
3. 'Ilm of recitations of Qur'an.
4. 'Ilm al-Hadith (the tradition of the prophet).
5. 'Ilm Usul al-Fiqh (Principles of Jurisprudence).
   a. Ilm al-Jadal (Argumentation).
   b. Ilm al-Khilaf (Disputation).
6. 'Ilm al-Fiqh (Jurisprudence). Major part of it is 'Ilm al-Fara'd, which requires rational knowledge such as

---

[43] Ibn Khaldun (1993): P. 345.

mathematics and al-gebra, in order to deal with the commands of Shari'ah.
7. 'Ilm al-Kalam (Scholastic Theology).
8. 'Ilm al-Tasawwuf (Mysticism).
9. 'Ilm Ta'beer al-Ru'iah (Interpretation of Dreams).

Ibn Khaldun also mentioned that the above sciences are specific to the Islamic Civilization and Islamic Religion. Other cultures might have some of these fields of knowledge too, but Islamic civilization shares only in general with other cultures of these fields in regard to its source as received from God. However, these Islamic Sciences (al-'Ulum al-Naqliyah) are in specific distinguished from all other types of religious belief.

These sciences deal with Qur'an and Sunnah and since Islamic Divine Law is comprehensive and abrogates any previous kind of beliefs, the prophet (Pbuh) said advising all Muslims: "Do believe in what the people of the book (Jews and Christian) say, and shall not tell them that they are lying, but say we believe in what had revealed to us and what was revealed to you, and our Lord and your Lord is One".

27.2. Rational Sciences:
Based on both sensory experience and pure rationality, rational sciences are divided into:

1. Logic
2. Mathematics, includes many fields one of them al-Jabra which is established by al-Khawarismi in his book *al-Jabr wal Muqabala* in which he intended to facilitate the issues of Islamic Shari'ah in regard to inheritance.
3. Physics
4. Astronomy
5. Chemistry
6. Biology
7. Medicine

I will discuss Kalam, Philosophy, Algebra, and Interpretation of Dreams as an example.

28. 'ILM AL-KALAM

(Scholastic Theology)

Definition: Kalam is a field of Islamic study that is intended to defend the Islamic creed against the infidels. However, the Mutakallimun were involved in logical and philosophical arguments on God's existence and similar issues. We will discuss only one of these arguments.

28. 1. Kalam Argument: The Universe Must have a Cause

The Qur'an advises people to understand the Creator through observing His miraculous creation. It is a method of reasoning by which we reach an understanding of the cause by reflecting upon the effects. Allah says:

"Do they not look in the dominion of the heavens and the earth and all things that Allah has created?" (Qur'an, 7:185)

"We will show them Our Signs in the universe, and in their own sleves, until it becomes manifest to them that this (the Qur'an) is the truth. Is it not sufficient in regard to your Lord that He is a Witness over all things?" (Qur'an, 41:53)

The Mutakallimun (Muslim Theologians) decided to follow the teaching of the Qur'an in constructing arguments to prove the existence of Allah; they also noticed that the very essence of Allah is beyond human understanding, while observation of the universe and the creation of Allah is possible. The Prophet (pbuh) said:

"Do not reflect upon the essence of God, instead, reflect on the creation of God."

Mutakallimun offered some arguments in proving the existence of Allah through cause and effect, going from creation and the created things to the Creator Himself. Imam al-Ghazali (1058-1111) in his book *Ihya 'Ulum al-Deen (Revival of the Religious Sciences)* said:

"[B]y way of preparation and following the example of the learned theologians, we say: One of the obvious logic of the mind is that:

1. an originated phenomenon cannot come into existence without a cause.
2. Since the world is an originated phenomenon,
3. [Therefore,] it cannot come into existence without a cause."[44]

We can clarify this argument further as follows:

1. Everything that is originated (has a beginning in time) cannot come into existence without a cause.
2. The world is an originated thing (began to exist in time).
   ----
3. Therefore, the world cannot come into existence without a cause.

The conclusion of this argument negates the possibility of an effect to exist without a cause. This argument is valid and consists with the rules of syllogism. Since one of its premises is negated, the conclusion has to be negated too. Al-Ghazali tried to explain each part of it thoroughly:

Regarding the first premise: the originated world cannot come into existence without a cause, because every originated phenomenon belongs to a certain definite time the precedence or the subsequence of which may be assumed. Its being definite in time and distinct from what preceded it and what succeeded it, will naturally require one who renders things definite, and this is the cause.[45]

As in regard to the second premise: that the world is an originated phenomenon and began to exist, its proof is found in the fact that:

Bodies are not independent of motion and rest.
Both states (motion and rest) are originated phenomena;
Whatever is not independent of originated things is itself originated.[46]

Another way to support the second premise is to say that:

---

[44] Al-Ghazali (1987): Vol. 1. p.126.
[45] Al-Ghazali (1987): Vol. 1. p. 126.
[46] Al-Ghazali (1987): Vol. 1. p. 126.

- if the universe has no beginning in time, then it existed eternally and it is infinite in time (meaning that an actual series of infinite events existed)
- But actual infinity is impossible (al-Kindi will offer an argument to prove that actual infinity is impossible.)
- Therefore, the universe cannot be eternal.

28.2. Schools of 'Ilm al-Kalam:
Al-Mu'tazilah

1. Established in Iraq, first in Basra and moved to Baghdad, the capital of the Islamic Caliphate at that time.

Wasil Ibn 'Ata' was accompanying other students in a circle (Halqa) studying religious topics and discussing a crucial issue about the person who commits a grave sin, whether he is going to be a believer or non-believer. Wasil was not satisfied with the answer from his master, thus he withdrew from this circle and established a circle on his own to teach his own ideas. His master said: "E'tazalana Wasil" meaning: "Wasil separated himself from us". (E'tazala means he isolated himself). And thus the word E'tizal and Mu'tazila came into existence to refer to the school.[47]

Al-Ash'ariyyah:

Derives its name from its founder Abul Hasan al-Ash'ari (d.935) who was a Mu'tazali first and then after a short period of solitude in Basra devoted totally to the careful examination of the theology of Mu'tazilah and their principles, al-Ash'ari reached revolutionary ideas and decided to end his solitude and decided to announce to the public his conclusion.

---

[47] The most distinguished theologian in this school are:
In Basra-Iraq:
Wasil Ibn 'Ata' (d. 748).
Abu'l-Hudhaiyel al-'Allaf (d. 841).
Ibrahim al-Nazzam (d. between 835-845).
'Amer Ibn Bahr al-Jahid (d. 868).
Abu Ali al-Jubba'i (d. 915).
Abu Hashim al-Jubba'i (the son of Abu Ali al-Jubba'i) (d. 933).
In Baghdad-Iraq:
Bishr Ibn al-Mu'tamir (d.825).
Al-Iskafi (d. 855).
Abul-Hassain al-Khayyat (d.902).(his book *al-Entisar*)
Al-Qadi Abdul-Jabbar (d.1025)

Al-Ash'ari went to the Mosque in Basra wearing two sets of clothes, one on top of the other, and stood on a chair announcing that: "I denounce the Mu'tazilah as I take off my dress." And he took off one of his dresses.[48]

Al-Ash'ari's new theology became the most dominant in the Islamic world up to our time. Al-Ash'ari was not satisfied intellectually with Ahlul-Hadith and their literal position in dealing with the text, at the same time he was intellectually bothered by the audacious rationalism of the Mu'tazilah, as a result he emerged with a type of scholastic theology presented as a golden mean to be abided by Qur'an and Sunnah, at the same time to give reason the place it deserves according to Shari'ah.

▼	▼	▼
Ahlun-Nass	al-Ash'ariyyah	al-Mu'tzilah
Scripture first	Scripture and Reason	Reason first
Text Literal interpretation	Reason used within the	Reason with no
(Qur'an and Sunnah)	limits of Shari'ah	limits

There are a few characteristics might be considered as a contribution of Ash'ariyyah:

1- To Utilize the capabilities of human reason.
2- To realize the limitations of human reason.
3- To lay down the foundation of Islamic Logic.

This logic will reach its peak with Ibn Taimia although he is not an Ash'ari. Also they have a method of presenting an issue and have the debater answer by yes or no, which reduces both answers to contradictions.

Ash'ariyyah developed a theory of causality related to their idea of Kasb. This theory also presented by al-Ghazali in his book *The Incoherence of The Philosophers*, chapter 17.

---

[48] The most famous scholars in this school are:
Al-Ash'ari, Abu Al-Hasan (d.935)
Al-Baqillani (d. 403 A.H.)
Imam al-Haramain al-Juwaini (d.1085)
Imam Abu Hamed al-Ghazali (d.1111)

29. ISLAMIC PHILOSOPHY

(FALSAFA)

29.1. Islamic Theory of Knowledge (Ma'rifah)
The epistemology of Islam is based on the Islamic ontology and Qur'anic presentation of reality. Reality in Islam consists of different levels; this is why the Islamic theory of knowledge also consists of stages.

The different levels and stages of knowledge are:

- **Fitra**
- **Sensory experience**
- **Rationality**
- **Revelation**

We discussed Fitra before, thus we will cover briefly sensory experience and rationality.

Contrary to Western philosophy, Muslim philosophers hold sensory experience as neither reliable nor deniable.
It is not solely reliable as the only source of knowledge and experience as John Locke (1632-1704) and the empiricists claimed. It is also not deniable as Rene Descartes (1596-1650) and the rationalists claimed. Sensory experience in Islamic philosophy is being positioned in its domain; which is the natural and physical stage of reality. In this stage knowledge is gained by observation and experimentation, by means of imperfect induction and generalization, in which the results are measured by degrees of probability instead of certainty. Nature is not the ultimate reality it is only the physical manifestation of one level of it. To reduce reality to what we see, hear, and touch… is to beg the question: how do we know that what we see is the total reality? We can only confirm, verify or falsify what we see but we cannot confirm that what we see is the entire reality, and we cannot dismiss everything beyond sensation as superstitious.

In fact to reduce reality to the surface of what we can experience by sensation is a fairly new philosophy that came about 300 years ago from the empiricism of John Locke and other British philosophers who took a simple approach to reality. Contrary to the empiricists, many philosophers thought of reality as something more cohesive, substantial and intrinsic than the outside shell.

Al-Kindi was the first Muslim philosopher to give an appropriate account to the limitations of sensory experience in the context of reality, comparing it with the ability of reason.

29.2. Al-Kindi; (805-873)[49]

Al-Kindi ranked philosophy as the highest level and noblest of human efforts, he defines it as:

"Knowledge of the essence of things, insofar as is possible for man."[50]

This definition immediately causes us to think that philosophy according to al-Kindi must pass from the natural, phenomenological aspects of existence to a more essential level that is the cause and the very essence of everything. In order to *"understand"* the truth rationally, we must know the meaning of

---

[49] Al-Kindi is the first philosopher in Islam. He was a mathematician first of all, physicist, astronomer, physician, geographer, plus an expert in music.
He wrote many books and treatises in many different fields of knowledge - the sum of which is over 350 treatises, 11 of them on Arithmetic, 32 on Geometry, 22 on Philosophy, and the rest of his writing are on physics, astronomy, medicine, psychology, meteorology, topography, alchemy, and music. Al-Kindi was known to the western medieval world as al-Kindus, many of his books were translated into Latin by Gerard of Cremona (1114-1187), and made available to scientists and philosophers in the West. His work was very impressive, to the point that Cardan considered him one of the twelve greatest minds. According to al-Kindi seeking truth was his first priority, regardless where truth comes from:
"We ought not to be embarrassed of appreciating the truth and of obtaining it wherever it comes from, even if it comes from races distant and nations different from us. Nothing should be dearer to the seeker after truth than the truth itself."
See Al-Kindi (1948): p. 81. This book was translated by Alfred L. Ivry, (see Ivry: 1974). However, I will retranslate some important passages because al-Kindi's philosophical language is difficult even for those who speak Arabic as a native tongue. In some other passages I will quote Ivry (1974).
[50] Al-Kindi (1948): p77. Author's translation.

"stand – under". That which stands under is the true cause of every thing that comes to be. Understanding the effects is only possible through knowing their causes, which, in turn, will help in achieving the truth, al-Kindi said:

"It is impossible to find the truth that we are seeking without finding a cause."[51]

Natural sciences deal with causes and effects, and our understanding of the effects is enhanced by more theoretical descriptions and explanations of the causes, this type of knowledge is presented in physics, chemistry, biology, etc... But this is only one level of knowing reality. Sensory experience is not reliable because it is not the ultimate extent of philosophizing. In knowing the truth al-Kindi said that we could only go as far as our rational capability can go. In his definition of philosophy al-Kindi realized not only the limitation of sensory experience, but also the limitation of the pure reason. This point will gain great importance and emphasis by al-Ghazali, and Ibn Taimia, who articulate this thesis in showing the limited domain of philosophy and bringing revelation as another level of reality.

Al-Kindi on Sense Data and Reason

Al-Kindi's main goal of philosophy was to know Allah the creator of this world. A second goal, that is related to the first, was to prove in metaphysics *creation ex nihilo* or that the world is not eternal. But what sources of knowledge shall we use to achieve these goals?

Al-Kindi furnishes some epistemological premises to start with before getting into his metaphysics. He stated that human perceptions and knowledge are of two kinds:

- Perception of the senses, and
- Knowledge of the intellect.

The existents are of two kinds:

- Particulars, which are perceived by the senses, and
- Universals, that exist in the mind.

---

[51] Al-Kindi (1948): p. 77.

The sensory perception is usually achieved through the contact of the senses with the sensible particular objects. And since the sensible objects are in continuous motion and in a constant changing, therefore knowledge based on sensations is unstable and localized to the perceiver.[52]

The sensory perceptions take images of the sensory objects and send them to our mind, which establishes them in the area of imagination, then the imagination conveys them to the memory; and thus the sensible object is represented in our soul. For this reason sense perception is closer to the perceiver himself, and far from the essential nature of the object we sense, also it is subjected to the contributing factors of perception.

Another reason that al-Kindi gave about the limitations of sense experience is that since sense-able materials exist in bodies, thus our perception, which is related to them, basically deals with that particular object. According to al-Kindi knowledge of the particulars cannot help to establish philosophical insights, because philosophy aims at knowing universal concepts, such as: species, genera, human soul, infinity, God, etc…

The mind, or the intellect, is more qualified in establishing such philosophical knowledge in dealing with universal concepts. This knowledge is superior to that of the senses, because it is possible to be validated and rendered certain by the intellectual principles that are necessarily true, such as the law of non-contradiction.[53]

Al-Kindi gave an example:[54]

If the universe is a body, then:
    either the universe is infinite in quantity, or
    it is quantitatively finite.
The universe cannot be quantitatively infinite, (al-Kindi will prove later on how actual infinity is impossible.)

Therefore, the universe is quantitatively finite.

---

[52] Al-Kindi (1948): p 85.
[53] Al-Kindi (1948): p 87.
[54] Al-Kindi (1948): p 87.

Al-Kindi concluded from this form of reasoning that we reached the conclusion here with some kind of necessity. Its form does not exist in the soul as sense perception exists in it, in sensation there is no necessity only probability. Thus the intellect, but not sensory perception, is more entitled to study the subject of metaphysics. Al-Kindi realized that there is a limited domain for sensation, which is natural sciences, while in non-physical subjects or in mathematical sciences proves by demonstrative reasoning, is necessary.

Al-Kindi's solution to the conflict between rationalism and empiricism came from his hierarchical conception of reality and from his realization of the importance of physics, mathematics, and metaphysics to reach the truth.

His example mentioned above is based on disjunctive syllogism in the form:

Either P, or Q
Not P

Therefore, Q

This form is only valid when one of the disjunct is denied in the second premise. It is a deductive form of reasoning and its validity is based on the necessary connection between the premises and the conclusion. Of course this form of reasoning has nothing to do with observation and sense experience thus it is formal and has certainty. Al-Kindi said:

"...whoever examines things which are beyond nature, i.e., those which have no matter and are not joined to matter, will not find for them a representation in the soul, but will perceive them by means of intellectual inquiries."[55]

Al-Kindi thinks that different fields of knowledge, since they have different subject matter, must have different methods of study too. The perception and understanding of fields such as linguistics, physics, mathematics, and metaphysics, is different because their

---

[55] Al-Kindi (1974): p 64.

subject matter is not similar. Al-Kindi's methodological classification of sciences is based on the subject matter of study:

"We ought, however, to aim at what is required for each pursuit, and not pursue probability in the science of mathematics, nor sensation or exemplification in the science of the metaphysical; nor conceptual generalization in the principles of the science of the physical; nor demonstration in rhetoric, nor demonstration in the principles of demonstration. Surely if we observe these conditions the pursuits which are intended will become easy for us but if we disobey this, we will miss the objectives of our pursuits, and the perception of our intended objects will become difficult."[56]

---

[56] Al-Kindi (1974): p 66.

29.3. The Model of Islamic Conception of Reality

Islamic Conception of Reality

Ontological Levels of reality	Epistemology Levels of Knowing
Religious Reality	Revelation, Prophecy
Metaphysical Reality	Human Intellect (Abstraction and Logical reasoning)
Mathematical Reality	Human Intellect (Abstraction, logical reasoning and demonstration)
Physical Reality	Human Senses and Intellect (Observation, experimentation, generalization, and abstraction)
Fitra Reality (Instilled in man by Allah since first creation)	Human reasoning in the ability of knowing Allah, it is also internal and intuitively learned, Religious experience.

Metaphysics

29.4. The Universe is Not Eternal

Infinity: Case Study
Nada is a four year old girl, who loves physical education, her favorite exercise is to jump, but to jump on numbers, especially the series of natural numbers; 12345.... If she decided to jump on all of them, then when do you think that her exercise will *actually* be finished?

...-8 -7 -6 -5 -4 -3 -2 -1 0 1 2 3 4 5 6 7 8 ...

You might answer: that she will finish her exercise when she finishes the whole series of natural numbers, but we know that this series of numbers is infinite, thus she might actually finish her exercise when she actually finishes infinity, but the problem is that we know that infinity has no end and can not be finished in actuality.

Al-Kindi furnished an argument to prove that *actual* infinity is impossible. He did not know Nada but his attempt was to prove that Allah creates the world. As an implication, his main thesis is to prove first that God is the only eternal being and the ultimate cause of existence, and second to prove, as a result, that the world is not eternal. The core emphasis of al-Kindi's philosophy is Islamic in essence, which reflects the teachings of the Qur'an and the tradition of the Prophet Muhammad (pbuh).

Al-Kindi tried to show that matter, motion and time are inseparable from each other. If one of them is eternal, then the rest are eternal as well. Al-Kindi presented some arguments to prove that the eternity of any of these three is "impossible" and in fact, self-contradictory.

The eternal is necessary in the sense that it must never have been a non-existent being, and "before" does not apply because in actual infinity "before" and "after" make no sense. The eternal has no cause, has neither subject nor predicates. Al-Kindi said:

"The eternal is that which must never have been a nonexistent being, the eternal having no existential "before" to its being; the eternal's subsistence is not due to another; the eternal has no cause; the eternal has neither subject nor predicate, nor agent nor reason,... The eternal has no genus, for if it has a genus, then it is species, ... Now, inasmuch as a body has genus and species, while the eternal has no genus, a body is not eternal."[57]

29.5. Actual Infinity is Impossible:
Al-Kindi's first step in disproving the eternity of the world can be summarized in his statements as follows:

"It is not possible, either for an eternal body or for other objects which have quantity and quality, to be infinite in actuality, infinity being only in potentiality."[58]

What he is saying is: *Actual infinity is impossible.* Why? And how?

Al-Kindi constructed an argument that is heavily based on mathematics:
First, he thought it necessary to appeal to some of the axioms in mathematics. He called these axioms: "the true first premises which are thought with no mediation." By this he probably meant that the mind could grasp their truth immediately, without demonstration or need of proof. These premises need no mediation because they are self-evident, and these are called axioms. He stated the axioms that he needs to disprove the eternity of the world as follows:[59]

1. **All bodies of which one is not greater than the other are equal;**
2. **Equal bodies are those where the dimensions between their limits are equal in actuality and potentiality;**
3. **That which is finite is not infinite;**

---

[57] Al-Kindi (1974): pp. 67-68.
[58] Al-Kindi (1974): p 68.
[59] Al-Kindi (1974): p 68.

4. When a body is added to one of equal bodies it becomes the greatest of them, and greater than what it had been before that body was added to it;
5. Whenever two bodies of finite magnitude are joined, the body which comes to be from both of them is of finite magnitude, this being necessary in (the case of) every magnitude as well as in (the case of) every object which possesses magnitude;
6. The smaller of every two generically related things is inferior to the larger, or inferior to a portion of it.

Arguments Against the Eternity of the World
After stating his thesis as: actual infinity is impossible, and after supporting it with six mathematical axioms that their truth is self-evident, al-Kindi tried to present his refutation of the Aristotelian theme that the world is eternal in a logical argument which is closer to a mathematical theorem. The following is the argument as Al-Kindi stated it:

"Now, if there is an infinite body, then whenever a body of finite magnitude is separated from it, that which remains of it will either be a finite magnitude or an infinite magnitude. If that which remains of it is a finite magnitude, then whenever that finite magnitude which is separated from it is added to it, the body which comes to be from them both together is a finite magnitude; though that which comes to be from them both is that which was infinite before something was separated from it. It is thus finite and infinite, and this is an impossible contradiction."[60]

Structuring al-Kindi's Argument:
If there is an infinite body, then after separating a finite magnitude from it, the remaining of it will:

        A- either be a finite magnitude, or
        B- an infinite magnitude.

Al-Kindi refutes both of them as necessarily contradictory. Let us start with A.

---

[60] Al-Kindi (1974): pp 68-69.

A. The Remaining is a Finite Magnitude.

1. If the remaining is a finite magnitude, then whenever that finite magnitude (which is already separated from it) is added back to it, then the body, which comes to be from both of them together, is a finite magnitude. (Axiom # 5)

2. However, that which comes to be from them both (the remaining plus the separated together) is that which was infinite before something was separated from it.

3. Therefore, it is finite and infinite,

4. We know from the axiom # 3 that that which is finite is not infinite,

5. Therefore, a finite infinity is an impossible contradiction.

6. Thus, actual infinity is impossible.

7. Therefore, the existence of an infinite body in actuality (such as an eternal world) is self-contradictory.

----

8. Therefore, the world is not eternal.

Let us move now to the second part of the argument (part B). Al-Kindi refuted this part as follows:

B. The Remaining is an Infinite Magnitude.
If the remainder is an infinite magnitude, then whenever that which was taken from it is added back to it, it will:

> B1-either be greater than what it was before the addition, or
> B2-equal to what it was before the addition.

B1- To be greater than what it was before the addition.
1. If it is greater than what it was before the addition, then that which has infinity will be greater than that which has infinity.

2. However, according to axiom # 6: the smaller of two things is inferior to the greater, or inferior to a portion of it.

Therefore, the smaller of two bodies which have infinity is inferior to the greater of them or inferior to a portion of the greater (if the smaller body is inferior to the greater, then it most certainly is inferior to a portion of it) and thus the smaller of the two is <u>equal</u> to a portion of the greater.

3. However, according to axiom # 2: two equal things are those whose similarity is that the dimensions between their limits are the same, and

4. Therefore, the two things possess limits, and they are both finite, and

5. Thus, the smaller infinite object is finite, and this is an impossible contradiction. One of them is not greater than the other.

6. Therefore, the remainder cannot be an infinite magnitude.

7. Therefore, actual infinity is impossible.

8. Therefore, the world is not eternal.

B2- To be equal to what it was before the addition.
   1. If it is equal to what it was before the addition, then this means that a body has been added to a body and has not increased anything,
   2. However, premise one contradicts axiom # 4.
   3. Also, the whole of this addition is equal to it alone and to its own part, then the part is like the whole, and this is an impossible contradiction.
   4. Therefore, the remainder cannot be an infinite magnitude.
   5. Therefore, actual infinity is impossible.
   6. Therefore, the world is not eternal.

Al-Kindi concluded:
"It has now been explained that it is impossible for a body to have infinity, and in this manner it has been explained that any quantitative thing cannot have infinity in actuality."[61]

---

[61] Al-Kindi (1974): p 69.

29.6. Al-Kindi and David Hilbert On Infinity
Clarification:
Al-Kindi aimed at a mathematical contradiction in the heart of the issue of actual infinity. In other words, actual infinity is self-canceling, and the only thing left is infinity on the potential level. Consider this example for the sake of simplification:
When we count from number 1 to number 2, we can count fractions in between such as: 1.1, 1.12, 1.13, 1.14, 1.2, 1.3, 1.9, 1.91, 1.92, 1.99, 1.999, 1.9999, and we can count 1.9n as many as we can count to almost infinity (of course, without reaching it), but no matter how many 1.99n we can count, we know that the actual end is number 2, and we are only <u>potentially</u> going between [1-----and-----2], and what <u>actually</u> exists is the finite limit of number 1 and that is number 2. The counting of 1.99n to infinity is unachievable and is actually impossible to reach; however, we can potentially assume the process of counting to go evermore.

Al-Kindi's notion of mathematical infinity is what relinquished Aristotelian cosmology as contradictory. Bodies that exist in actuality have a finite magnitude, and if we think about a body as infinite, that is only because it happens on the level of ideas but not in reality. Magnitudes are necessarily finite.

Al-Kindi was one of the mathematicians who singled out the notion of infinity in its relation to metaphysics and natural philosophy. Not many philosophers or mathematicians followed up as deeply on the notion of "infinity" until the twentieth century when a great mathematician, David Hilbert, published his paper "On The Infinite" 1925, in which he said:

"[T]he definitive clarification of the *nature of the infinite* has become necessary, not merely for the special interests of the individual sciences, but rather for the *honor of the human understanding* itself."[62]

Hilbert discussed infinity in two fields: microphysics and macrophysics. After he mentioned physics and the divisibility of atoms, particles, electrons, quanta, and how none of these permits infinite division in an absolute and unrestricted way, he said:

---

[62] Hilbert, D (1925): pp. 370-371.

"And the net result is, certainly, that we do not find anywhere in reality a homo-geneous continuum that permits of continued division and hence would realize the infinite in the small. The infinite divisibility of a continuum is an operation that is present only in our thoughts; it is merely an idea, which is refuted by our observation of nature and by the experience gained in physics and chemistry."[63]

The infinite cannot be actually found "anywhere in reality," especially in physics. It exists only on the level of potentiality, "in our thoughts"; it is an idea. As a physical object or body that exists outside the mind, it is finite. Thus, the body of the world that exists outside is finite, and thus it cannot be eternal. At the end of his paper Hilbert said:

"The final result then is: nowhere is the infinite realized; it is neither present in nature nor admissible as a foundation in our rational thinking-a remarkable harmony between being and thought."[64]

Hotel of Infinity
If there is a hotel of infinity in which there is infinite number of rooms, a vacant room must be available anytime you want a room, then do you think that there will be time when you call the hotel of infinity to reserve a room and find that there is no room and the hotel is actually full? According to Hilbert the hotel of infinity will never be *actually* full.

---

[63] Hilbert, D. (1925): p. 371.
[64] Hilbert, D. (1925): p. 392.

Metaphysics

29.7. Proofs of the Existence of Allah (The God)

If you are not satisfied with al-Kindi's account of creation, nor with that of Hilbert on infinity, then you may hold the idea that the universe is eternal or came into existence without a Creator and with no need for a god. This view seems to be acceptable by some people; however, according to al-Kindi it is contradictory. It states one of these two things:

- Either the universe as a magnitude is infinite, which is contradictory.

- Or the universe originated itself and gave itself existence which is contradictory too according to al-Kindi based on the following argument:

Al-Kindi's Argument on Essence and Generation
According to al-Kindi it is impossible for a thing to be the cause of the generation of its essence. In the third chapter of his book *On First Philosophy*, al-Kindi argued that:

It is not possible for a thing to be the cause of the generation of its essence, its becoming a being is either from something or from nothing. Thus, there are four possibilities:[65]

First:	a non-existent thing and its essence is non-existent.
Second:	a non-existent thing and its essence is existent.
Third:	an existent thing and its essence is non-existent.
Fourth:	an existent thing and its essence is existent.

The first is impossible, because it is nothing and its essence is nothing.

"Nothing" is neither a cause nor an effect, (cause and effect are predicated only of something).

Therefore, it is not the cause of the generation of its essence.

---

[65] Al-Kindi (1974): p.76.

The second, of course, with a similar proof, is impossible. The second is also impossible by another proof based on the law of identity. Al-Kindi said:[66]

1. If it is non-existent and its essence is existent, then its essence is different from the thing.
2. Thus, its essence would not be it (it = the thing).
3. However, the essence of everything is that thing itself.
4. Therefore, a thing would not be itself and it would be itself, but this is an impossible contradiction (according to the law of identity).
5. Therefore, a thing cannot be the cause of the generation of its essence.

The third is impossible (an existent thing and its essence is non-existent) for the same reason above based on the law of identity.

The fourth (an existent thing and its essence is existent) is also impossible, al-Kindi said:[67]

1. If the thing is an existent thing and its essence is existent, and it were the cause of the generation of its essence, then its essence would be its effect.

2. But the cause is different from the effect.

3. Therefore, it would be the cause of its essence while its essence would be its effect.

4. Thus, its essence would not be it (it=the thing).
However, the essence of every thing is that thing itself (according to the law of identity).

5. But from this argument it follows that it would not be itself, and that it would be itself. This is an impossible contradiction.

6. Therefore, a thing cannot be the cause of the generation of its essence. The Universe must have a cause.

---

[66] Al-Kindi (1974): p.77.
[67] Al-Kindi (1974): p.77.

30. Algebra (al-Jabr wal-Muqabalah)[68]

30.1. How to Divide Inheritance?
A woman[69] went, with her two daughters, to the Prophet (pbuh) complaining that her husband died and his brother (the two daughters' uncle) took all the estate of her dead husband, leaving the family with no money. The Prophet (pbuh) said that only Allah-the Exalted could legislate this issue. Then Allah revealed this aya:

"Allah instructs you concerning your children [i.e., their portions of inheritance]: for the male, what is equal to the share of two females. But if there are [only] daughters, two or more, for them is two thirds of one's estate. And if there is only one, for her is half. And for one's parents, to each one of them is a sixth of his estate if he left children. But if he [the deceased] had no children and the parents [alone] inherit from him, then for his mother is one third. And if he had brothers [and/or sisters], for his mother is a sixth, after any bequest he [may have] made or debt. Your parents or your children—you know not which of them are nearest to you in benefit. [These shares are] an obligation [imposed] by Allah. Indeed, Allah is ever Knowing and Wise." (Qur'an 4:11)

After receiving this revelation the Prophet (pbuh) sent for the brother of the deceased and instructed him: "give the two daughters two third of the inheritance, and give their mother (the wife of the deceased) one eighth, and the remainder is your portion from his estate." (al-Tirmithi)

How much is the share of the brother from the inheritance?

---

[68] In this section I should refer to an important article by Dr. Yasin Khalil called: "Al-Khawarizmi's Logic in al-Jabr wal-Muqabalah. Published in Baghdad, Afaq 'Arabiyya, No. 5, 1979.
Dr. Khalil applied his method of symbolic logic in structuring and rewriting the logic of al-Khawarizmi. He also proved that al-Khawarizmi is the founder of the mathematical logic, contrary to the opinion of some historians of logic who thought R. Lulus was the contributor in this field.
[69] This woman is the wife of Sa'd ibn al-Rabee'.

The Islamic Divine Law (Shari'ah) is very specific when it comes to the rights and properties of others. Dividing inheritance is one of these detailed fields of Islamic Law. It is called *'ilm al-Fara'idh* or the law of descent and distribution. This field is part of Islamic jurisprudence and it discusses the distributive shares in an estate. In order to divide the inheritance (assets) properly the jurist needs accurate mathematics to achieve justice in distributing shares.

Muhammad ibn-Musa al-Khawarizmi (778-840), a Muslim mathematician and astronomer, thought about a mathematical method to facilitate these issues. He wrote a book in Arabic about 830 A.D. called **Hisab al-Jabr wal-Muqabala**. *(Transposition and Balancing* or *Restoration and Opposition)* In the introduction al-Khwarizmi mentioned that the purpose of developing this mathematical method and equations of al-Jabr wal-Muqabala, was to facilitate dealing with issues that people constantly need in cases of inheritance, legacies, separation, lawsuits, trade, etc.[70] Thus al-Jabr intended to deal with practical problems.

His mathematical method became what we call today the science of algebra. The science of algebra is based on the work of al-Khawarizmi and the word "algebra" came from the Arabic word "al-Jabr" in the title of al-Khawarizmi's book *Hisab al-Jabr wal-Muqabala*. The word "algorithm" was also named after al-Khawarizmi's name.

Al-Khawarizmi's book **Hisab al-Jabr waI-Muqabala** was translated in 1140 A.D. into Latin and the title became **Liber algebrae et almucabala.** In the 16th century, the Arabic word "al-Jabr" appeared in the English language as "algebra"[71]

---

[70] Al-Khawarizmi (1968): The Introduction.
[71] 'Umar al-Khayyam (1050-1130) who was a poet and a mathematician made significant contributions to algebra especially the solution of cubic equations by geometric methods involving the intersection of conics.
Raymandus Lulus (1232-1316) used the book of *al-Jabr wal-Muqabala*. Lulus learned the Arabic language in Spain and he published in the Arabic and Latin languages. Germo Cordano (1501-1576) was also aware of this field when he published in 1545, his *Ars Magna*. In the 16th century, the Arabic word "al-Jabr" appeared in English language as "algebra" in the writing of the mathematician Robert Recorde (1510-1558) in his book *Pathway of Knowledge,* printed in 1551. Recorde studied and taught mathematics at both Oxford and Cambridge.

Back to the Example of the Woman and her Two Daughters

With al-Khawarizmi's method of algebra we can solve the problem of inheritance in this case as follow:

The wife takes 1/8, each daughter takes 1/3, and the brother of the deceased takes the remainder.

$1/8 + 1/3 + 1/3 + x = 1$ (1 is the total amount of the asset)
$3/24 + 8/24 + 8/24 + x = 1$
$19/24 + x = 1$
$x = 1 - 19/24$
$x = 24/24 - 19/24$
$x = 5/24$

If the husband left $48,000, then the share of each daughter is $16,000, the share of the wife is $6,000, and the share of his brother is $10,000.[72]

30.2. Al-Khawarizmi's Logical System of Algebra

Al-Khawarizmi set the foundation of algebra in his book. These basics can be summarized in a few categories:

1. Three basic concepts or terms of the science of algebra: units, roots and squares.
A unit according to al-Khawarizmi is any number.
A root is anything that is referred to symbolically as x or y.
While a square is the power x^2.

Al-Khawarizmi called these three terms:
'Adadd   (number),
Jathr   (root), and
Mal   (square)

2. Six forms of equations. These six equations are linear or quadratic.

3. In addition to the four basic operations of arithmetic: addition, subtraction, division, and multiplication.

---

[72] For cases related to dividing inheritance see al-Buti (1996): pp. 106-113.

4. The method of dealing with and solving these equations was called: al-Jabr wal-Muqabala. To explain al-Jabr, al-Khwarizmi gave examples similar to the following:

If we have $3x - x^2 = x$
Then we should restore or complete the solution by adding ($-3x$) to both sides of the equation:
$(-3x) + 3x - x^2 = x + (-3x)$
$-x^2 = -2x$
$x = 2$ *dividing both terms by $-x$*

To explain al-Muqabala:
If we have $2x + x^2 = 5x$
$x^2 + 2x - (2x) = 5x - (2x)$
Then we should balance the equation by reducing positive terms of the same power when they occur on both sides.
$x^2 = 3x$
$x^2 = 9$

The six standard forms of linear equations were reduced by al-Khawarizmi into two groups:

The first group has three equations of two terms:
1. Squares equal to roots (amwal equal juthor) $x^2 = \sqrt{9}$, $x = 3$
2. Squares equal to numbers (amwal equal 'adadd) $x^2 = 4$, $x = 2$
3. Roots equal to numbers (juthor equal 'adadd) $\sqrt{x} = 9$, $x = 3$

The second group has three equations of three terms:
4. Squares and roots equal to numbers
   (amwal and juthor equal 'adadd): $x^2 + 9x = 35$
5. Squares and numbers equal to roots
   (amwal and adadd equal juthor): $x^2 + 35 = 9x$
6. Roots and numbers equal to squares
   (juthor and 'adadd equal amwal): $3x + 4 = x^2$.

The method of *al-Jabr* and *al-Muqabala* implies some axioms applied by al-Khawarizmi in the operations of solving problems. His method of al-Jabr (completion) implies the axiom of addition:
$10x - x^2 = 21$
$10x - x^2 + (x^2) = 21 + (x^2)$
$10x = 21 + x^2$

This operation of al-Jabr implies the axiom of adding equal quantities to equal quantities gives equal results.

While the operation of al-Muqabala (balancing) implies the axiom of subtraction:

$$x^2 + 5x = 7x$$
$$x^2 + 5x - (5x) = 7x - (5x)$$
$$x^2 = 2x$$

Al-Khawarizmi also used laws of arithmetic such as:
The commutative law: $x + y = y + x$
The distributive law: $Q(x + y) = Qx + Qy$

Al-Khawarizmi presented a logico-mathematical method that is neither Euclidian nor Aristotelian. He did not use axioms and postulates as Euclid did in geometry; instead al-Khawarizmi presented standard forms of algebraic equations to be used in solving mathematical problems. Also al-Khawarizmi did not follow Aristotelian logic because Aristotelian syllogism proves that the conclusion is true only if the premises were true. While in algebra al-Khawarizmi discovers the value of the unknown by the known variables.

Example:
Divide 10 into two parts, multiply one of these two parts by the other, then multiply one of them by itself, the one that is multiplied by itself becomes *equal* to one of the parts multiplied by the other four times.

Solution:
One part will be x, the other will be $10 - x$
Then multiply x by $10 - x$
$$x(10 - x) = 10x - 4x^2$$
$$4(10x - x^2) = 40x - 4x^2$$
$$x \times x = x^2$$
$$x^2 = 40x - 4x^2$$

By al-Jabr:
$$x^2 + 4x^2 = 40x - 4x^2 + 4x^2$$
$$x^2 + 4x^2 = 40x$$
$$5x^2 = 40x$$
$x = 8$ This is one part of the 10, The other part is: $10 - 8 = 2$

31. Interpretation of Dreams

31.1. The Dream of the King of Egypt
The King of Egypt (Pharaoh) had a dream, the king said:

"Indeed, I have seen [in a dream] seven fat cows being eaten by seven [that were] lean, and seven green spikes [of grain] and others [that were] dry. O eminent ones, explain to me my vision, if you should interpret visions." (Qur'an, Chapter 12)

Dreams, or dream visions, are one of the normal human activities that take place in sleep. Dreams manifest themselves mostly in a symbolic way, and they reflect the very mystery of human nature. The importance of dreams comes from the fact that they are closely connected to prophecy.[73]

Prophet Muhammad (pbuh) said:

"A good dream vision is the forty-sixth part of prophecy."

Some dreams bring information about the future. They are a kind of supernatural perception of the unknown; this is probably why we are concerned about them. The prophet (pbuh) also said:

"The only remaining bearer of glad tidings is a good dream."

The Qur'an acknowledges the reality of dreams, their prophetic role, and their symbolism, Allah –The Exalted- mentioned in the Qur'an that the prophet Joseph has given the ability to interpret dreams. In Surat Yusuf which is chapter 12 of the Qur'an, Joseph was able to interpret the dream of the king of Egypt about the seven cows by saying:

"You will plant for seven years consecutively; and what you harvest leave in its spikes, except a little from which you will eat.

---

[73] The revelation given to the Prophet began with a dream vision. Every dream vision he saw appeared to him like the break of dawn, as 'Aisha said.

Then will come after that seven difficult [tears] which will consume what you advanced [i.e., saved] for them, except a little from which you will store.

Then will come after that a year in which the people will be given rain and in which they will press [olives and grapes]."

31.2. Different Kinds of Dreams

Prophet Muhammad said that dreams are of three kinds: one from Allah, the second from the angel, and the third is from Satan.

The first kind needs no interpretation, it should be clear, the second kind needs interpretation, while the last one is a nightmare or nonsense.

Since dreams happen in a symbolic way, they need interpretation. The interpretation of dreams is an established field of Islamic sciences. It is based solely on knowledge of the Qur'an and the Sunnah of the Prophet (pbuh). This field can be learned, however an interpreter of dreams is also a gifted or talented person. This ability of interpretation is mentioned in the Qur'an as a gift from Allah –The all Knowing-.

I will leave the description of how dreams take place to the scientists and psychologists, but I will shed some light on the interpretation of dreams.

31.3. Rules of Interpretation

Muslim scholars authored many books in this field. Haji Khalifa, in his book *Kashf al-Dhunoon,* mentioned more than thirty books in this field.

One of the most famous scholars in this field is Muhammad Ibn Sereen (33-110 A. H. / 653-729 A.D.) who belongs to the generation of the successor of the companions of the Prophet. He was very well known for his righteous manner and good deeds.

Ibn Sereen set some of the general rules and principles of the science of dream's interpretation, such as:

If the dream has different features of interpretation, then the interpreter must tend toward the most positive of these features.

Some dreams could be interpreted according to the dreamer's relevant factors such as his or her habits, practice, health, age, and time.

The same thing in a dream could refer to different interpretations with different people. The Pomegranate in dreams carry different interpretations, as in the case of the ruler's dreams being interpreted differently from that of a pregnant woman or a trader or a scholar or a single person.

Shared interpretation is only possible in two cases: First, if the two persons share the same lineage, as brothers, or sisters, or brother and sister. Second, if they share the same name or they are neighbors, or very similar to each other in many aspects.

Interpretation could be based on the Qur'an and Sunnah.
Interpretation could be based on the language and linguistics.
Interpretation could be based on semantics.
Interpretation of the dream by the opposite meaning. Laughing, for example, might be interpreted as sadness.
Interpretations by the increasing or the decreasing of the things happening. For example, the decreasing of laughter to the level of smiling might not be sadness; instead it will be interpreted as something good.

31.4. Good Dreams and False Dreams
There are differences between true dream visions and false dreams, or confused dreams. Good dream vision should be told to those you love and have good attachment with. Bad dreams are best not told to others.

Ibn Sereen also mentioned that some dreams are more truthful than others. For example, the time of the dream has great impact on its truthfulness. Dreams of early morning, before dawn, are more true than other times.

Ibn Khaldun mentioned that true dream visions have some signs that indicate their truthfulness and attest to their soundness; by these signs the person who has the dream vision becomes conscious of the glad tidings from God given to him in sleep.

"The first of these signs is that the person who has the dream vision awakes up quickly, as soon as he has perceived it. It seems as if he is in a hurry to get back to being awake and having sensual perception.

Another sign is that the dream vision stays and remains impressed with all its details in the memory. Neither neglect nor forgetfulness affects it. No thinking or remembering is required, in order to have present to one's mind. The dream vision remains pictured in the mind of the dreamer when he awakes.... However, if it requires thinking and application to remember a dream vision after a sleeper is awake, and if he has forgotten many of its details before he can remember them again, the dream vision is not a true one but a 'confused dream'."[74]

31.5. Some Requirements for a True Dream Vision
Ibn Sereen said that there are some etiquettes and conditions to help a person to have a true dream. These are:

1. The person should train himself or herself in telling the truth. A truthful person seldom has a false or confused dream. The prophet said: " The most truthful amongst you in having a dream vision is the most truthful in his speech."

2. The person should sleep with the state of physical purity. This purity can be achieved by performing Wudu' or Ghusl. These two mentioned in Salat discussion. Abu Tharr said that the Prophet commanded him three things, one of them is to sleep with the state of purity.

3. The person should sleep on his right side. This is also the practice and the tradition of the Prophet Muhammad (pbuh).

4. The person should sleep on the right side putting his right hand under his right cheek. Should also say: "O Allah protect me from Your punishment on the day Your servants are resurrected." (al-Tirmithi and Abu Dawood)
It has also been narrated that 'Aisha when she is about to sleep supplicates by saying: " O Allah I ask you a good dream vision,

---

[74] Ibn Khaldun (1989): p. 369.

true and not false, beneficial and not harmful, and make me able to remember it instead of forgetting it."

5. The person should make sure that he or she had clipped their nails, and kept them clean. The dirt under the nails is a temptation to Satan.

Ibn Sereen said some dreams might not need interpretation, because they are so evident and the happening in reality comes very similar to the course of happening in the dream vision.

31.6. Examples of Dreams
Examples from Ibn Sereen:
1. To see yourself shaking hands and hugging your enemy, that means the enmity between the two is ended.
2. The old woman in the dream is life; if she was with good appearance then it is a good life, if she was angry then the person loses his or her position and prestige, if she is naked then secrets will be uncovered, and so on. If an old woman entered the house of a person, then life will be improved.
3. A person went to Ibn Sereen telling him this dream: he saw a big ox came out from a small hole, the person was very surprised, then when the ox tried to go back to his hole, could not enter in it. Ibn Sereen said: this is dangerous word that comes out from the mouth and a person cannot get it back.

Examples from the Qur'an about the dreams of two young men who were in prison with prophet Joseph:

1. "One of them said, "Indeed, I have seen myself [in a dream] pressing wine."
2. The other said, "Indeed, I have seen myself carrying upon my head [some] bread, from which the birds were eating."

The interpretation was given to them by prophet Joseph (pbuh):

He said, "I have followed the religion of my fathers, Abraham, Isaac and Jacob. And it was not for us to associate anything with Allah. That is from the favor of Allah upon us and upon the people, but most of the people are not grateful.

O [my] two companions of prison are separate lords better of Allah. The One, the Prevailing?

You worship not besides Him except [mere] names you have named them, you and your fathers, for which Allah has sent down no authority. Legislation is not but for Allah. He has commanded that you worship not except Him. That is the correct religion, but most of the people do not know.

O two companions of prison, as for one of you, he will dive drink to his master of wine; but as for the other, he will be crucified, and the birds will eat from his head. The matter has been decreed about which you both inquire." (Qur'an, chapter 12)

The Dream of Eleven Stars, The Sun, and The Moon prostrating
One of the most wonderful dreams is that of prophet Joseph mentioned in the Qur'an at the beginning of chapter 12:

Joseph said to his father:

"O my father, indeed I have seen [in a dream] eleven stars and the sun and the moon; I saw them prostrating to me."

To know the interpretation of this dream, you need to read the Qur'anic Sura or chapter 12 listed in this book under Qur'anic stories in part seven.

PART SIX

THE ISLAMIC STATE

32. The Supreme Authority of The Islamic State

The Islamic state derives its legitimacy from Islamic Divine Law (Shari'ah). Muslims consider the Shari'ah as a vital and valid source for all aspects of life and politics is one of these aspects. The Shari'ah is also considered by Muslims as a valid source for all times, thus an Islamic state is an appropriate form of government in modern times. The Islamic Divine Law (Shari'ah) regulates human affairs on earth including political affairs. It prescribes laws for human conduct. The Qur'an and Sunnah set the main rules and principles of the Islamic government. Minor details must be worked out in consistency with the Qur'an and Sunnah.

In Islam Allah is the lawgiver and the only authority of legislation:

"Legislation is for none but Allah." (Qur'an, 12: 40)

Following any law other than Shari'ah makes the Muslim a disbeliever, Allah –the Exalted- said:

"And whoever does not judge by what Allah has revealed- then it is those who are the disbelievers" (Qur'an, 5: 44)

"And whoever does not judge by what Allah has revealed- then it is those who are the wrong-doers [i.e. the unjust]." (Qur'an, 5:45)

"And whoever does not judge by what Allah has revealed- then it is those who are the defiantly disobedient." (Qur'an, 5: 47)

Things and issues that were not mentioned in the Qur'an with details or not in a definitive text then must be searched in the tradition of the Prophet Muhammad (pbuh).

Obeying the teaching and the commands of Allah and His Messenger are obligatory in the political realm and in all aspects of

Muslims' lives. This is the real meaning of Islam in submitting the will of man to the will of Allah:

"It is not fitting for a Believer, man or woman, when a matter has been decided by Allah and His Messenger, to have any option about their decision: if anyone disobeys Allah and His Messenger, he is indeed on a clearly wrong Path." (Qur'an, 33:36)

Thus the main source of political legislation is Allah. The commands of Allah as stated in the Qur'an are definitely binding in the political-legal sense.

The second source of political obligation is the Sunnah or the tradition of the Prophet that is manifested in his sayings or commands and in his deeds.

If the specific benefits were not clearly regulated in Qur'an and Sunnah, then a jurist who is also called a Mujtahid can derive the appropriate legal rule within the spirit of the Shari'ah teaching, as we will explain later.

The third source of political authority and legislation is people whom Allah called "Ulul Amr" or those charged with authority. Those people are those whose views and knowledge manage Muslims' affairs. The rest of the nation usually refers to them because they reflect their interest and their views. Those people who are "charged with authority" are those rulers, scholars, and officials who supervise the public in their affairs seeking their well-being. Those people also should be known for their piety and following the religion and obey Allah and His Messenger. Also they must do this work for the sake of others voluntarily.

Such authorized people might be called: Supreme board of the nation, whose vision on public issues is binding for all, even to the ruler himself, otherwise his refusal to their decision might lead to his dismissal.

The proof of these three sources is from the Qur'an:

"O you who believe! obey Allah, and obey the Messenger, and those charged with authority among you." (Qur'an, 4:59)

How Legislation was Formed after the Qur'an and Sunnah?

The Prophet Muhammad (pbuh) spent his entire time after revelation in explaining the Shari'ah and applying it. All Muslims used to asked him and refer to him about issues that were related to religion and worldly affairs. After his death his companions, especially those of great knowledge, used to answer the public in regard to legal opinions that concerned religious or general affairs. The authority of the companions and the successors of the Prophet (pbuh) was based first on their understanding the Qur'an and Sunnah. Second, on their ability in deriving judgments through independent interpretation, which is called Ijtihad, especially in cases for which there is no definitive text in commanding or forbidding, this is an area we discussed before and is called al-Masalh al-Mursala or the unregulated benefits in regard to things that might happen in the future such as cloning, or organ transplant, or computer ethics, etc.

The companion of the Prophet spread in many countries to teach Islam. Around those companions many students gathered to learn from them, among those students the more intelligent became scholars of Ijtihad.

Those scholars of Ijtihad acquired their knowledge and skills and authority through these avenues: Understanding the Qur'an and Sunnah, experience by dealing with many cases in light of Islamic Shari'ah, and through their own intelligence and talents in interpreting the texts.

Thus Muslims usually refer to those scholars who exist in every Islamic country to perform this legislative duty.

Some of those scholars, by studying Shari'ah, came up with their own independent interpretation. These independent jurisprudential interpretations were recorded and considered as laws only inasmuch as they stemmed out of, and were based on the Qur'an and Sunnah.

The recording of the Ijtihadats or independent jurisprudential interpretations, of those scholars and their own technical way in deriving them in addition to the sources on which they relied in deriving their legal opinions gave appearance to what we called before schools of jurisprudence such as: Hanafi, Maliki, Hanbali, and others. All this work is performed in light and frame of Islamic Shari'ah. Thus, following any of these schools is not only beneficial in religious and worldly affairs but also in enhancing intellectuality and better understanding the Islamic Divine Law.

Ijtihad must be continuously practiced in dealing with new issues in our modern time to show how Shari'ah is actively relevant to our time and to manifest its workability.

Is Islamic Government a Theocracy or Democracy?
In Islam there is no clergy system. No one in Islam should claim that his authority is granted to him from Allah. Every one is equally responsible and equally accountable before Allah, so the ultimate authority is for the Divine Law itself. The ruler is no more than a guardian who assures the application and the practice of the divine law in daily life in order to achieve the benefits of people. The Muslim ruler is the representative and the guardian of justice and equality. In this sense the Prophet (pbuh) was the first Muslim leader who assured the best application of the Islamic Shari'ah. Any one who follows him in this regard is only a successor (Khalifa = Caliph) of the Prophet in assuring this application of Islamic Shari'ah. Allah said:

"And when your Lord said to the angels: 'Indeed I will make upon the earth a successive authority." (Qur'an, 2:30)

Thus the source of legislation is the Qur'an and not the clergy. There is no religious class to claim any governmental authority based on religion. Islamic state is not theocratic.

However, the Islamic government is not democratic in the western sense of democracy. Because people are not the source of legislation rather Allah is. However, Muslim people should practice their political rights through democratic procedures called Shura or consultation, and voting or taking part in an election.

Islam, as a realistic religion, states that the entire public cannot hold governmental responsibilities, and a group of people should be doing this political task. Those people are the people who are charged with authority (Ulul Amr) and must be chosen by the nation in order to apply Islamic Divine law, and only by this application of Shari'ah Muslims will be satisfied with them since Shari'ah achieves the benefits of people equally.

33. Legal Steps and Procedures in Establishing the Islamic State

There are some procedures that are followed in establishing the Islamic state, these are:

1. Shura (Consultation),
2. Musawat (Equality), and
3. 'Adl (Justice)

33.1. Shura (Consultation)

Shura or consultation is one of the most important politic-legislative principles in the Islamic Shari'ah. In fact one entire chapter or sura in the Qur'an is called: Surat al-Shura (consultation), as a reference to emphasize the importance of this principle. The Muslim ruler must act according to the dictates of the Shari'ah, but he must gain the consent of the Muslim community. This consent is earned through consultation. In this Sura Allah –the Exalted- said:

"Those who hearken to their Lord, and establish regular prayer; who (conduct) their affairs by mutual Consultation; who spend out of what We bestow on them for Sustenance." (Qur'an, 42:38)

" So by mercy from Allah, [O Muhammad], you were lenient with them. And if you had been rude [in speech] and harsh in heart, they would have disbanded from about you. So pardon them and ask forgiveness for them and consult them in the matter. And when you have decided, then rely upon Allah. Indeed, Allah loves those who rely [upon Him]." (Qur'an, 3:159)

Consultation or Shura helps people to control community affairs through two ways: in choosing the Muslim ruler himself first, and second in examining all decisions that are made by the Islamic state.

The second source of Shari'ah that emphasizes the importance of Shura or consultation is Sunnah or the tradition of the Prophet Muhammad (pbuh). He personally practiced shura with his companions in many different occasions in peace and war. Practicing Shura was the command of Allah that His Messenger applied successfully, and by doing so the Prophet set an example to be followed after him by all Muslims.

Practicing Shura requires the knowledge of the Qur'an and Sunnah, and this might not be the state of the entire majority of people. And what is meant from Shura is a constructive advice and active pointing out what is good based on the teaching of Islamic Shari'ah. Opinions of those who do not know the religion might be destructive. This is why Allah said:

"When there comes to them some matter touching (public) safety or fear, they spread it around. If they had only referred it to the Messenger or to those charged with authority among them, the proper investigators would have tested it from them (direct)." (Qur'an, 4:83)

Obeying Ulul Amr or those people who are "charged with authority" is obligatory in Islam in order to achieve the general welfare. Obeying in Islam is not blindly following them; it is rather consciously observing them by the light of the religion and within the framework of Shari'ah. This involvement of people in the state is to assure the rights and duties and to achieve the prosperity. For this reason Allah legislates a practice called Shura or consultation.

Those people "charged with authority" that the Qur'an is referring to are those who have knowledge and wisdom of the Shari'ah and are capable of making sound judgment based on Shari'ah. Allah made clear a distinction between people of knowledge and the ignorant, Allah said:

"Say: "Are those equal, those who know and those who do not know?" (Qur'an, 39:9)

33.2. Musawat (Equality)

Equality is one of the most superior aspects of Islam. The legislation of equality in the Qur'an and Sunnah is so clear and evident that it leaves no room for oppression or injustice.

In Islam all people are equal before the law. All enjoy same political rights and duties:

Regardless of race:	no Arab surpasses a non-Arab,
Regardless of skin color:	no white surpasses a black,
Regardless of wealth:	no rich one surpasses a poor one,
Regardless of social classes:	no notable person surpasses a beggar

And any other aspect of superiority or inferiority is nullified in Islam. The source of this law of equality is the Qur'an and Sunnah:

Allah –the Exalted– says:

"O mankind! We created you from a single (pair) of a male and a female, and made you into nations and tribes, that ye may know each other (not that ye may despise each other). Verify the most honored of you in the sight of Allah is (he who is) the most righteous." (Qur'an, 49: 13)

Notice that in this Aya Allah –the Creator– addresses all mankind, not just Muslims, attracting their attention to the fact that there are no races. And that type of creation that called mankind is descended from one pair of parents (Adam and Eve). It is clear that equality will be destroyed if some humans claimed racial superiority.

In fact the term "human races" (in the plural sense) is contradictory and self-canceling. Human nations might be distant form each other in geography however; they are indeed very close to each other in humanity. Allah created them as one race but He made them different nations because diversity is beauty and has an aesthetic dimension. Also diversity is a great motivation for knowledge, it touches the essence of man which is reason, and it initiates the curiosity of knowing that who is not like us in the outside appearance, however he is exactly the same in the hidden essence, i.e., being human. This is why Allah said: "you may know each other."

Knowing each other is an effort initiated from love and curiosity to know that who is us but seems not. Islam encourages people to know each other for love and experience what we learn from others in dealing with problems. Human beings are equal however; they are sublime in as much as they do good things to the rest of human beings.

The other source of the legislation of equality is coming from the tradition of the Prophet (pbuh). In his Farewell Pilgrimage, the Prophet (pbuh) said:

"O people! Your Lord is One, and your father is one. So let no Arab be favored over a non-Arab, or the latter over the former, or a Black over a Red, or the Red over a Black - except in Righteousness."

The Prophet used to socialize with all kinds of people; the poor, the rich, slaves, masters, Christians, Jews, Arab, non-Arab, foreigner...etc. The nobles of Quraish blamed him and refused to sit with him until he left those people, but he refused to do so, then they asked him to set one day for them and another day for the lower class, and revelation came down to reject such inequality.

The Prophet (pbuh) put equality in practice commanding Muslims to apply it. When he heard Abu Tharr Al-Ghafari disputing an issue with a Negro slave, telling him: 'son of the Negro woman' is a title of humiliation.

The Prophet rejected such humiliation, and he said to Abu Tharr:

'No White should be favored over a Black, except in piety and good deeds!'

When Abu Tharr heard this statement he put his cheek on the ground and asked the slave, in atonement for his misbehavior, to put his foot on his cheek.

A freeman is not better than a slave, in fact the Prophet appointed Bilal, a black and former slave as a ruler of Medina for a period of time, Bilal also was the first person to call for prayer.

33.3. 'Adl (Justice)

Applying justice in Islam is unconditional, meaning it should be achieved among all people equally. And it must be applied even though it conflicts with one's own interest. Allah –the Exalted- said:

"O ye who have believed, be persistently standing firm for justice, as witnesses for Allah, even if it be against yourselves or parents and relatives. And whether it be (against) rich or poor; for Allah is more worthy of both. Follow not the lusts (of your hearts) lest you, Swerve, and if you destroy (justice) or decline to do justice, verily Allah is well-acquainted with all that you do." (Qur'an, 4: 135)

Since justice is unconditional it must be applied even with enemies of Muslims. Allah commanded Muslims to do so:

"Let not the hatred of others to you prevent you from being just." (Qur'an, 5: 8)

Allah also said:

"When you judge between mankind, judge with justice." (Qur'an, 4: 58)

Allah urges people to be just also in speech: "Whenever you speak, speak justly, even if a near relative is concerned." (Qur'an, 6: 152).

Allah -the Exalted- also clarified in Qur'an the purpose of revelation as he –the Exalted- said:

"We have already sent Our messengers with clear evidences and sent down with them the Scripture and the Balance (of Right and Wrong), that men may stand forth in justice." (Qur'an, 57: 25)

Al-Ghazali said in his book *al-Mustasfa min 'Ilm al-Usul* that the purpose of revelation is to achieve the benefits of people. The

Islamic Divine Law seeks the realization of the welfare of people. Ibn Taimia said in his *Fatawa* that the goal of Shari'ah is to achieve justice. In fact there is no contradiction as I explained before, since justice is one of the benefits of people.

Other scholars of Shari'ah realized the importance of achieving benefits in the Islamic Divine Law. Imam Al-Shatibi, from a city in Spain near Granada, followed al-Ghazali by saying in his book *Al-Mowafaqat (the Agreements)*:

"The decrees of Shari'ah were set only for the welfare of people; and wherever such a welfare exists, we find a divine decree of Shari'ah."

Imam Ibn al-Qayyem al-Jawziah, in his book *Al-Turoq Al-Hikamiyah (The Wise Procedures)*, said:

"Almighty Allah sent His messenger and revealed His Books to establish justice among people, the same justice on which the earth and heavens have been founded. When justice reveals itself, no matter how, there is divine law and religion."

In fact the ultimate goal of Shari'ah is to achieve every good possible for people and to forbid evil of all kinds. Allah –the Exalted- said in describing what the Prophet Muhammad (pbuh) is teaching people through revelation:

"Who enjoins upon them what is right and forbids them what is wrong and makes lawful for them the good things and prohibits for them the evil and relieves them of their heavy burdens," (Qur'an, 7:157).

From the above explanation of these three procedures and principles we can say that the triangle of political reality in Islam cannot be established without consultation, equality, and justice.

33.4. The Auxiliary but Essential Principle:
Prescribing what is Right and Forbidding what is Evil
Enjoining the good and forbidding evil is an auxiliary principle to aid establishing consultation, equality, and justice. It also assures the proper practice and exercise of such principles.

"Islam requires that in an Islamic State there should be a group of people with authority who represent the nation, act on its behalf, and keep a careful watch over its affairs. God refers to this group of people saying: "Let there arise out of you a band of people inviting to all that is good, enjoining what is right, and forbidding what is evil; they are the ones to attain felicity." (Qur'an: 111:104) The duty of such people is to supervise rulers, be their reference of legislation, recommend good deeds, prevent acts of evil, and advise the people.

Such a responsibility, however, is not limited to this group of people; The Qur'an extends this to all believers: "The Believers, men and women, are protectors, one of another. They enjoin what is just, and forbid what is evil; they observe regular prayers, practice regular charity, and obey God and His Apostle. On them will God pour His Mercy" (Qur'an: 9: 71). The promise of mercy which God makes to those believers, who carry out this obligation, is a promise of Divine Care and Assistance.

God further reveals the importance of enjoining righteousness, saying: "By (the Token of) Time (through the Ages), verily- Man is in loss, except such as have Faith, do righteous deeds, and (join together) in the mutual teaching of Truth, and of Patience and Constancy." (Qur'an: sura 103)

The whole community would commit sin if evil spreads among its members with none to denounce it.

God considers the enjoining of right and the forbidding of evil as a special attribute that raises the Islamic nation above other nations: "Ye are the best of Peoples, evolved for mankind, enjoining what is right, forbidding what is evil, and believing in God." (Qur'an: 3: 110).

The Prophet Muhammad (pbuh) instructed the believers to this same effect; he says:

"When one of you sees an evil committed, let him change it by hand; if it is beyond his ability, let him do so by his tongue (by persuasion); if still it is beyond his ability, let him do so by his heart (by wish), which is the least bit of faith."

In this way, Islam seeks to form a general, unified view toward a very noble goal: uprooting corruption wherever it may be, and never letting it dominates. Nothing, in fact, is more harmful to a people than the acts of aggression committed by some of its members against the sanctities of religion, the State, and common rights, with none to move a limb to condemn their acts and, in one way or another, make them refrain from the evils they have indulged themselves in."[75]

The Legal Steps and Procedures in Establishing the Islamic State

1. Consultation or Shura

2. Equality

3. Justice

4. Commanding the good and forbidding evil

---

34. Legality and the General Political Principles from Jurisprudence

Muslim scholars who are talented and trained in the field of jurisprudence and the field of the principles of Islamic jurisprudence derived from the Qur'an and the Sunnah general legislative principles that achieve the benefits of people equally. Those scholars also set rules of derivation by which they can derive more and legislate further. The total of such legislative work constitute the legal heritage of Islam.

---

[75] Tabbarah (1993): pp. 301-303.

These legislative principles have the ability to be applied to all people equally - in other words they transcend space and time, although the particular instances of such is specific to certain cases and specific individuals.

These general principles were classified under four major categories. These categories are:

1. Principles Set for the Aversion of Harm
2. Principles Devised to Avoid Corruption
3. Relief from Difficulties
4. The Principle of Necessities Justifying Prohibition

Under each of the above four categories there are a set of principles that legislate further with more specification. The following is a brief explanation of the principles of each category.[76]

34.1. Principles set for the Aversion of Harm

Muslim Scholars of Shari'ah based this category, and consequently derived all its principles from a famous saying of the Prophet Muhammad (pbuh) who said in regard of achieving the benefits of all people equally and avoiding harm the following:

"Let no harm be done unto others, and never pay off a harm with another".

From this prophetic saying the scholars of Ijtihad derived the following principles:

> **First. Harm is to be legally removed**
> Under this heading go the right or preemption to the partner and neighbor, the obligation of responsibility or guarantee on the part of those who spoil the property of others, and the obligation of protection and medication against disease.
>
> **Second. Harm is never removed by harm**

---

[76] For the explanation of these principles please see the useful book of Tabbarah (1993): pp. 305-308.

Hence, one should not let harm befall others in order to avoid it himself, or spoil the property of others so as to save his.

Third. Personal harm should be tolerated to avoid general harm
Accordingly, a killer may be killed so that people may live in security, and a shaky wall bordering on a public street may be pulled down before it collapses.

Fourth. In a state of exigency or urgency, the least harmful act may be done to avoid a severer one
So a wife, for instance, may be divorced to avoid further harm or when her husband is totally insolvent; and, similarly, financial support becomes an obligation on the rich relatives of the poor.

Fifth. The avoidance of harm should come before the seeking of benefit
In this connection, the property owner is not allowed to dispose of his property the way he chooses, if this leads to the harm of others.

34.2. Principles Devised to Avoid Corruption
Scholars derived these principles from the Qur'an, Allah –The Exalted- says:

"And do not insult those they invoke other than Allah, lest they insult Allah in enmity without knowledge." (Qur'an, 6: 108).

Along this line, scholars derived the following principles:

First. That which leads to what is prohibited is prohibited itself.

Second. That which is the only means of fulfilling an obligation is an obligation.

Third. That which in large quantity is harmful is prohibited though only in little quantity.

Fourth. The avoidance of corruption should be worthier of attention than the securing of personal welfare.

There are about ninety-nine illustrations in proving the above principles all brought forth by Ibn al-Qayyem al-Jawziah in his book *A'lam Al-Muwaqi'in*, who made a thorough interpretation of such principles. For instance, he reports that the Prophet prohibits marriage between a woman and her aunt on the one hand, and the same man on the other, saying "if you do this, you would break the ties of kinship among you. It should never be permitted, though the woman accepts it, because this would be a pretext to the prohibited breaking of kinship".

In another place, Ibn al-Qayyem al-Jawziah explains that the Shari'ah refuses the acceptance of a person's testimony against his enemy, lest the former take advantage of this to achieve his aim against his enemy through false testimony.

He also explains that the Prophet prohibits the man to pass the night at a woman's lodging, unless he be her husband or one who is legally forbidden to get married to her (for close kinship relations), because passing the night at such a woman's lodging might lead to adultery.

34.3. Principles for Relief from Difficulties
The source of this principle lies in God's words:

"[Allah] has not placed upon you any difficulty in the religion." (Qur'an, 22: 78)

"Allah intends every facility for you. He does not want to put you to difficulties." (Qur'an, 2: 185)

"On no soul does Allah place a burden greater than it can bear." (Qur'an, 2: 286).

From these verses, scholars have derived the following principles:

First. Hardship requires facilitation
On this basis, the Shari'ah allows the faster to break his fast while on a long travel or during sickness; it also permits

short prayers during travel, and releases the weak and the sick from going on pilgrimage to Mecca.

Second. Difficulty is legally removed
Here, for instance, the testimony of women is the only one accepted in cases of feminine defects and matters which men should have no information about.

Third. Needs take the same standing of necessities in justifying what is prohibited
From this principle stems a wide range of transactions and ties of partnership that take effect among people as business necessitates. If true evidence shows that some of these transactions or dealings are so urgent for the proper running of people's affairs that difficulty might arise if such dealings were forbidden, a fair allowance is granted to remove difficulty.

34.4. The Principle of Necessities Justifying Prohibition
Muslim Scholars derived this principle from the Qur'an, Allah – The Exalted- says: :

"But whoever is forced [by necessity], neither dressing [it] nor transgressing [its limit], there is no sin upon him. Allah is forgiving and merciful." (Qur'an, 2:173).

In this connection in sura 16: 106, Allah includes those whom He forgives for expression of disbelief in cases of necessity; under compulsion while their hearts remain firm in faith.

That is why Allah also permits people, in cases of compulsion, to eat the prohibited meat of dead animals or drink wine in order to save life, because life is one of the five main objectives of the Islamic Shari'ah. It is on such grounds that scholars based a number of conclusions:

First. Necessities should be given their due value only
And in this connection, one should not go to extremes; for when danger disappears, prohibition becomes applicable.

Second. Necessity does not nullify the rights of others
Here, if one has to eat the food of another person, lest he should die, he has to pay its value.

35. Characteristics of Islamic Legislative System (Shari'ah)

The spread and acceptance of Islam in many diverse and different cultures on the globe gave the Islamic Shari'ah an excellent realm to manifest itself as a successful law that its application achieves the benefits, justice and equality for people. From the Far East cultures and countries such as Indonisia, Malaysia, and from China, Tibet, to the Indian Peninsula, to the Middle East and Europe, the Islamic Shari'ah are applied to assure the benefits of people and achieves equality and justice. There are some characteristics that made the Islamic Shari'ah acceptable and adaptable in these different cultures:

1. Comprehensivity: Islamic Divine Law transcends space, time and cultural differences, it is not for a specific culture or specific time, rather it is for all cultures and all time, it is not for a specific race it is rather for mankind, and it is not for middle ages it is rather for all ages, it is not for the past rather it is for the future. Its comprehensivity comes from its source of legislation from The God who legislates not for Arabs or a specific community, He legislates for mankind.

Professor Santinnala, for instance, in his *Avant-Projet du Code Civil et Commercial Tunisien*, says: "Islamic jurisprudence encompasses all that meets the needs of Muslims in their civil legislations, not to mention its satisfaction of the needs of all humanity."[77]

2. Applicability: It is easy to apply on individual levels, community, and society. Tabbara in his book (1993) said that professor Hawking who singled out a thoroughly developed chapter on 'The Future of Islamic Culture' in his book *The Spirit of Universal Politics*, said: "The achievement of progress in the Islamic kingdoms has not been through the adoption of Western ideas which claim that religion should have nothing to do with the individual's daily life, nor with laws and divine regulations; instead,

---

[77] See Tabbarah (1993): p. 309.

one should find in religion a source of development and progress. Sometimes people question whether the system of Islam could generate new ideas and issue independent regulations-which go in harmony with modern life. The answer is that Islam covers all the potential readiness for development, and its adaptability and ability to progress surpass by far the rest of similar doctrines. The difficulty was not in the non-availability of the means for development and Advancement in the Shari'ah but in the non-existence of the inclination toward using such means. I feel I am right when I ascertain that the Islamic Shari'ah includes, abundantly, all the principles required to achieve advancement."[78]

3. Workability: when it applies it does achieve the benefits of people and it works for all. Dr. Levy Olman said: "The Islamic Shari'ah in the domain of dealings and transactions, should be considered as a vital source of modern law and jurisprudence and the comprehensive origin of the concept of right in its various stages."[79]

Dr. Enrico I. Touhin said: "Islam suitably harmonizes with the requirements of people's visible needs; it can develop without weakening with the passage of time, and can keep all its vitality and flexibility... It was Islam that gave the world the firmest set of laws, and its Shari'ah, in many of its details, surpasses the European constitutions."[80]

36. Islamic State and Leadership

The Muslim ruler is usually called Caliph (the Arabic word "Khalifa" is derived from Khalafa meaning to succeed someone in something) or Imam (derived from the Arabic word Amma meaning to lead). The ruler is called caliph because he succeeded the Prophet Muhammad (pbuh) in the leadership of Muslims in religious and worldly affairs, after the Prophet's death. The Muslim ruler is then the successor of Allah's Prophet (Khalifat Rasulil-lah).

The Muslim ruler has a principal task, which is to apply the Islamic Shari'ah and assure that people abide by its legal principles, in order to achieve their welfare, both in this life and in the Hereafter.

---

[78] See Tabbarah (1993): p. 310.
[79] Tabbarah (1993): p. 310.
[80] See Tabbarah (1993): P. 310.

36.1. Who Appoints the Muslim Ruler (Caliph)?

Since this sensitive position requires religious and political requirements, those who nominate him should have higher knowledge in religion and must be acquainted with social and political affairs. Those scholars called Ulul Amr or those who are charged with authority in the nation. With this knowledge they will be able to nominate a person who is qualified and meets the conditions and the requirements of Muslim ruler.

Any one who seeks this position for the sake of honor and wealth, his request must be denied, because the religion commands Muslims not to give those people such a position. The Prophet once said to two people who asked him to appoint them as emirs or rulers:

"We never appoint as an emir him who desires such a post or is covetous about it."

But what are the qualifications and conditions of such a position?

36.2. The Conditions and Requirements of the Ruler

Scholars set a number of conditions for the holder of the office of Caliph or ruler. Of these, one may mention those set by al-Mawardi in his book *al-Ahkam as-Sultaniah (Royal Principles)*. He says,

"As for those qualified for the Caliphate, they have to meet seven conditions:

1. Justice, in accordance with its definitive conditions.

2. Enough knowledge that enables one to exercise acts of Ijtihad (independent judgments based on interpretation).

3. Sound hearing, vision and speech so that one's perception may meet the conditions he faces.

4. Absence of bodily handicaps that might hinder one from exercising a readiness of movement.

5. Sound reason that enables one to lead and guide the people and manage their affairs.

6. Courage and bravery to protect the nation's territories and fight the enemy.[81]

Duty of the Caliph Toward the Nation
The Caliph has to propagate the call of Islam, establish justice, protect religion against offence and heresy, and consult others on points not settled by The Koran. He is responsible for all the measures he takes, should accept the advice and instruction of his subjects when they discover a mistake he makes, and in this case he is held accountable before those charged with authority. To this effect, Muhammad (pbuh) explains:

"The Imam is a guardian, and (as such) he is responsible for his subjects."

Allah –The Exalted- says:

"Indeed Allah commands you to render trusts to whom they are due and when you judge between people to judge with justice." (Qur'an: 4: 58).

The "trusts" meant here, include all that must be kept and rendered to those who deserve them. Public posts are a trust put under the charge of the Iman who has to entrust them to those fit for them; public funds are also a trust to be spent in the proper way. Individual and group legal rights should likewise be rendered to their holders - and the established principle of justice here is to apply God's revealed decrees, and to render quickly unto people all their dues."[82]

36.3. How was the First Muslim Caliph Elected?
"The Prophet died leaving behind a nation managing its affairs according to the word of The Qur'an and the Sunnah. He did not name his successor, from among his distinguished Companions, to the leadership of Muslims.

---

[81] There is another condition about the ruler to be a descent from the tribe of Quraish for it has been reported that the Prophet said so, and consensus seems to stress this point. In fact the last condition is disputable among scholars. The famous Muslims scholars thought that it is not necessary, among those scholars: Abu Bakr al-Baqillani, al-Juwaini, and al-Ghazali.
[82] See Tabbarah (1993): p. 313-314.

His death was an unexpected occurrence that perplexed his people for a while, and the loss was so huge that some of them were about to give up Islam. In such a critical situation, Abu Bakr (a leading Companion) took a stand in front of the people and addressed them, saying:

'O people! Those of you who have been worshipping Muhammad, should know that Muhammad is dead; but those who have been worshipping Allah, certainly know that Allah is Alive and never dies!'

Then he quoted Allah's words:

"Muhammad is no more than a messenger. [other] messengers have passed on before him. So if he were to die or be killed, would you turn back on your heels [to unbelief]? And he who turns back on his heels, will never harm Allah at all; but Allah will reward those who (serve Him) with gratitude." (Qur'an, 3: 144).

With these words, the Companions regained their morale, left Muhammad's body lying down in his chamber, held a meeting somewhere else, and consulted with one another on who to appoint for the succession of Muhammad. Not later than an hour, they unanimously agreed to appoint Abu Bakr for the succession of Muhammad. When the people's pledge of allegiance was made to him, he took a stand in front of them and addressed them, saying:

'O people! I have been appointed as your Imam, and I know I am not the best among you. My request, however, is that you offer me your support as long as I properly carry out my office, and correct my mistakes when I depart from right and justice. Truthfulness is fidelity, and falsehood a betrayal. The weak among you shall be strong until I restore their right, and the strong shall be weak in my view until I take away the rights of others from them, if God so wills. Let no one forsake the Way of Jihad, for God strikes with humiliation all those who forsake the Way of Jihad. Obey me as long as I have obeyed God and His Apostle, and if I should disobey God you are free of my obedience. Now, stand up for prayer, that God may have mercy on you!'

If we consider closely this speech - the first speech the Muslims heard from an authorized person after the death of Muhammad - we could discover the principles of democracy in full bloom. In those times, there was a huge gap between nations and democracy. The appointment of Abu Bakr as the "Head of State" after meetings and consultations as one who best deserved to head the government, and the people's pledge of allegiance offered to him after his appointment- indicate clearly that the final word of authority is for the nation as a whole, and Muhammad's not naming his successor to the leadership of Muslims does support such a right on the part of the public.

In Abu Bakr's words: 'My request, however, is that you offer me your support as long as I properly carry out my office, and correct my mistakes when I depart from right and justice', there is a clear evidence that the nation has the right to supervise governmental practices, offer support to those who work well, and call others to account or depose them.

When Abu Bakr says, 'Obey me as long as I have obeyed God and His Apostle, and if I should disobey God you are free of my obedience', he makes a definite declaration that the Islamic government has an established law: The Qur'an and the Sunnah; and Abu Bakr undertakes in public to follow the line of Allah's established law. He makes it clear that the nation has the right to remove the government if it fails to fulfill what the constitution and laws require. Such rights constitute today basic standards of true democracy."[83]

36.4. Should Muslims Obey the Rulers Regardless?
The Prophet (pbuh) explains:

"No obedience is due to anyone if it be against Allah's Commandments; it is due only when goodness be its purpose."

Based on this prophetic tradition the ruler must assure people the application of Shari'ah which indicates the achievement of their benefits. If the ruler does not follow and apply the Shari'ah he will be considered as one of the people mentioned above, as the Qur'an

---
[83] See Tabbarah (1993): pp. 314-316.

states about those who judge not by that which Allah revealed such ruler become: "disbelievers", "wrong-doers", and "rebellious".

As a result the ruler loses credit and authority in political-religious sense.

The Four Rightly Guided khalifas after the Prophet Muhammad (pbuh)

Abu Bakr as-Siddiq	(d. 13 A.H./634 A.D.)
Umar Ibn al-Khattab	(d. 23 A.H./644 A.D.)
Uthman Ibn 'Affan	(d. 35 A.H./656 A.D.)
Ali Ibn Abi Talib	(d. 40 A.H./661 A.D.)

Then:
The Umayyads (41-132 A.H./ 661-750 A.D.)
(al-Dawla al-Umawiyya)

The Abbasids (132-656 A.H./ 750-1258 A.D.)
(al-Dawla al-Abbasiyya)

PART SEVEN

ISLAMIC STORIES AND POETRY

37. A Qur'anic Story: The Story of Prophet Joseph

This story is from the Qur'an. It covers the life of prophet Joseph (Yusuf) in his relation to his family and his obedience to Allah. It is called in Qur'an Surat Yusuf. It is chapter 12 of the Qur'an.

SURAT YUSUF

Bismillahir-Rahmanir-Raheem

"1. Alif, Lam, Ra. These are the verses of the clear book.

2. Indeed, We have sent it down as an Arabic Qur'an that you might understand.

3. We relate to you, [O Muhammad], the best of stories in what We have revealed to you of this Qur'an although you were, before it, among the unaware.

4. [Of these stories mention] when Joseph said to his father, "O my father, indeed I have seen [in a dream] eleven stars and the sun and the moon; I saw them prostrating to me."

5. He said, "O my son, do not relate your vision to your brothers or they will contrive against you a plan. Indeed Satan, to man, is a manifest enemy.

6. And thus will your Lord choose you and teach you the interpretation of narratives [i.e., events or dreams] and complete His favor upon you and upon the family of Jacob, as He completes it upon you fathers before, Abraham and Isaac. Indeed, your Lord is Knowing and Wise.

7. Certainly were there in Joseph and his brothers signs for those who ask, [such as]

8. When they said, "Joseph and his brother are more beloved to our father then we, while we are a clan. Indeed, our father is in clear error.

9. Kill Joseph or cast him out to [another] land; the countenance [i.e., attention] of your father will [then] be only for you, and you will be after that a righteous people."

10. Said a speaker among them, "Do not kill Joseph but throw him into the bottom of the well; some travelers will pick him up- if you would do [something]."

11. They said, "O our father, why do you not entrust us with Joseph wile indeed, we are to him sincere counselors?

12. Send him with us tomorrow that he may eat well and play. And indeed, we will be his guardians."

13. [Jacob] said, Indeed, it saddens me that you should take him, and I fear that a wolf would eat him while you are of him unaware."

14. They said, "If a wolf should eat him while we are [strong] clan, indeed, we would then be losers."

15. So when they took him [out] and agreed to put him into the bottom of the well... But We inspired to him, "You will surely inform them [someday] about this affair of theirs while they do not perceive [your identity]."

16. And they came to their father at night, weeping.

17. They said, "O our father, indeed we went racing each other and left Joseph with our possessions, and a wolf ate him. But you would not believe us, even if we were truthful."

18. And they brought upon his shirt false blood. [Jacob] said, "Rather, your souls have enticed you to something, so patience is most fitting. And Allah is the one sought for help against that which you describe."

19. And there came a company of travelers; then they sent their water drawer, and he let down his bucket. He said, "Good news! Here is a boy." And they concealed him, [taking him] as merchandise; and Allah was Knowing of what they did.

20. And they sold him for a reduced price- a few dirhams- and they were, concerning him, of those content with little.

21. And the one from Egypt who bought him said to his wife, "Make his residence comfortable. Perhaps he will benefit us, or we will adopt his as a son." And thus, We established Joseph in the land that We might teach him the interpretation of events [i.e., dreams]. And Allah is predominant over His affair, but most of the people do not know.

22. And when he [i.e., Joseph] reached maturity, We gave him judgment and knowledge. And thus We reward the doers of good.

23. And she, in whose house he was, sought to seduce him. She closed the doors and said, "Come, you." He said, "[I seek] the refuge of Allah. Indeed, he is my master, who has made good my residence. Indeed, wrongdoers will not succeed."

24. And she certainly determined [to seduce} him, and he would have inclined to her had he not seen the proof [i.e., sign] of his Lord. And thus [it was] the We should avert form him evil and immorality. Indeed, he was of Our chosen servants.

25. And they both raced to the door, and she tore his shirt from the back, and they found her husband at the door. She said, "What is the recompense of one who intended evil for your wife but that he be imprisoned or a painful punishment.

26. [Joseph] said, "It was she who sought to seduce me." And a witness from her family testified, "If his shirt is torn from the front, then she has told the truth, and he is of the liars.

27. But if his shirt is torn from the back, then she has lied, and he is of the truthful."

28. So when he [i.e., her husband] saw his shirt torn from the back, he said, "Indeed, it is of your [i.e. women's] plan. Indeed your plan is great [i.e., vehement].

29. Joseph, ignore this. And, [my wife], ask forgiveness for your sin. Indeed, you were of the sinful."

30. And women in the city said, "The wife of al-'Azeez is seeking to seduce her slave boy; he has impassioned her with love. Indeed, We see her [to be] in clear error."

31. So when she heard of their scheming, she sent for them and prepared for them a banquet and gave each one of them a knife and said [to Joseph], "Come out before them." And when they say him. They greatly admired him and cut their hands and said, "Perfect is Allah! This is not a man,; this is none but a noble angel."

32. She said, "That is the one about whom you blamed me. And I certainly sought to seduce him, but he firmly refused; and if he sill surely be imprisoned and will be of those debased.

33. He said, "My Lord, prison is more to my liking than that to which they invite me. And if You do not avert from me their plan, I might incline toward them and [thus] be of the ignorant.

34. So his Lord responded to him and averted from him their plan. Indeed, He is the Hearing, the Knowing.

35. Then it appeared to them after they had seen the signs the he [i.e., al-Azeez] should surely imprison him for a time.

36. And there entered the prison with him two young men. One of them said, "Indeed, I have seen myself [in a dream] pressing wine." The other said, "Indeed, I have seen myself carrying upon my head [some] bread, from which the birds were eating, Inform us of its interpretation; indeed, we see you to be of those who do good."

37. He said, "You will not receive food that is provided to you except that I will inform you of its interpretation before it

comes to you. That is from what my Lord has taught me. Indeed, I have left the religion of a people who do not believe in Allah, and they. In the Hereafter, are disbelievers.

38. And I have followed the religion of my fathers, Abraham, Isaac and Jacob. And it was not for us to associate anything with Allah. That is from the favor of Allah upon us and upon the people, but most of the people are not grateful.

39. O [my] two companions of prison, are separate lords better of Allah. The One, the Prevailing?

40. You worship not besides Him except [mere] names you have named them, you and your fathers, for which Allah has sent down no authority. Legislation is not but for Allah. He has commanded that you worship not except Him. That is the correct religion, but most of the people do not know.

41. O two companions of prison, as for one of you, he will dive drink to his master of wine; but as for the other, he will be crucified, and the birds will eat from his head. The matter has been decreed about which you both inquire."

42. And he said to the one whom he knew would go free, "Mention me before you matter." But Satan made him forget the mention [to] his master, and he [i.e., Joseph] remained in prison several years.

43. And [subsequently] the king said, "Indeed, I have seen [in a dream] seven fat cows being eaten by seven [that were] lean, and seven green spikes [of grain] and others [that were] dry. O eminent ones, explain to me my vision, if you should interpret visions."

44. They said, "[It is but] a mixture of false dreams, and we are not learned in the interpretation of dreams."

45. But the one who was freed and remembered after a time aid, "I will inform you of its interpretation, to send me forth."

46. [He said],"Joseph, O man of truth, explain to us about seven fat cows eater by seven [that were] lean, and seven green spikes [of grain] and others [that were] dry-that I may return to the people [i.e., the king and his court]; perhaps they will know [about you]."

47. [Joseph] said, "You will plant for seven years consecutively; and what you harvest leave in its spikes, except a little from which you will eat.

48. Then will come after that seven difficult [tears] which will consume what you advanced [i.e., saved] for them, except a little from which you will store.

49. Then will come after that a year in which the people will be given rain and in which they will press [olives and grapes]."

50. And the king said, "Bring him to me.' But when the messenger came to him. [Joseph] said, "Return to your master and ask him what is the case of the women who cut their hands, Indeed, my Lord is Knowing of their plan."

51. Said [the king to the women], "What was you condition when you sought to seduce Joseph?" They said, "Perfect is Allah! We know about no evil" The wife of al-Azeez said, "Now the truth has become evident, It was I who sought to seduce him. And indeed, he is of the truthful.

52. That is so he [i.e., al-Azeez] will know that I did not betray him in [his] absence and that Allah does not guide the plan of betrayers.

53. And I do not acquit myself. Indeed, the soul is a persistent enjoiner of evil, except those upon which my Lord has mercy. Indeed, my Lord is Forgiving and Merciful."

54. And the king said, "Bring him to me; I will appoint him exclusively for myself." And when he spoke to him, he said, "Indeed, you are today established [in position] and trusted.

55. [Joseph] said, "Appoint me over the storehouses of the land. Indeed, I will be a knowing guardian."

56. And thus We established Joseph in the land to settle therein wherever he willed. We touch with Our mercy whom We will, and We do not allow to be lost the reared of those who do good.

57. And the reward of the Hereafter is better for those who believed and were fearing Allah.

58. And the brothers of Joseph came [seeking food], and they entered upon him; and he recognized them, but he was to them unknown.

59. And when he had furnished them with their supplies. He said. "Bring me a brother of yours from your father. Do not you see that I give full measure and that I am the best of accommodators?

60. But if you do not bring him to me, no measure will there be [hereafter] for you from me, nor will you approach me."

61. They said, "We will attempt to dissuade his father from [keeping] him, and indeed, we will do [it]."

62. And [Joseph] said to his servants, "Put their merchandise into their saddlebags so they might recognize it when they have gone back to their people that perhaps they will [again] return.

63. So when they returned to their father, they said, "O our father, [further] measure has been denied to us, so send with us our brother [that] we will be given measure. And indeed, we will be his guardian.

64. He said, "Should I entrust you with him except [under coercion] as I entrusted you with his brother before? But Allah is the best guardian, and He is the most merciful of the merciful.

65. And when they opened their baggage, they found their merchandise returned to them. They said, "O our father what

[more] could we desire? This is our merchandise returned to us. And we will obtain supplies [i.e., food] for our family and protect our brother and obtain an increase of a camel's load, that is an easy measurement."

66. [Jacob] said, "Never will I send him with you until you give me a promise [i.e., oath] by Allah that you will bring him [back] to me, unless you should be surrounded [i.e., overcome by enemies]." And when they had given their promise, he said, "Allah, over what we say. Is Witness."

67. And he said, "O my sons, do not enter from one gate but enter from different gates, and I cannot avail you against [the decree of] Allah at all. The decision is only for Allah' upon Him I have relied, and upon Him let those who would rely [indeed] rely."

68. And when they entered from where their father had ordered them, it did not avail them against Allah at all except [it was] a need [i.e., concern] within the soul of Jacob, which he satisfied. And indeed, he was a possessor of knowledge because of what We had taught him, but most of the people do not know.

69. And when they entered upon Joseph, he took his brother to himself, he said, "Indeed, I am your brother, so do not despair, over that they used to do [to me]."

70. So when he had furnished them with their supplies, he put the [gold measuring] bowl into the bag of this brother. Then an announcer called out, "O caravan, indeed you are thieves."

71. They said while approaching the, "What is it you are missing."

72. They said, "We are missing the measure of the king. And for he who produces it is [the reward of] a camel's load, when I am responsible for it."

73. They said, "By Allah, you have certainly known that we did not come to cause corruption in the land, and we have not been thieves."

74. They [the accusers] said, "Then what would be its recompense if you should be liars?"

75. [The brother] said, "Its recompense is that he in whose bag it is found-he [himself] will be its recompense. Thus do we recompense the wrongdoers.

76. So he began [the search] with their bags before the bag of his brother, then he extracted it from the bag of his brother. Thus did We plan for Joseph. He could not have takes his brother within the religion [i.e., law] of the king except that Allah willed. We raise in degrees whom We will, but over every possessor of knowledge in one [more] knowing.

77. They said, "If he steals-a brother of his has stolen before." But Joseph kept it within himself and did not reveal it to them. He said, "Your are worse in position, and Allah is most knowing of what you describe."

78. They said, "O 'Azeez, indeed he has a father [who is] an old man, so take on of us in place of him. Indeed, we see you as a doer of good."

79. He said, "[I seek] the refuge of Allah [to prevent] that we take except him with whom we found our possession. Indeed, we would then be unjust."

80. So when they had despaired of him, the secluded themselves in private consultation. The eldest of them said, "Do you not know that your father has take upon you an oath be Allah and [that] before you failed in [your duty to] Joseph? So I will never leave [this] land until my father permits me or Allah decides for me, and He is the best of judges."

81. Return to your father and say, 'O our father, indeed your son has stolen, and we did not testify except to what we knew. And we were not witnesses of the unseen.

82. And ask the city to which we were and the caravan in which we came-and indeed, we are truthful."

83. [Jacob] said, "Rather, your souls have enticed you to something, so patience is most fitting. Perhaps Allah will bring them to me all together. Indeed, it is He who is the Knowing. The Wise."

84. And he turned away from them and said, "Oh, my sorrow over Joseph," and his eyes became white from grief, for he was [of that] a suppressor.

85. They said. "By Allah, you will not cease remembering Joseph until you become fatally ill or become of those who perish."

86. He said, "I only complain of my suffering and my grief to Allah, and I know form Allah that which you do not know.

87. O my sons, go and find out about Joseph and his brother and despair not of relief from Allah. Indeed, no one despairs of relief from Allah except the disbelieving people.

88. So when they entered upon him [i.e., Joseph], they said, "O Azeez, adversity has touched us and our family, and we have come with goods poor quality, but give us full measure and be charitable to us. Indeed, Allah rewards the charitable.

89. He said, "Do you know what you did with Joseph and his brother when you were ignorant?

90. They said, "Are you indeed Joseph?" He said, I am Joseph, and this is my brother. Allah has certainly favored us. Indeed, he who fears Allah and is patient, then indeed, Allah does not allow to be lost the reward of those who do good/"

91. They said, "By Allah, certainly has Allah preferred you over us, and indeed, we have been sinners."

92. He said, "No blame will there be upon you today. Allah will forgive you, and He is the most merciful of the merciful.

93. Take this, my shirt and cast it over the face of my father; he will become seeing. And bring me your family, all together.

94. And when the caravan departed [from Egypt], their father said, "Indeed, I find the smell of Joseph [and would say that he was alive] if you did not think me weakened in mind."

95. They Said, "By Allah, indeed you are in your [same] old error."

96. And when the bearer of good tidings arrived, he cast it over his face, and he returned [once again] seeing. He said, "Did I not tell you that I know from Allah that which you do not know?"

97. They said, "O our father, ask for us forgiveness of our sins, indeed, we have been sinners."

98. He said, "I will ask forgiveness for you from the Lord. Indeed, it is He who is the Forgiving, the Merciful.

99. And when they entered upon Joseph, he took his parents to himself [i.e., embraced them] and said, "Enter Egypt, Allah willing, safe [and secure].

100. And he raised his parents upon the throne, and they bowed to him in prostration. And he said, "O my father, this is the explanation of my vision of before. My Lord has made it reality. And He was certainly good to me when H took me out of prison and brought you [here] from Bedouin life after Satan had induced [estrangement] between me and my brothers. Indeed, My Lord is Subtle in what He will. Indeed, it is He who is the Knowing, the Wise.

101. My Lord, You have given me [something] of sovereignty and taught me of the interpretation of dreams. Creator of the heavens and earth. You are my protector in this world and the Hereafter. Cause me to die a Muslim and join me with the righteous.

102. That is from the news of the unseen which We reveal. [O Muhammad], to you. And you were not with them when they put together their plan while they conspired.

103. And most of the people, although you strive [for it], are not believers.

104. And you do not ask of them for it any payment. It is not except a reminder to the worlds.

105. And how many a sign within the heavens and earth do they pass over while they, therefrom, are turning away.

106. And most of them believe not in Allah except while they associate others with Him.

107. Then do they feel secure that there will not come to them an overwhelming [aspect] of the punishment of Allah or that the Hour will not come upon them suddenly while they do not perceive?

108. Say, "This is my way, I invite you Allah with insight, I and those who follow me. And exalted is Allah, and I an not of those who associate others with Him."

109. And We sent not before you [as messengers] except men to whom We revealed from among the people of cities. So have they not traveled through the earth and observed how was the end of those before them? And the home of the Hereafter is best for those who fear Allah; they will not reason?

110. [They continued] until, when the messengers despaired and were certain that they had been denied, there came to them Our victory, and whoever We willed was saved. And Our punishment cannot be repelled from the people who are criminals.

111. There was certainly in their stories a lesson for those of understanding. Never was it {i.e., the Qur'an} a narration invented, but a confirmation of what was before it and a detailed explanation of all things and guidance and mercy for a people who believe." (Qur'an, Sura 12)

38. Stories of the Companions of the Prophet

38.1. The Story of Umm Salamah

Her real name was Hind. She was the daughter of one of the notables in the Makhzum clan. Umm Salamah's husband was Abdullah ibn Abdulasad and they both were among the first persons to accept Islam. As soon as the news of their becoming Muslims spread, the Quraish reacted with frenzied anger. They began hounding and persecuting Umm Salamah and her husband. But the couple did not waver or despair and remained steadfast in their new faith.

The persecution became more and more intense. Life in Mecca became unbearable for many of the new Muslims. The Prophet, peace be upon him, then gave permission for them to emigrate to Abyssinia. Umm Salamah and her husband were in the forefront of these muhajirun, seekers of refuge in a strange land. For Umm Salamah it meant abandoning her spacious home and giving up the traditional ties of lineage and honor for something new, hope in the pleasure and reward of Allah.

Despite the protection Umm Salamah and her companions received from the Abyssinian ruler, the desire to return to Mecca, to be near the Prophet and the source of revelation and guidance persisted.

News eventually reached the muhajirun that the number of Muslims in Mecca had increased. Among them were Hamzah ibn Abdulmuttalib and Umar ibn al-Khattab. Their faith had greatly strengthened the community and the Quraish they heard, had eased the persecution somewhat. Thus a group of the muhajirun, urged on by a deep longing in their hearts, decided to return to Mecca.

The easing of the persecution was but brief as the returnees soon found out. The dramatic increase in the number of Muslims following the acceptance of Islam by Hamzah and Umar only infuriated the Quraish even more. They intensified their persecution and torture to a pitch and intensity not known before. So the Prophet gave permission to his companions to emigrate to Madina. Umm Salamah and her husband were among the first to leave.

The Hijra of Umm Salamah and her husband though was not as easy as they had imagined. In fact, it was a bitter and painful experience and a particularly harrowing one for her.
Let us leave the story now for Umm Salamah herself to tell.

When Abu Salamah (my husband) decided to leave for Madina, he prepared a camel from me, hoisted me on it and placed our son Salamah on my lap. My husband then took the lead end went on without stopping or waiting for anything. Before we were out of Mecca however some men from my clan stopped us and said to my husband:

"Though you are free to do what you like with yourself, you have no power over your wife. She is our daughter. Do you expect us to allow you to take her away from us?"
They then pounced on him end snatched me away from him. My husband's clan, Banu Abdulasad, saw them taking both me and my child. They became hot with rage.
"No! By Allah," they shouted, "We shall not abandon the boy. He is our son and we have a first claim over him."
They took him by the hand and pulled him away from me. Suddenly in the space of a few moments, I found myself alone and lonely. My husband headed for Madina by himself and his clan had snatched my son away from me. My own clan, Banu Makhzum, overpowered me and forced me to stay with them.

From the day when my husband and my son were separated from me, I went out at noon every day to that valley and sat in the spot where this tragedy occurred. I would recall those terrible moments and weep until night fell on me.
I continued like this for a year or so until one day a man from the Banu Umayyah passed by and saw my condition. He went back to my clan and said: "Why don't you free this poor woman? You have caused her husband and her son to be taken away from her." He went on trying to soften their hearts and play on their emotions. At last they said to me. 'Go and join your husband if you wish."

But how could I join my husband in Madina and leave my son, a piece of my own flesh and blood, in Mecca among the Banu Abdulasad?
How could I be free from anguish and my eyes be free from tears were I to reach the place of Hijra not knowing anything of my little son left behind in Mecca?
Some realized what I was going through and their hearts went out to me. They petitioned the Banu Abdulasad on my behalf and moved them to return my son.

I did not now even want to linger in Mecca till I found someone to travel with me and I was afraid that something might happen that would delay or prevent me from reaching my husband. So I promptly got my camel ready, placed my son on my lap and left in the direction of Madina.

I had just about reached Tanim (about three miles from Mecca) when I met Uthman ibn Talhah. (He was a keeper of the Ka'bah in pre-Islamic times and was not yet a Muslim.)

"Where are you going, Bint Zad ar-Rakib?" he asked.
"I am going to my husband in Madina."
"And there isn't anyone with you?"
"No, by Allah. Except Allah and my little boy here."
"By Allah. I shall never abandon you until you reach Madina," he vowed.

He then took the reins of my camel and led us on. I have, by Allah, never met an Arab more generous and noble than he. When we reached a resting place, he would make my camel kneel down, wait until I dismounted, lead the camel to a tree and tether it. He would then go to the shade of another tree. When we had rested he would get the camel ready and lead us on.

This he did every day until we reached Madina. When we got to the village near Quba (about two miles from Madina) belonging to Banu Amr ibn Awf, he said, "Your husband is in this village. Enter it with the blessings of God. "

He turned back and headed for Mecca.

Their roads finally met after the long separation. Umm Salamah was overjoyed to see her husband and he was delighted to see his wife and son.

Great and momentous events followed one after the other. Then there was the battle of Uhud in which the Muslims were sorely tested. Abu Salamah came out of this wounded very badly. He appeared at first to respond well to treatment, but his wounds never healed completely and he remained bedridden.

Once while Umm Salamah was nursing him, he said to her: "I heard the Messenger of Allah saying. Whenever a calamity afflicts anyone he should say,

"Surely from Allah we are and to Him we shall certainly return."
And he would pray,
'O Lord, give me in return something good from it which only You Exalted and Mighty, can give."

Abu Salamah remained sick in bed for several days. One morning the Prophet came to see him. The visit was longer than usual. While the Prophet was still at his bedside Abu Salamah passed away. With his blessed hands, the Prophet closed the eyes of his dead companion. He then raised these hands to the heavens and prayed:
"O Lord, grant forgiveness to Abu Salamah. Elevate him among those who are near to You. Take charge of his family at all times. Forgive us and him, O Lord of the Worlds. Widen his grave and make it light for him."

Umm Salamah remembered the prayer her husband had quoted on his deathbed from the Prophet and began repeating it, "O Lord, with you I leave this my plight for consideration . . ." But she could not bring herself to continue . . . "O Lord give me something good from it", because she kept asking herself, "Who could be better than Abu Salamah?" But it did not take long before she completed the supplication.
The Muslims were greatly saddened by the plight of Umm Salamah. She had no one in Madina of her own except her small children, like a hen without feathers.

Both the Muhajirun and Ansar felt they had a duty to Umm Salamah. When she had completed the Iddah (three months and ten days), Some proposed marriage to her but refused and declined the proposal. The Prophet then approached her and she replied:

"O Messenger of Allah, I have three characteristics:
I am a woman who is extremely jealous and I am afraid that you will see in me something that will anger you and cause Allah to punish me.
I am a woman who is already advanced in age, and
I am a woman who has a young family."
The Prophet replied:
"Regarding the jealousy you mentioned, I pray to Allah the Almighty to let it go away from you.

Regarding the question of age you have mentioned. I am afflicted with the same problem as you.
Regarding the dependent family you have mentioned, your family is my family."

They were married and so it was that Allah answered the prayer of Umm Salamah and gave her better than Abu Salamah. From that day on Hind al Makhzumiyah was no longer the mother of Salamah alone but became the mother of all believers, Umm al-Mumineen.

38.2. The Story of Abu al-Darda'

Early in the morning, Abu al-Darda' awoke and went straight to his idol which he kept in the best part of his house. He greeted it and made obeisance to it. Then he anointed it with the best perfume from his large shop and put on it new raiment of beautiful silk which a merchant had brought to him the day before from Yemen. When the sun was high in the sky he left his house for his shop.

His close friend Abdullah Ibn Rawaha went to the house of Abu al-Darda' and went to the room where Abu al-Darda' kept his idol. He took out an adz, which he had brought with him and began destroying the idol. When the idol was completely smashed, he left the house.

When Abu al-Darda' returned home, he looked at the broken idol and was horrified. He was consumed with anger and determined to take revenge. Before long however his anger subsided and thoughts of avenging the idol disappeared. Instead he reflected on what had happened and said to himself:

"If there was any good in this idol, he would have defended himself against any injury."

He then went straight to Abdullah and together they went to the Prophet, peace be on him. There he announced his acceptance of Islam. He was the last person in his district to become a Muslim.

A Governor in Syria

During the caliphate of 'Umar, 'Umar wanted to appoint Abu al-Darda' as a governor in Syria. Abu-d Darda' refused. Umar persisted and then Abu al-Darda' said:

"If you are content that I should go to them to teach them the Book of their Lord and the Sunnah of their Prophet and pray with them, I shall go."

'Umar agreed and Abu al-Darda' left for Damascus. There he found the people immersed in luxury and soft living. This appalled him. He called the people to the masjid and spoke to them:

"O people of Damascus! You are my brethren in religion, neighbors who live together and helpers one to another against enemies. "O people of Damascus! What is it that prevents you from being affectionate towards me and responding to my advice while I do not seek anything from you? Is it right that I see your learned ones departing (from this world) while the ignorant among you are not learning? I see that you incline towards such things which Allah has made you answerable for and you abandon what He has commanded you to do.
"Is it reasonable that I see you gathering and hoarding what you do not eat, and erecting buildings in which you do not live, and holding out hopes for things you cannot attain.
"Peoples before you have amassed wealth, made great plans and had high hopes. But it was not long before what they had amassed was destroyed, their hopes dashed and their houses turned into graves. Such were the people of 'Ad, O people of Damascus, They filled the earth with possessions and children.
"Who is there who will purchase from me today the entire legacy of 'Ad for two dirhams?"

The people wept and their sobs could be heard from outside the masjid. From that day, Abu al-Darda' began to frequent the meeting places of the people of Damascus. He moved around in their market places, teaching, answering questions and trying to arouse anyone who had become careless and insensitive. He used every opportunity and every occasion to awaken people, to set them on the right path.

Is it Possible to Love People and Hate their Evil Actions?
Once Abu al-Darda' passed a group of people crowding around a man. They began insulting and beating the man. Abu al-Darda' came up to them and said:

"What's the matter?"
"This is a man who has committed a grave sin," they replied.
"What do you think you would do if he had fallen into a well?" asked Abu al-Darda'.
"Wouldn't you try to get him out?"
"Certainly," they said.

"Don't insult him and don't beat him. Instead admonish him and make him aware of the consequences of what he had done. Then give praise to Allah Who has preserved you from falling into such a sin."

"Don't you hate him?" they asked Abu al-Darda'.
"I only detest what he had done and if he abandons such practice, he is my brother."
The man began to cry and publicly announced his repentance.

Advice

A youth once came up to Abu al-Darda' and said:
"Give me advice, O companion of the Messenger of Allah" and Abu al-Darda' said to him:
"My son, remember Allah in good times and He will remember you in times of misfortune.
"My son, be knowledgeable, seek knowledge, be a good listener and do not be ignorant for you will be ruined.
"My son, let the masjid be your house for indeed I heard the Messenger of God say: The masjid is the house of every God-conscious person and Allah Almighty has guaranteed serenity, comfort, mercy and staying on the path leading to His pleasure, to those for whom masjids are their houses."

While Abu al-Darda' was still in Syria, the Caliph 'Umar ibn al-Khattab came on an inspection tour of the region. One night he went to visit Abu al-Darda' at his home. There was no light in the house. Abu al-Darda' welcomed the Caliph and sat him down. The two men conversed in the darkness. As they did so, 'Umar felt Abu al-Darda's "pillow" and realized it was an animal's saddle. He touched the place where Abu al-Darda' lay and knew it was just small pebbles. He also felt the sheet with which he covered himself and was astonished to find it so flimsy that it couldn't possibly protect him from the cold of Damascus. 'Umar asked him:

"Shouldn't I make things more comfortable for you? Shouldn't I send something for you?"

"Do you remember, 'Umar," said Abu-d Darda', "a hadith which the Prophet, may God bless him and grant him peace, told us?"

"What is it?" asked 'Umar.

"Did he not say: Let what is sufficient for anyone of you in this world be like the provisions of a rider?"

"Yes," said 'Umar.

"And what have we done after this, O 'Umar?" asked Abu al-Darda'.

Both men wept no doubt thinking about the vast riches that had come the way of Muslims with the expansion of Islam and their preoccupation with amassing wealth and worldly possessions. With deep sorrow and sadness, both men continued to reflect on this situation until the break of dawn.

39. Parables from Al-Ghazali

First:

One of the "knowers" [Sufis] spoke the truth when one of the princes said to him:

"Ask me for what you need."

He replied:

"Do you say this to me, when I have two servants who are your masters?"

He said:

"Who are they?"

He replied:

"Greed and passion: I have indeed mastered them, but they have mastered you; and I rule them, but they rule you."

Second:

"Someone said to one of the Sheikhs [Masters: of Sufism]:

"Counsel me."

He replied:

"Be a king in this life and thou will be a king in the afterlife-i.e. cut off your need and your passion [appetite] from this life, for sovereignty or kingship is in freedom and independence."

Third:

One day, a poor person entered a royal court. When the king entered, the poor person, unlike others, did not bow to him. The king was shaken by such insolence and called out:

"How dare you not bow down before me. It is only God does not bow down before me, and there is *nothing* greater than God. Who then are you?"

The poor person replied with a smile: "I am that *nothing*."

40. POETRY

This is from Hafiz *The Gift* (1999). Hafiz is a Persian Sufi poet who lived 1320-1389.

This Sky

This Sky

Where we live

Is no place to lose your wings

So love, love
Love.

The Heart is Right

The Heart is right to cry

Even when the smallest drop of light,
Of love,

Is taken away.

Perhaps you may kick, moan, scream
In a dignified Silence,

But you are so right
To do so in any fashion
Untill God returns
To
You.

References

The Qur'an:

I used the Arabic edition of the Qur'an. I also used three translations of the meanings of the Qur'an in English language. For some verses I decided to give my own translation based on the readings of the original Arabic text and the different meanings of these three translations.

Yusuf Ali (No date):

The Holy Qur'an, English translation of the meanings. The custodian of the two Holy Mosques; King Fahd, al-Madina.

Al-Hilali, Muhammad Taqi-ud-Din **& Khan,** Muhammad Muhsin **(1417 A.H.):**

The Nobel Qur'an, English translation of the meanings and commentary, King Fahd Complex for The Printing of The Holy Qur'an, Madinah, K.S.A.

The Qur'an **(1997):**

Arabic Text With Corresponding English Meanings, Translated by Saheeh International, Riyadh, Al-Muntada Alislami.

The Hadith

Sahih al-Bukhari (No date): Arabic-English, 9 vol. Dar Ayha Us-Sunnah, al-Madina.

Sahih Muslim (1993): Dar El-Fiker, Bairut, Lebanon.

Al-Bayan (1996): *Al-Bayan fima Etafaqa 'Alaihi Al-Shaikhan* (Agreed Upon)**,** Sakhr Software Co. Nasr City, Cairo.

Forty Hadith Qudsi (1980):

Selected and translated by, Ezzeddin Ibrahim & Denys Johnson-davies, Dar A-Koran Al-Kareem, Beirut, Lebanon.

An-Nawawi (1976):

Forty Hadith, translated by, Ezzeddin Ibrahim & Denys Johnson-davies, Dar A-Koran Al-Kareem, Beirut, Lebanon.

References other than the Qur'an and Sunnah:

Al-Allaf, Mashhad (2003):

The Essence of Islamic Philosophy, IIC Classic Series, first edition, USA.

Al-Allaf, Mashhad (1988):

Dr. Yasin Khalil, His Philosophy and Scientific Works, Baghdad, Iraq.

Al-Buti, Muhammad Sa'id Ramadan (1996):

Al-Mar'ah, Dar al-Fikr, Damascus, Syria.

Al-Ghazali, Abu Hamed (1980):

Deliverance from Error (al-Munqidh min al-Dalal), translated by R.J.McCarthy as *Freedom and Fulfillment,* Fons Vitae, Louisville, KY.

Al-Ghazali (1987):

Ihya' 'Ulum al-Deen, 5 vols. Dar al-Rayyan lil Turath, al-Qahira.

Al-Ghazali (1988):

Al-Arba'een fi Usul Addeen, Darul Jeel, Bairut.

Al-Ghazali (1997):

Al-Mustasfa min 'Ilm al-Usul, two volumes. Al-Resalah Publishing House, Bairut.

Al-Ghazali (1997):

The Incoherence of The Philosophers, translated by Michael E. Marmura, Brigham Young University Press, Provo, Utah.

Al-Ghazali (2000):

Inner Dimensions of Islamic Worship, translated from the *Ihya'* by Muhtar Holland, The Islamic foundation.

Hafiz (1999): *The Gift,* trans by D. Ladinsky, Penguin Compass, UK.

Heijenoort, Jean van (1967): (Editor)

From Frege to Godel, A source book in Mathematical Logic, 1879-1931, Harvard University press. Cambridge. Third edition.

Hilbert, David (1925):

On The Infinite, in Heijenoort (1967).

Iqbal, Muhammad (1934):

The Reconstruction of Religious Thought in Islam, Oxford University Press. London.

Al-Jurjani, Ali Ibn Muhammad al-Shareef (1969):

Kitab Al-Ta'rifat, Maktabat Lebanon, Beirut.

Al-Kisa'i, Muhammad Ibn 'Abdullah (1997):

Tales of The Prophets (Qisas al-Anbiya'), translated by Wheeler M. Thackton Jr. Great books of The Islamic World.

Kamali, M. H. (1991):

Priciples of Islamic Jurisprudence, Islamic text society, Cambridge.

Ibn Khaldun (1989):

The Muqaddimah, An Introduction to History. Translated by Franz Rosenthal, Bolling series, Princeton.

Ibn Khaldun (1993):

Al-Muqaddimah, Dar al-kutub al-'Ilmiyya, Beirut, Lebanon.

Khalil, Yaseen (1979):

Al-Khawarizmi's Logic of al-Jabr Wal-Muqabalah, Afaq Arabiyya, No. 5. Baghdad, Iraq.

Al-Khawarizmi, Muhammad Ibn Musa (1968):

Kitab al-Jabr wal-Muqabalah, Dar al-Katib al-Arabi, Misr, thired edition.

Al-Kindi, Abu Yusuf Ya'qub bin Ishaq (1948):

Kitab al-Kindi ila Al-Mu'tasim Billah fil Falsafah al-Ula, Edited by al-Ahwani, first edition, Cairo.

Al-Kindi (1950):

Rasa'il al-Kindi al-falsafiyya, haqqaqaha wa-akhrajaha Muhammad 'Abd al-Hadi Abu Rida, Dar al-fikr al-Arabi, al-juz', 1, **Vol. 1,**1369/1950.

Al-Kindi (1953):

Rasa'il al-Kindi al-falsafiyya, haqqaqaha wa-akhrajaha Muhammad 'Abd al-Hadi Abu Rida, Dar al-fikr al-Arabi, al-juz', 2, **Vol. 2,** 1372/1953.

Al-Kindi (1974):

Fi al-Falsafah al-Ula, A Translation of Yaqub Ibn Ishaq Al-Kindi's Treatise *"On First Philosophy,"* In *al-Kindi's Metaphysics*, ed. and translated by Alfred L. Ivry, New York, Albany, 1974.

Al-Mubarakpury, Safiy al-Rahman (2000):

Al-Raheeq al-Makhtom, second edition, Maktabat al-Rasheed, al-Riyadh.

Al-Raheeq al-Makhtom (The Sealed Nectar), translated by Issam Diab, The Sunnah Islamic Page, Safat, Kuwait. See also al-sunnah.com.

This book was awarded First prize by the Muslim world league at worldwide competition on the biography of the Prophet held at Mecca Al-Mukarramah in 1399 A.H./1979 A.D.

Al-Razi, Muhammad Ibn Abi Bakr Ibn 'Abd al-Qader (1989):

Mukhtar al-Sihah, Maktabat Lebanon, Beirut.

Rescher, Nicholas (1964):

Al-Kindi: An Annotated Bibliography, University of Pittsburgh Press.

Ibn Sereen (1998):

Tafseer al-Ahlam al-Kabeer, Dar al-Iman, Tarabuls, Lebanon.

Tabbarah, Afif A. (1993):

The Spirit of Islam, Dar El-Ilm Lilmalayain, Beirut, Lebanon.

al-Uthaimeen, Muhammad Saleh (No date):

Explaining The Pillars of Iman, al-Riyadh, Saudia Arabia.

Zaidan, Abdul Karim (1987):

Al-Wajeez fi Usul al-Fiqh, Maktabat al-Quds, Baghdad, Iraq.